STAY

WRITTEN BY
LEWIS TRONDHEIM

ILLUSTRATED BY
HUBERT CHEVILLARD

TRANSLATION, LAYOUT, AND EDITING BY
MIKE KENNEDY

ISBN: 978-1-5493-0771-3
Library of Congress Control Number: 2019936687

Printed in China.

10 9 8 7 6 5 4 3 2 1

Thanks to Juan Marquez Jimenez, Lauriane Lamri, Wolf Wong, who lent their features to some of the characters in this story, and to Boyi Wong for his photos.

Thanks to LC for his friendly support, which I will never forget.

H. C.

Thanks to my sister, Elisabeth, for her technical advice.

L. T.

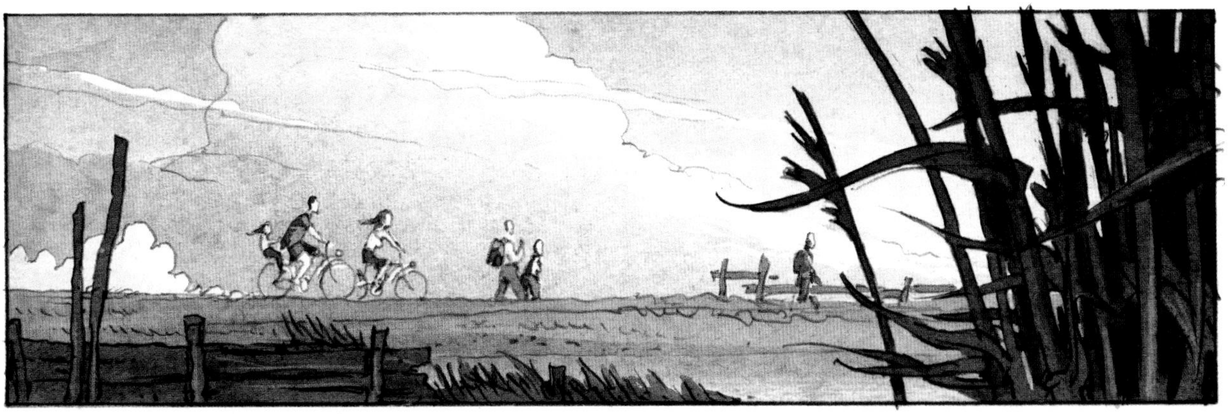

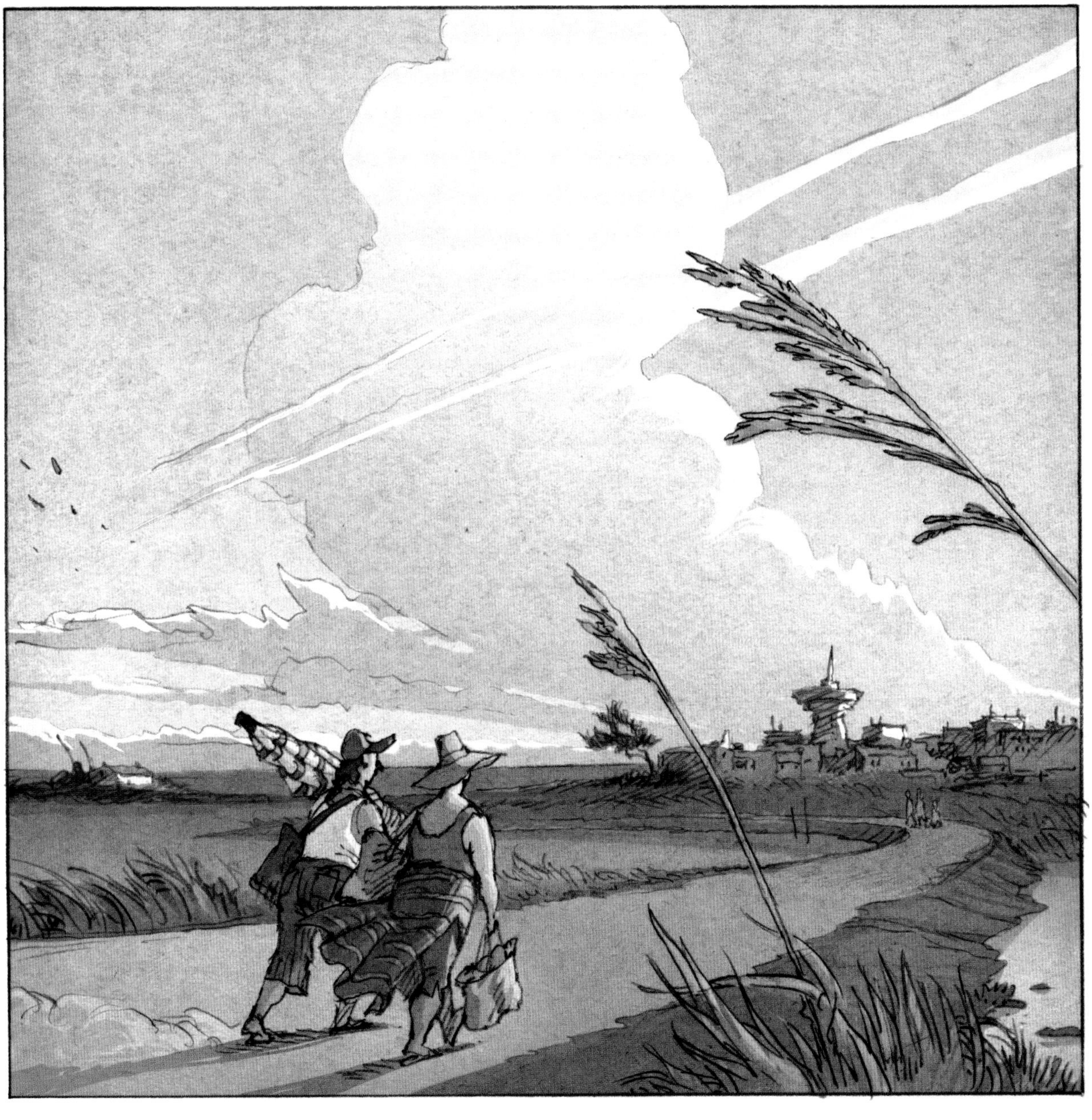

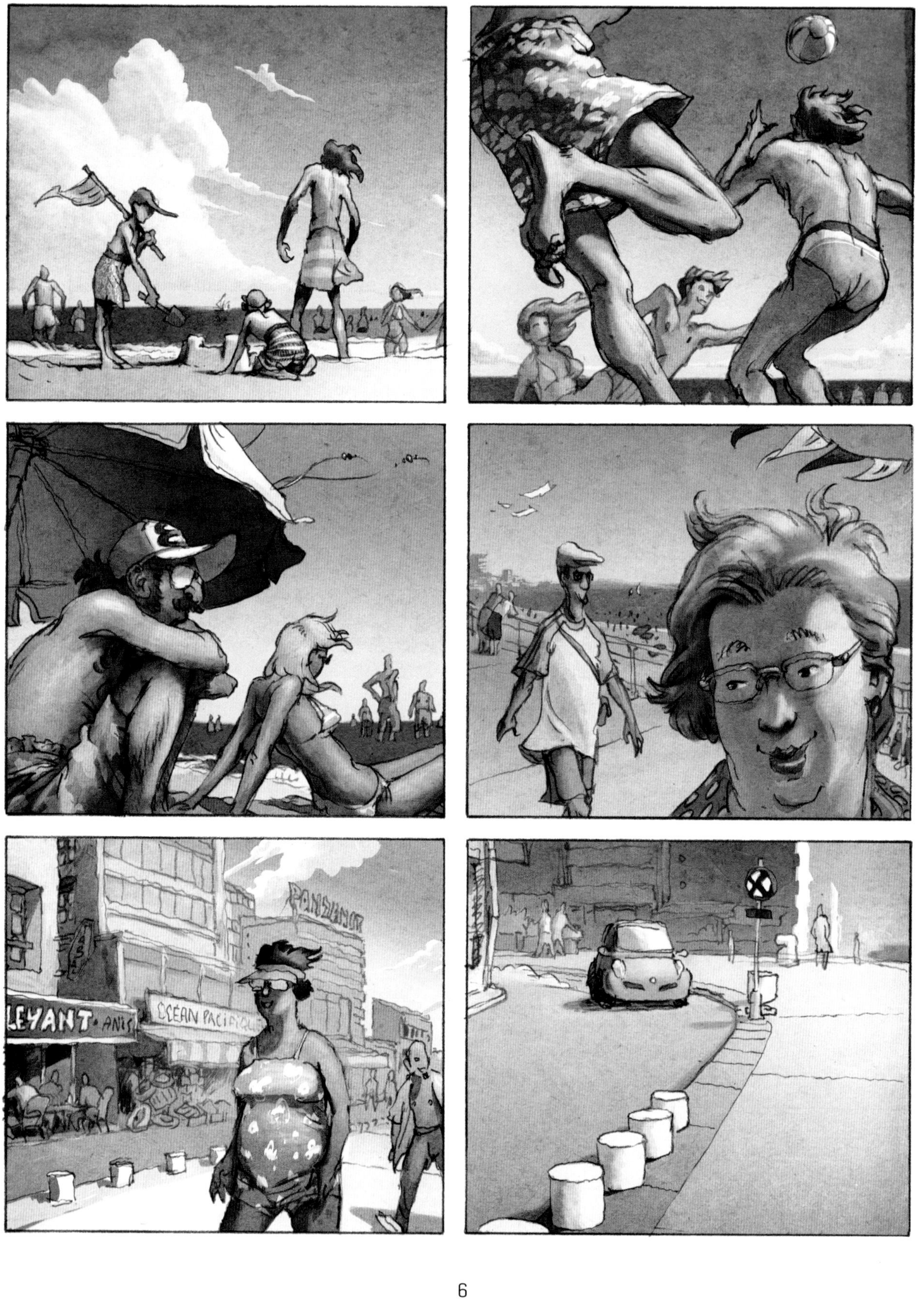
LEYANT · ANIS
OCÉAN PACIFIQU

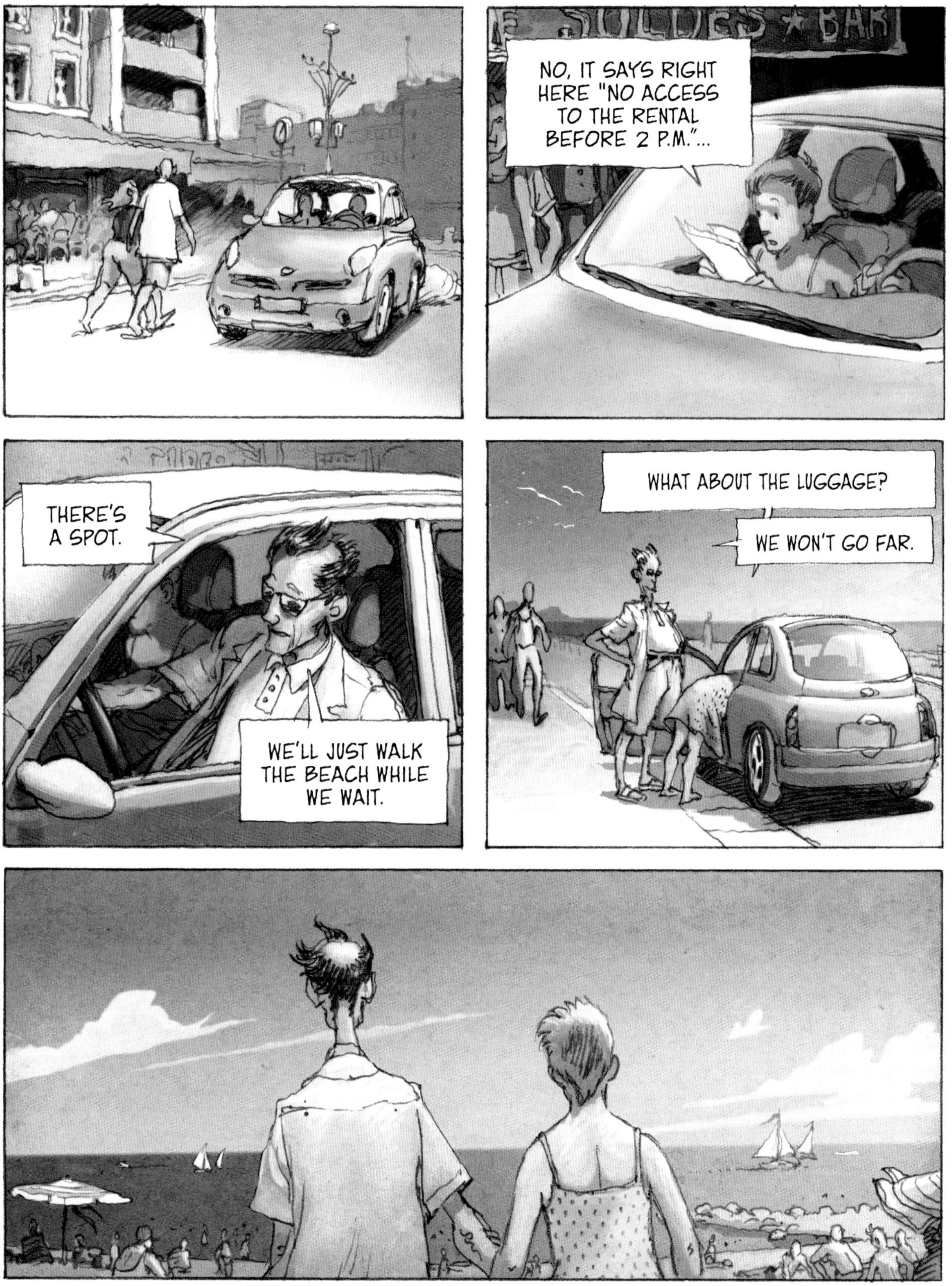
NO, IT SAYS RIGHT HERE "NO ACCESS TO THE RENTAL BEFORE 2 P.M."...
THERE'S A SPOT.
WE'LL JUST WALK THE BEACH WHILE WE WAIT.
WHAT ABOUT THE LUGGAGE?
WE WON'T GO FAR.

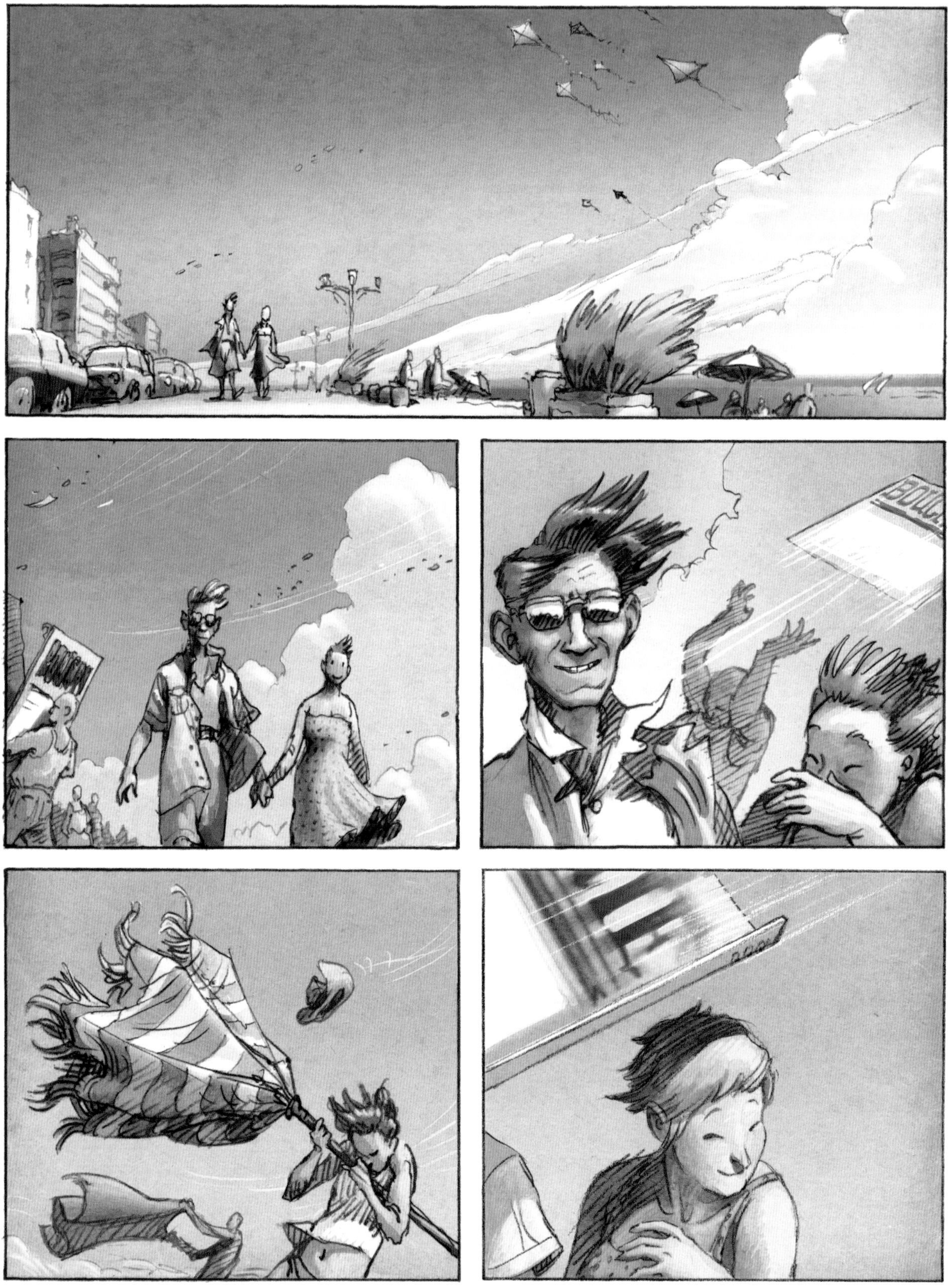

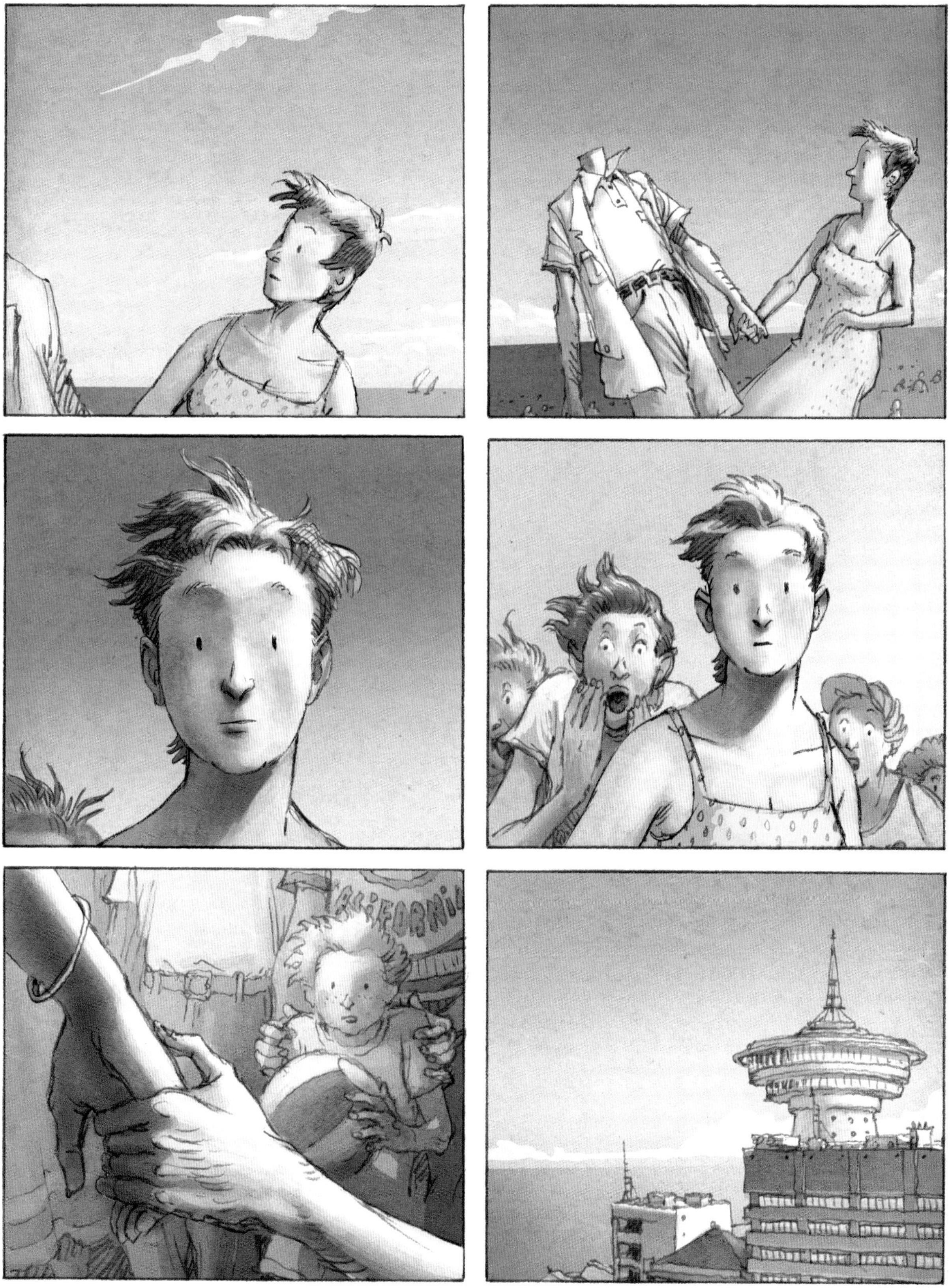

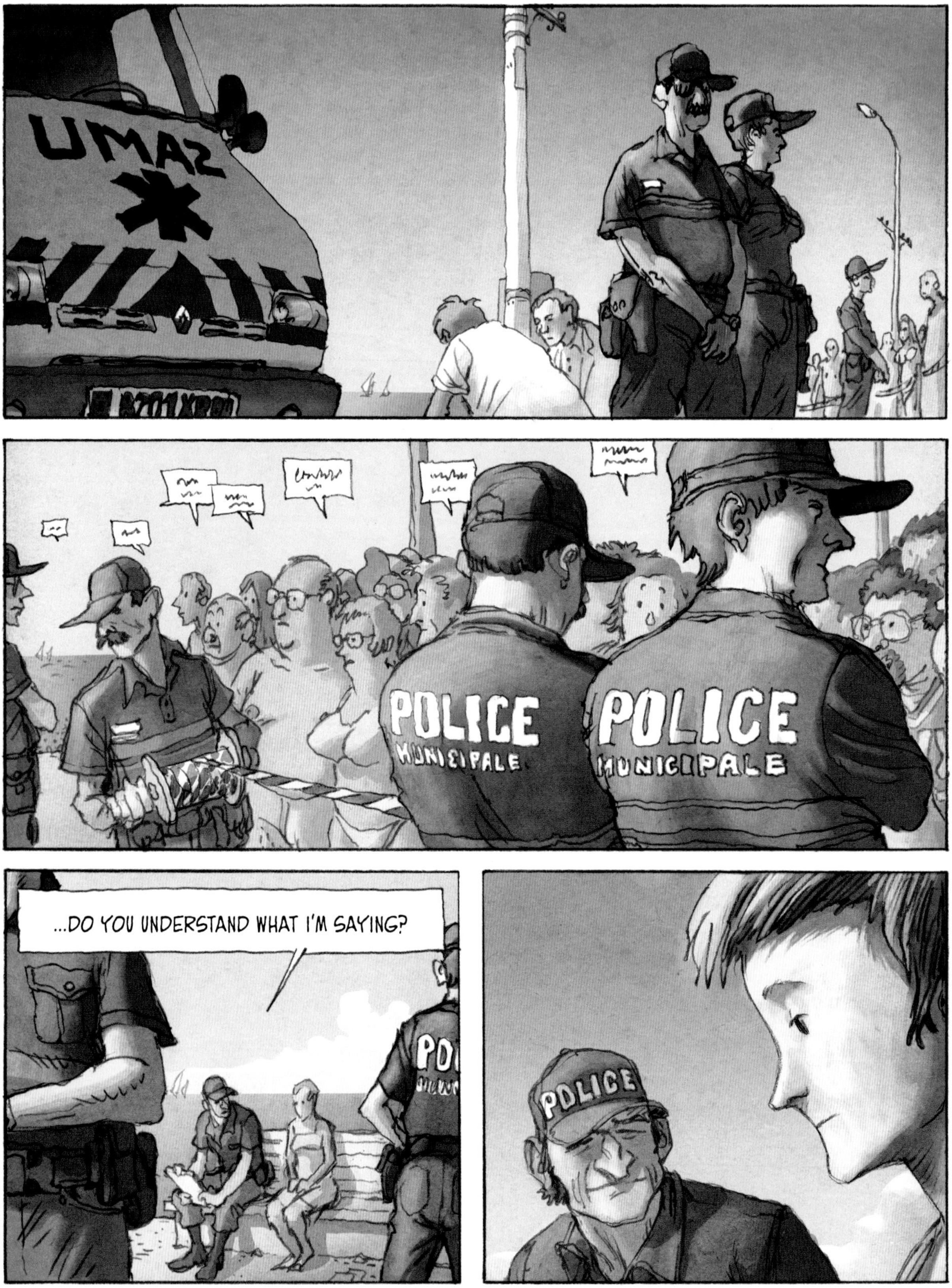
POLICE
MUNICIPALE
POLICE
MUNICIPALE
...DO YOU UNDERSTAND WHAT I'M SAYING?
POLICE

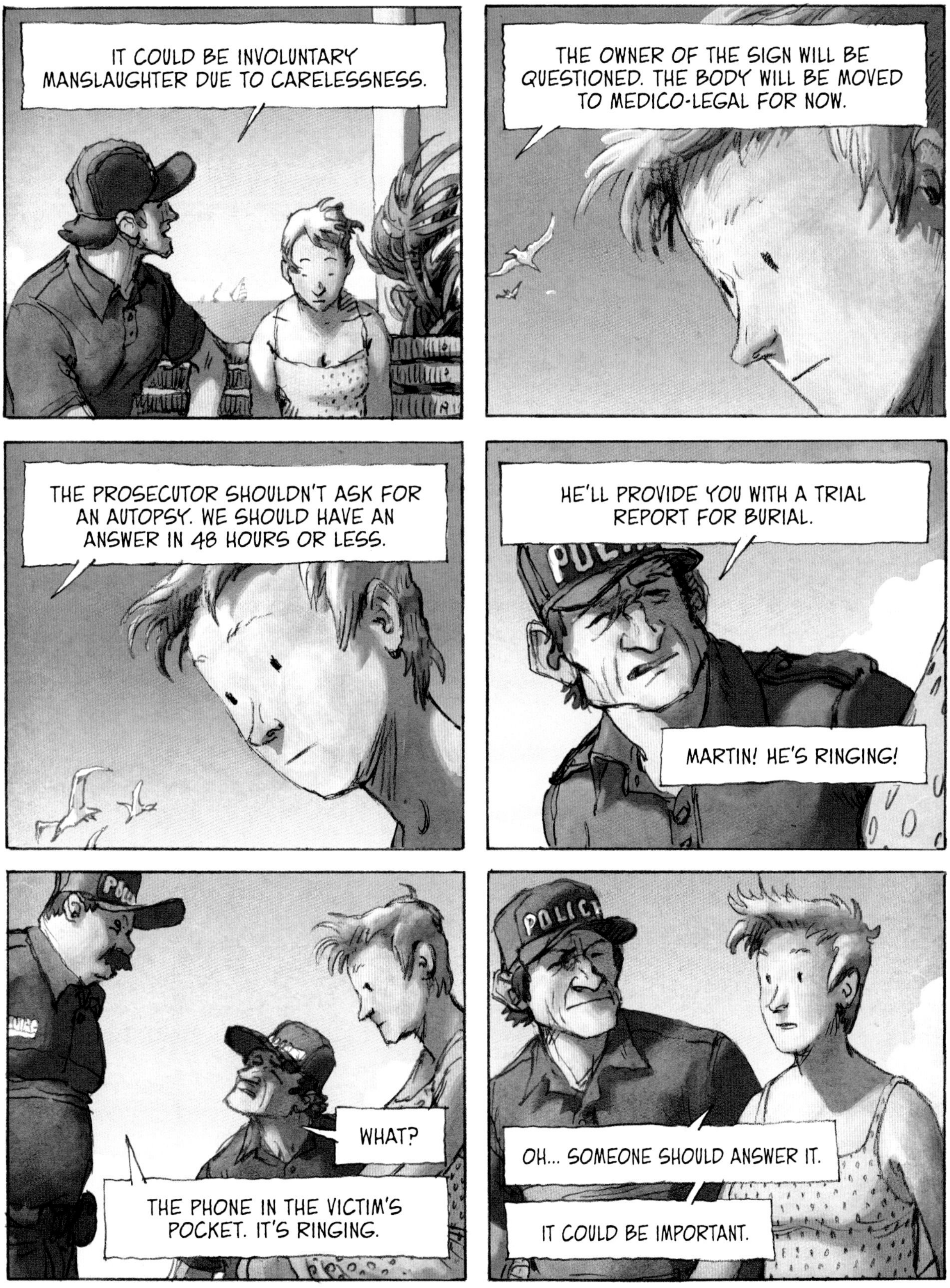
IT COULD BE INVOLUNTARY MANSLAUGHTER DUE TO CARELESSNESS.
THE OWNER OF THE SIGN WILL BE QUESTIONED. THE BODY WILL BE MOVED TO MEDICO-LEGAL FOR NOW.
THE PROSECUTOR SHOULDN'T ASK FOR AN AUTOPSY. WE SHOULD HAVE AN ANSWER IN 48 HOURS OR LESS.
HE'LL PROVIDE YOU WITH A TRIAL REPORT FOR BURIAL.
POLICE
MARTIN! HE'S RINGING!
WHAT?
THE PHONE IN THE VICTIM'S POCKET. IT'S RINGING.
POLICE
OH... SOMEONE SHOULD ANSWER IT.
IT COULD BE IMPORTANT.

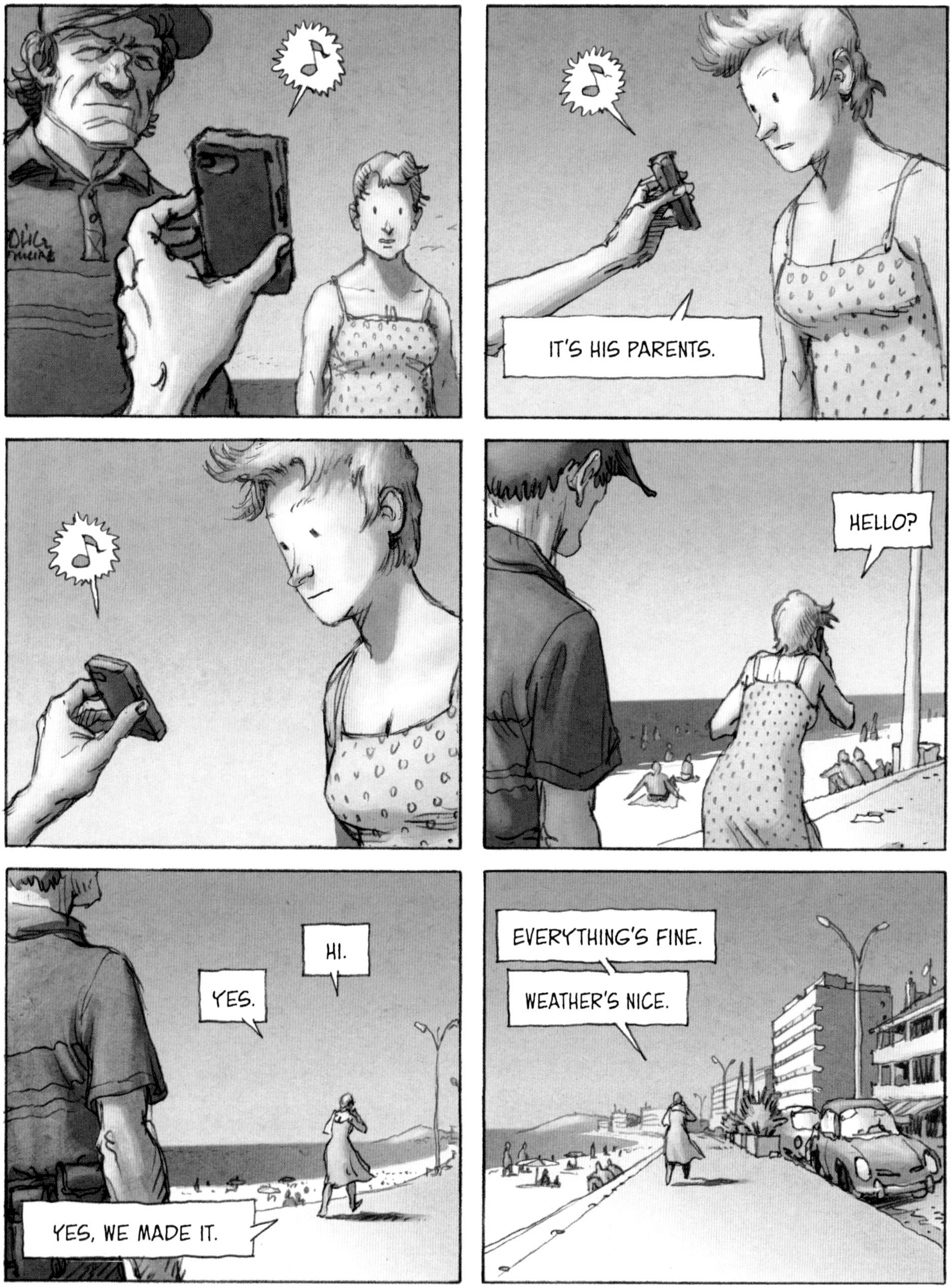
IT'S HIS PARENTS.
HELLO?
HI.
YES.
YES, WE MADE IT.
EVERYTHING'S FINE.
WEATHER'S NICE.

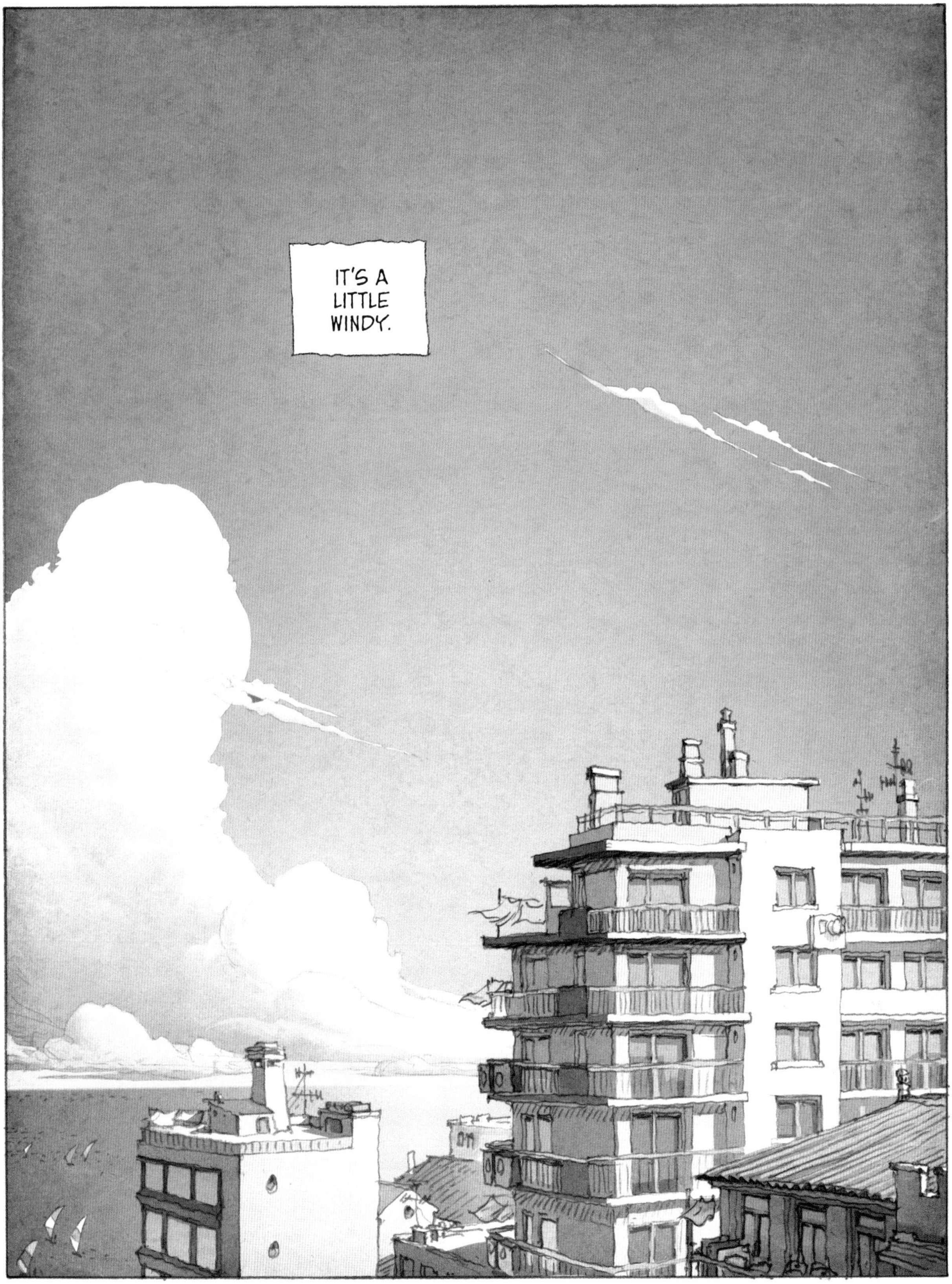
IT'S A LITTLE WINDY.

Wha Wha
Rwaf!!
Wha
wha! Wha!!
6
AOÛT
sem 33
7
les Acacias
Mme Moutin
14h -
8
10
11-12

* Les Acacias, Miss Moutin 2pm

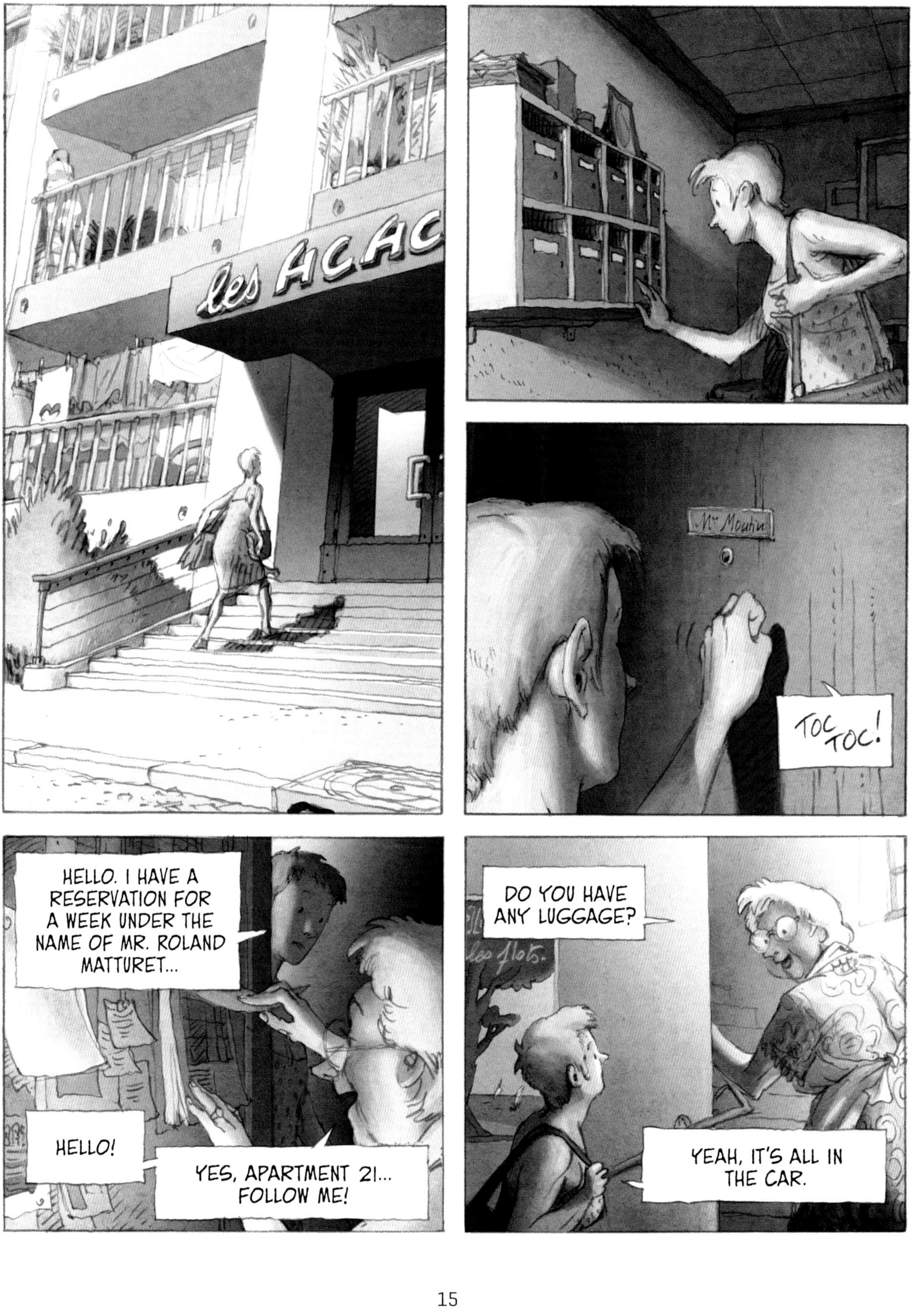
les ACAC
TOC TOC!
HELLO. I HAVE A RESERVATION FOR A WEEK UNDER THE NAME OF MR. ROLAND MATTURET...
HELLO!
YES, APARTMENT 21... FOLLOW ME!
DO YOU HAVE ANY LUGGAGE?
YEAH, IT'S ALL IN THE CAR.

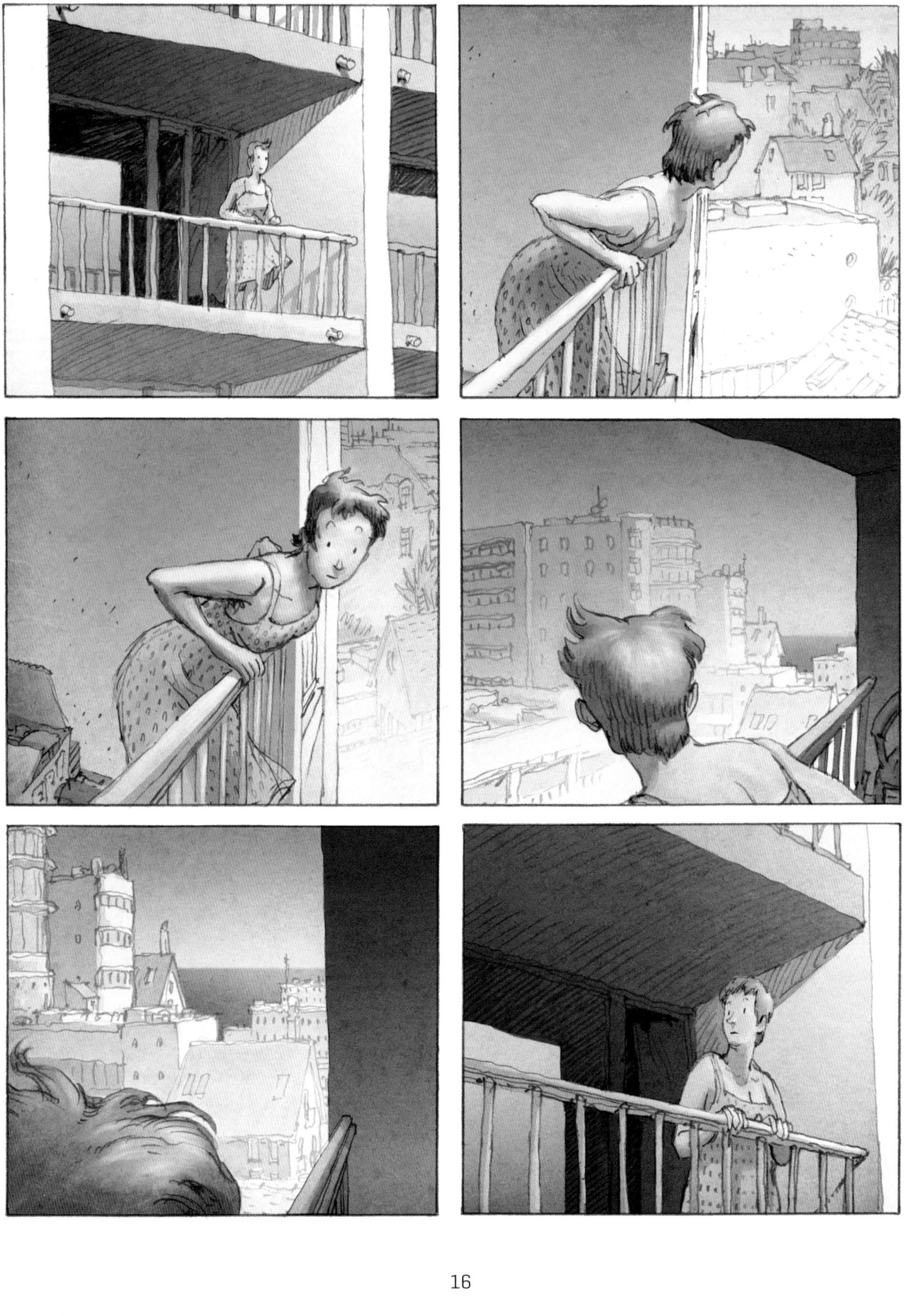

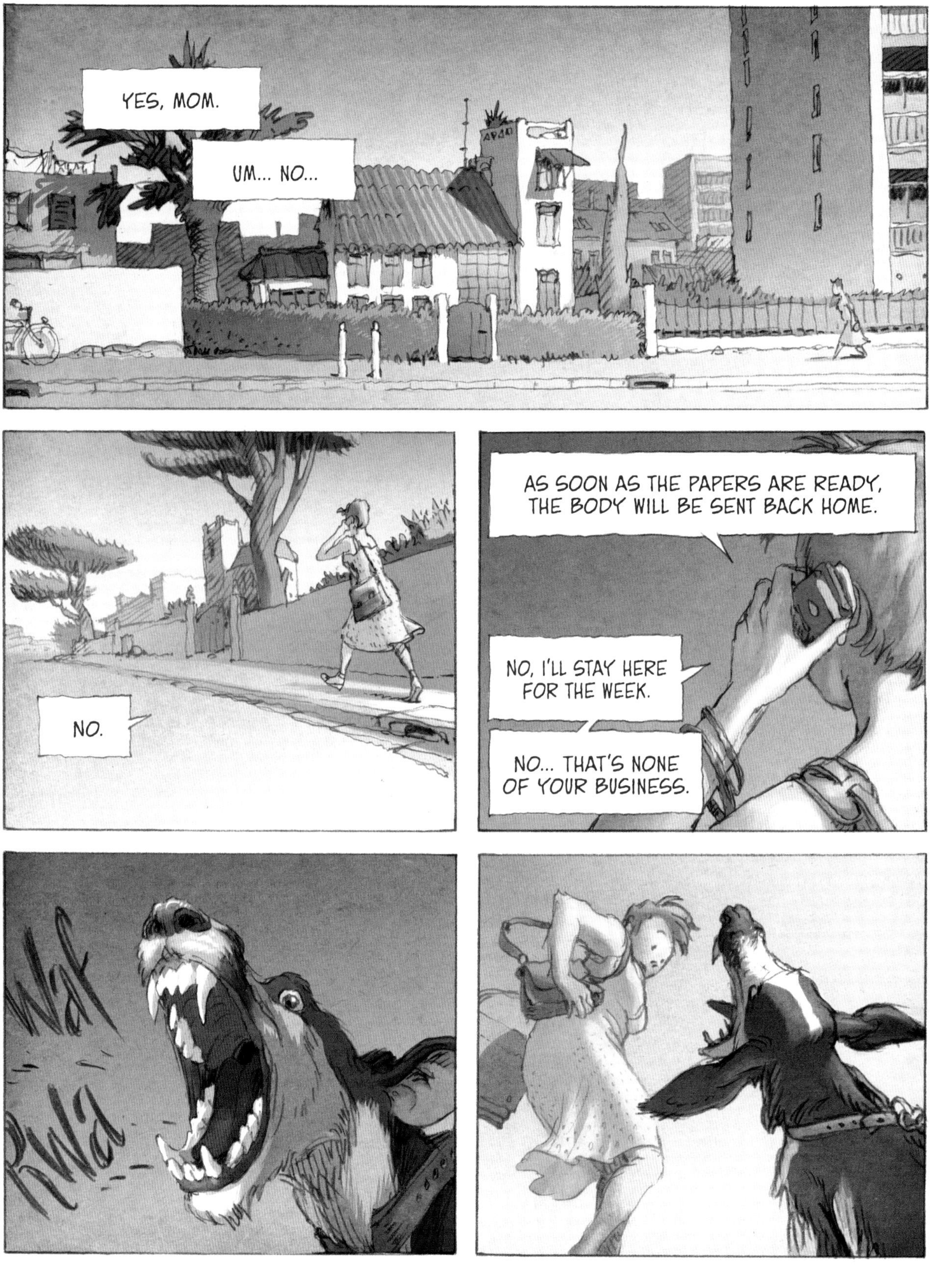
YES, MOM.
UM... NO...
NO.
AS SOON AS THE PAPERS ARE READY, THE BODY WILL BE SENT BACK HOME.
NO, I'LL STAY HERE FOR THE WEEK.
NO... THAT'S NONE OF YOUR BUSINESS.
Waf
Rwa

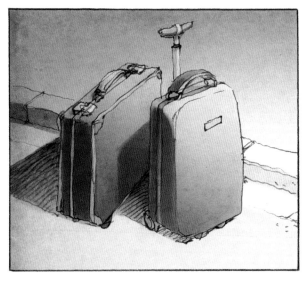

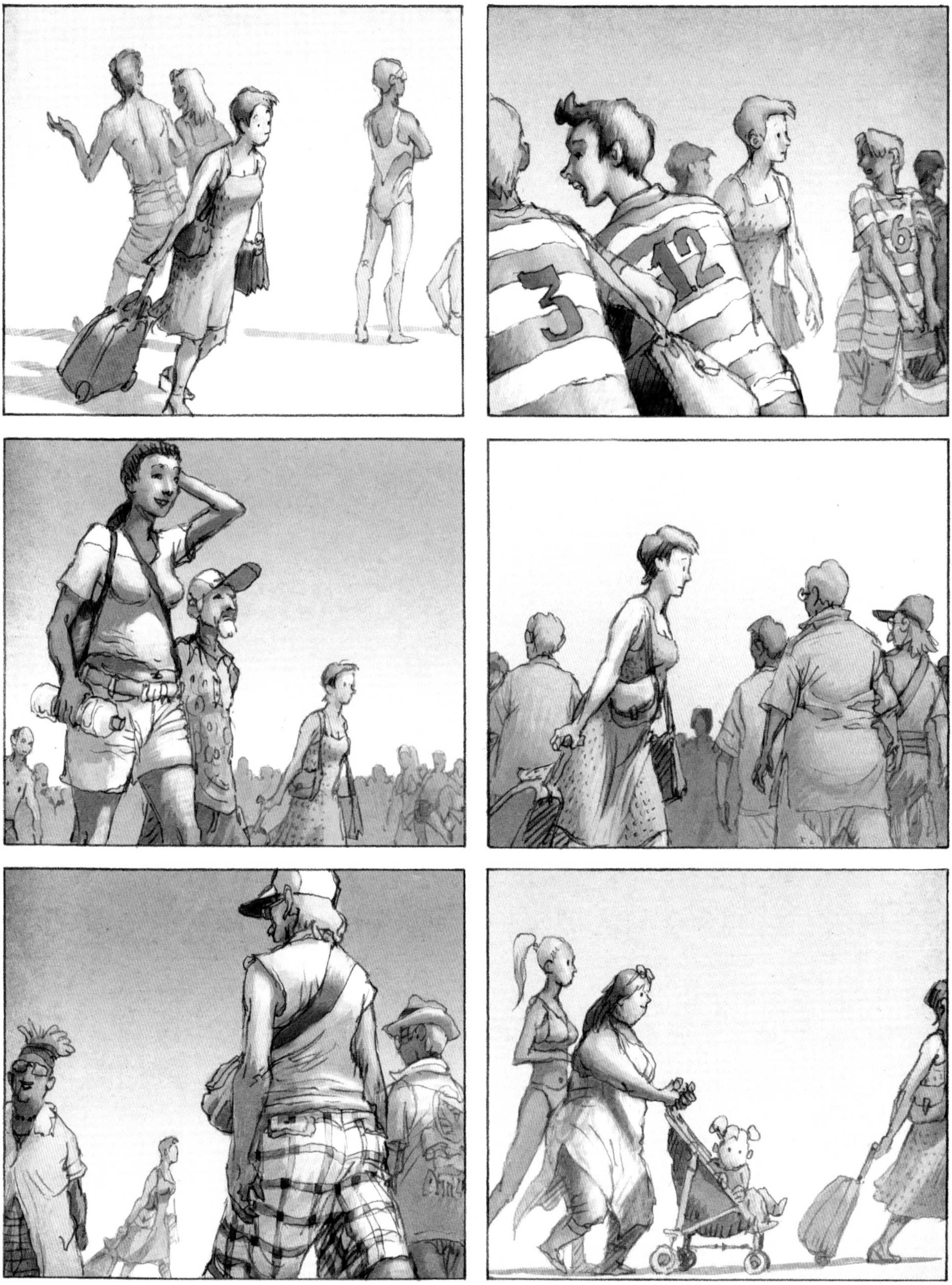

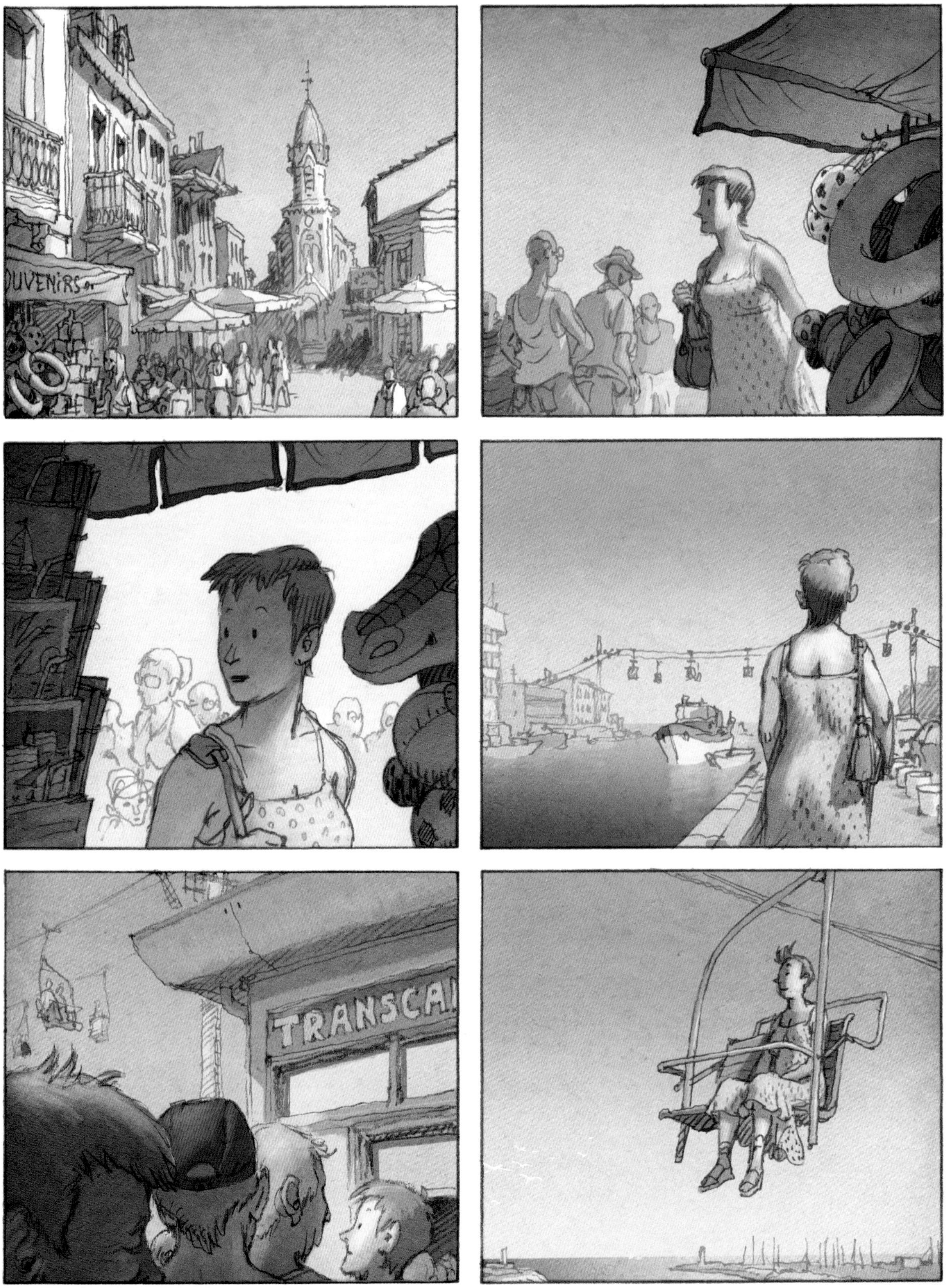
OUVENIRS
TRANSCA

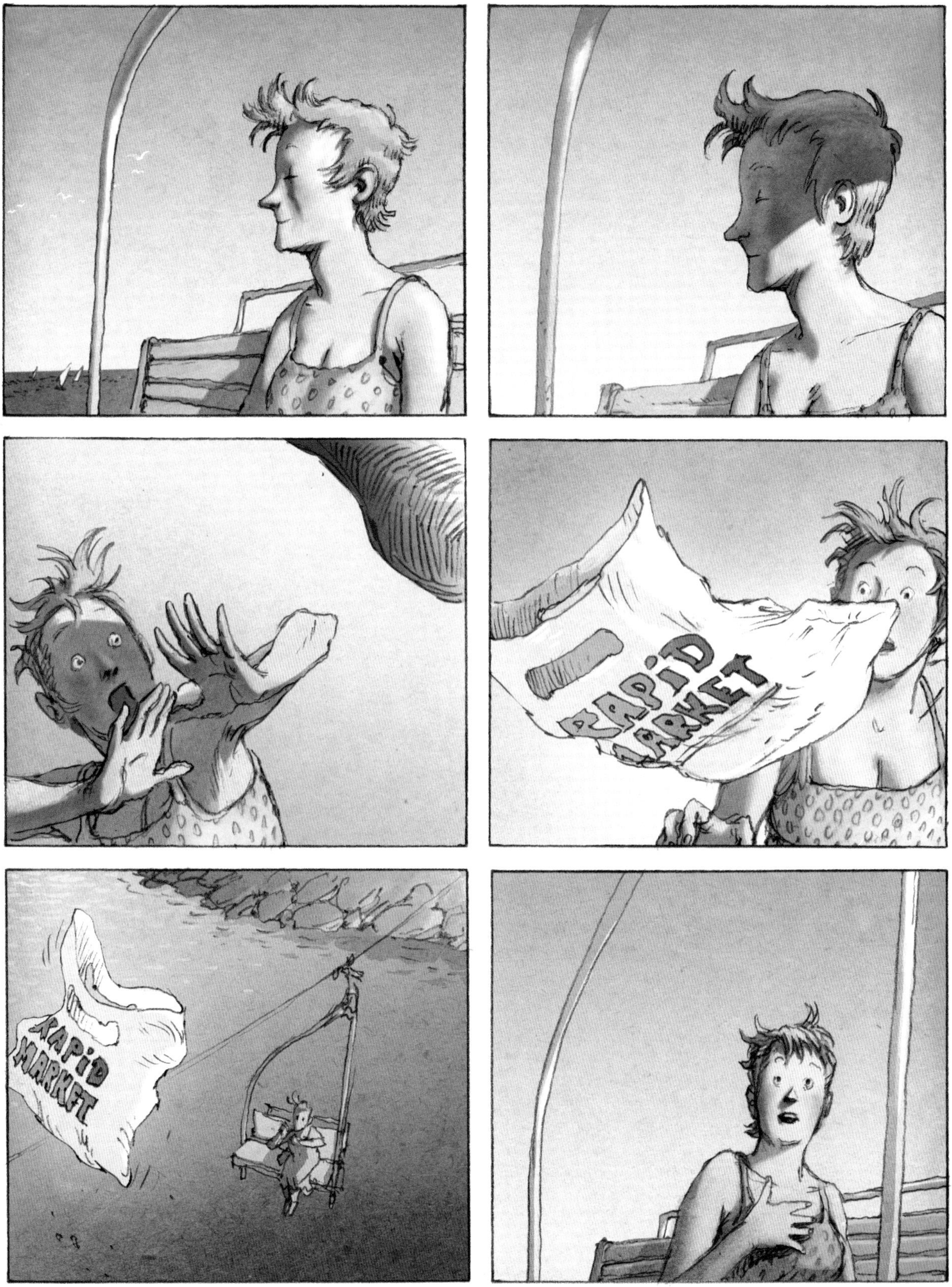
RAPiD
ARKET
RAPiD
MARKET

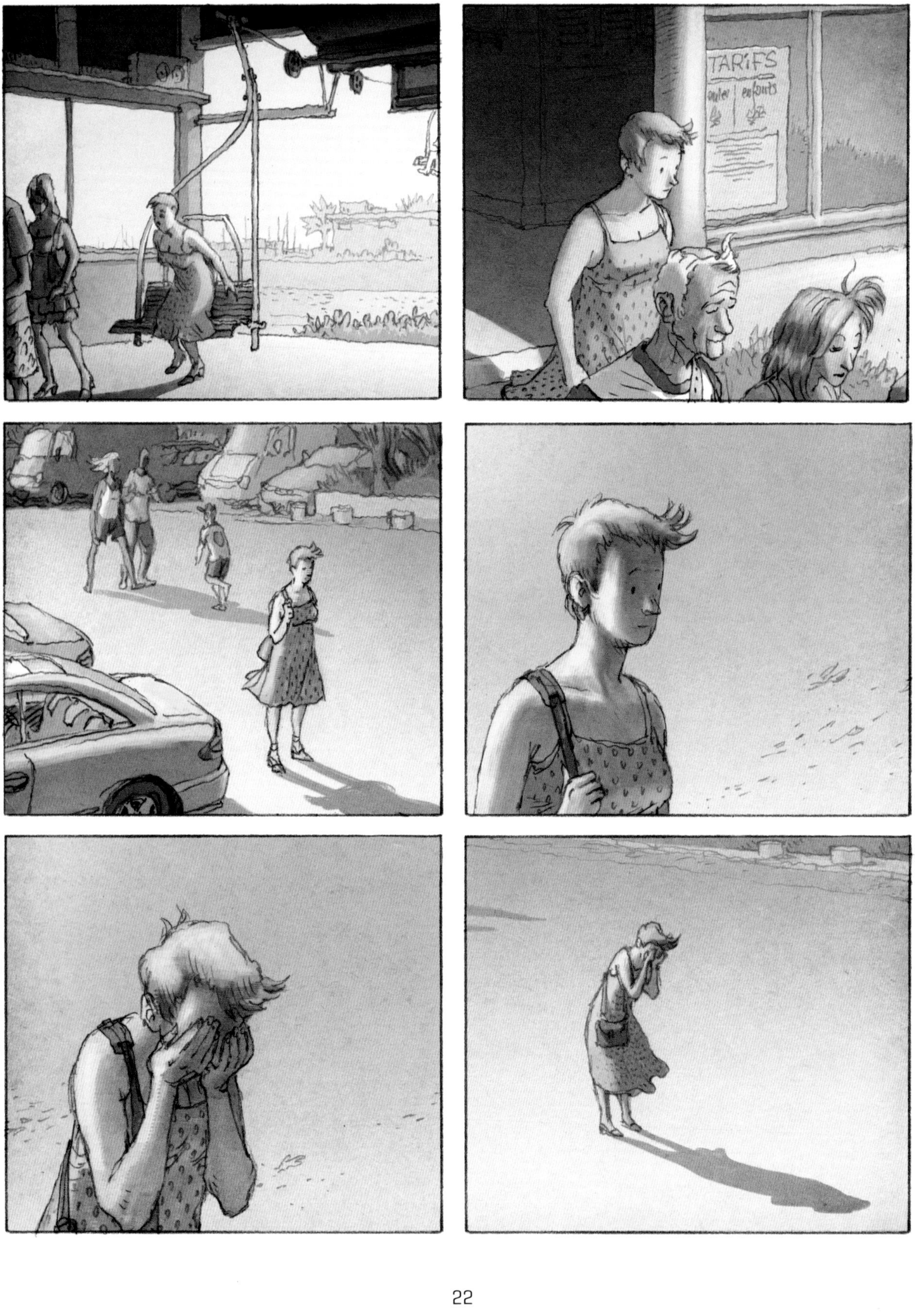
TARIFS
enfants

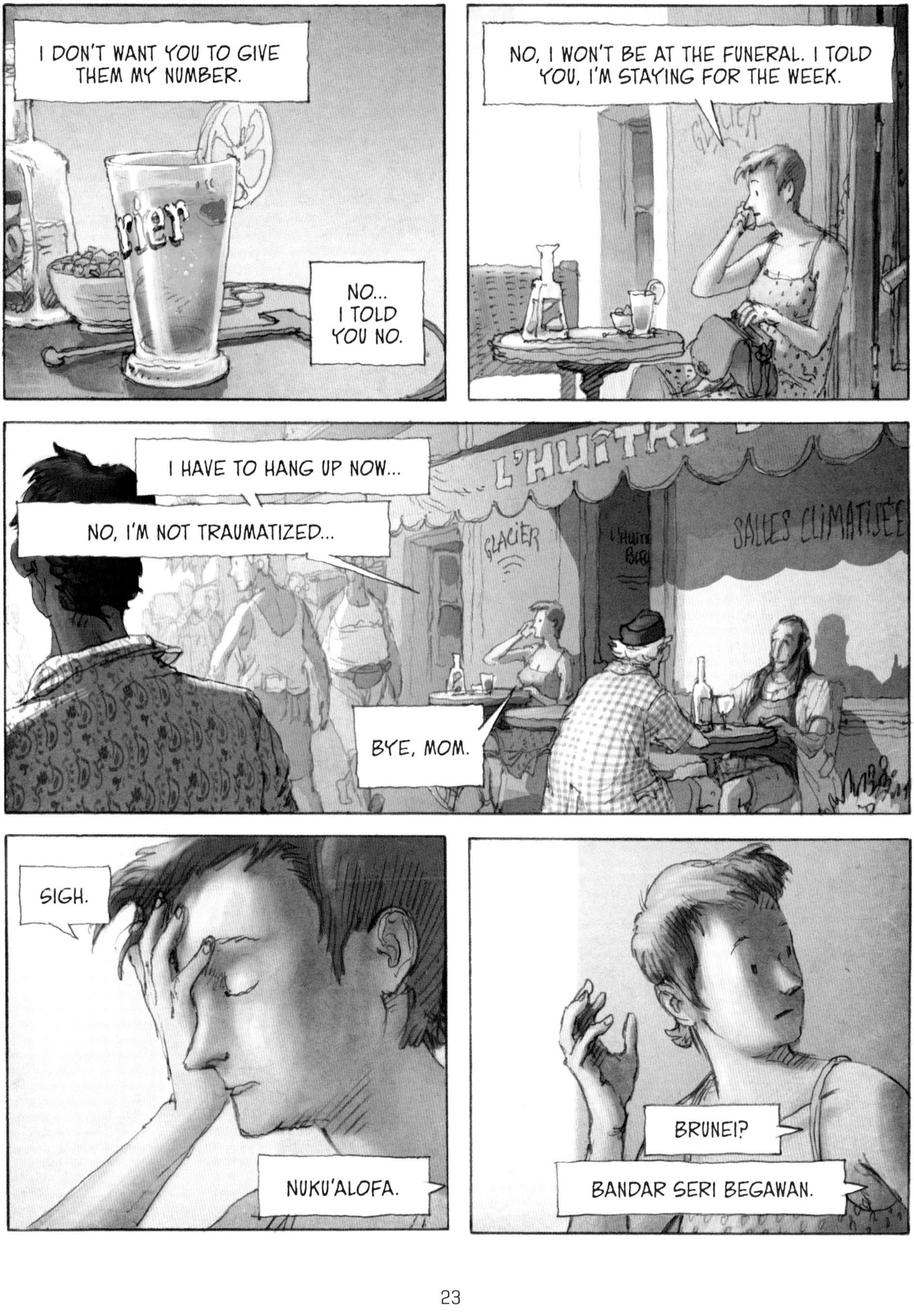
I DON'T WANT YOU TO GIVE THEM MY NUMBER.
NO... I TOLD YOU NO.
NO, I WON'T BE AT THE FUNERAL. I TOLD YOU, I'M STAYING FOR THE WEEK.
I HAVE TO HANG UP NOW...
NO, I'M NOT TRAUMATIZED...
L'HUITRE
GLACIER
SALLES CLIMATISÉE
BYE, MOM.
SIGH.
NUKU'ALOFA.
BRUNEI?
BANDAR SERI BEGAWAN.

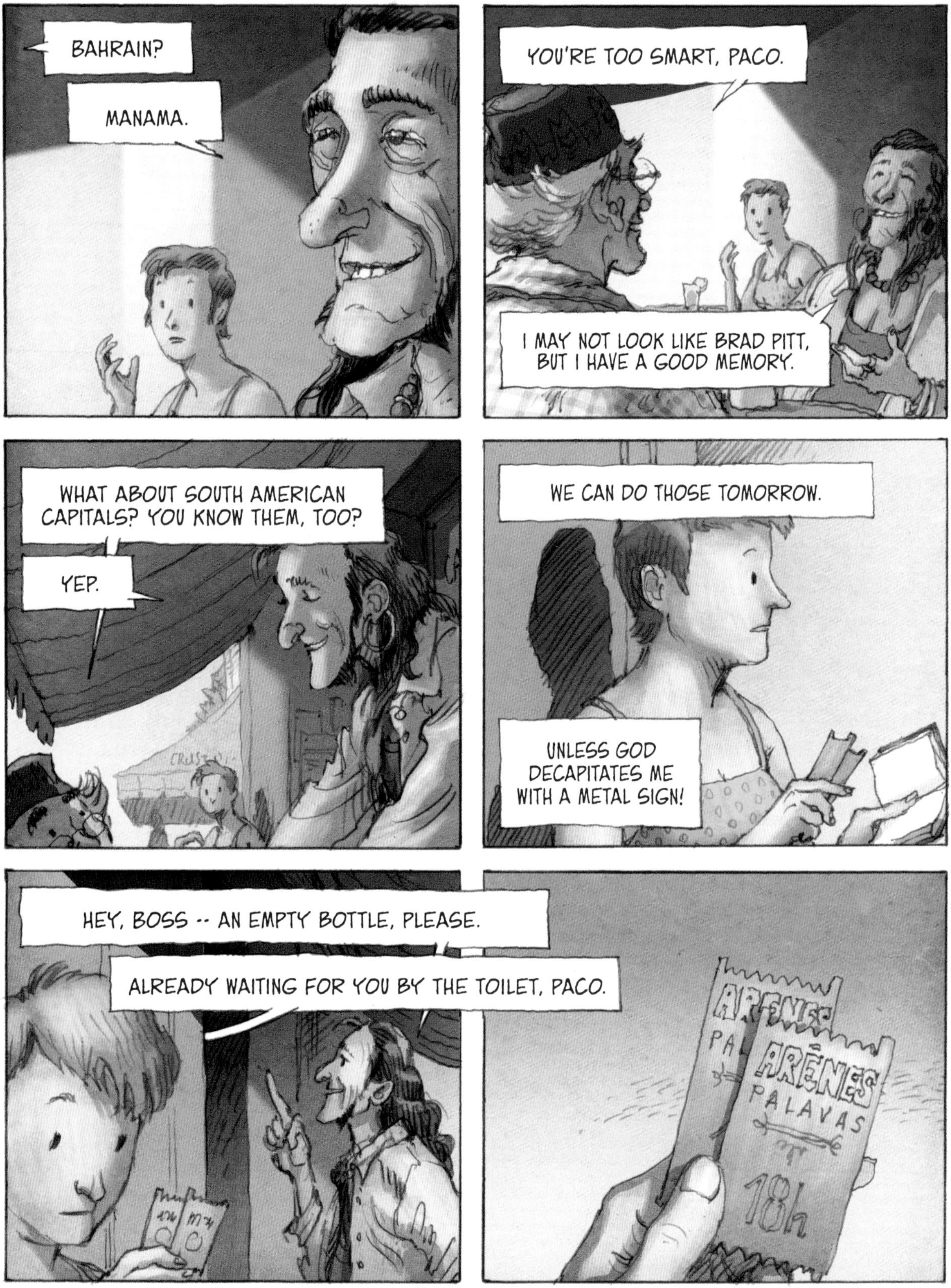
BAHRAIN?
MANAMA.
YOU'RE TOO SMART, PACO.
I MAY NOT LOOK LIKE BRAD PITT, BUT I HAVE A GOOD MEMORY.
WHAT ABOUT SOUTH AMERICAN CAPITALS? YOU KNOW THEM, TOO?
YEP.
WE CAN DO THOSE TOMORROW.
UNLESS GOD DECAPITATES ME WITH A METAL SIGN!
HEY, BOSS -- AN EMPTY BOTTLE, PLEASE.
ALREADY WAITING FOR YOU BY THE TOILET, PACO.
ARÊNES
PALAVAS
18h

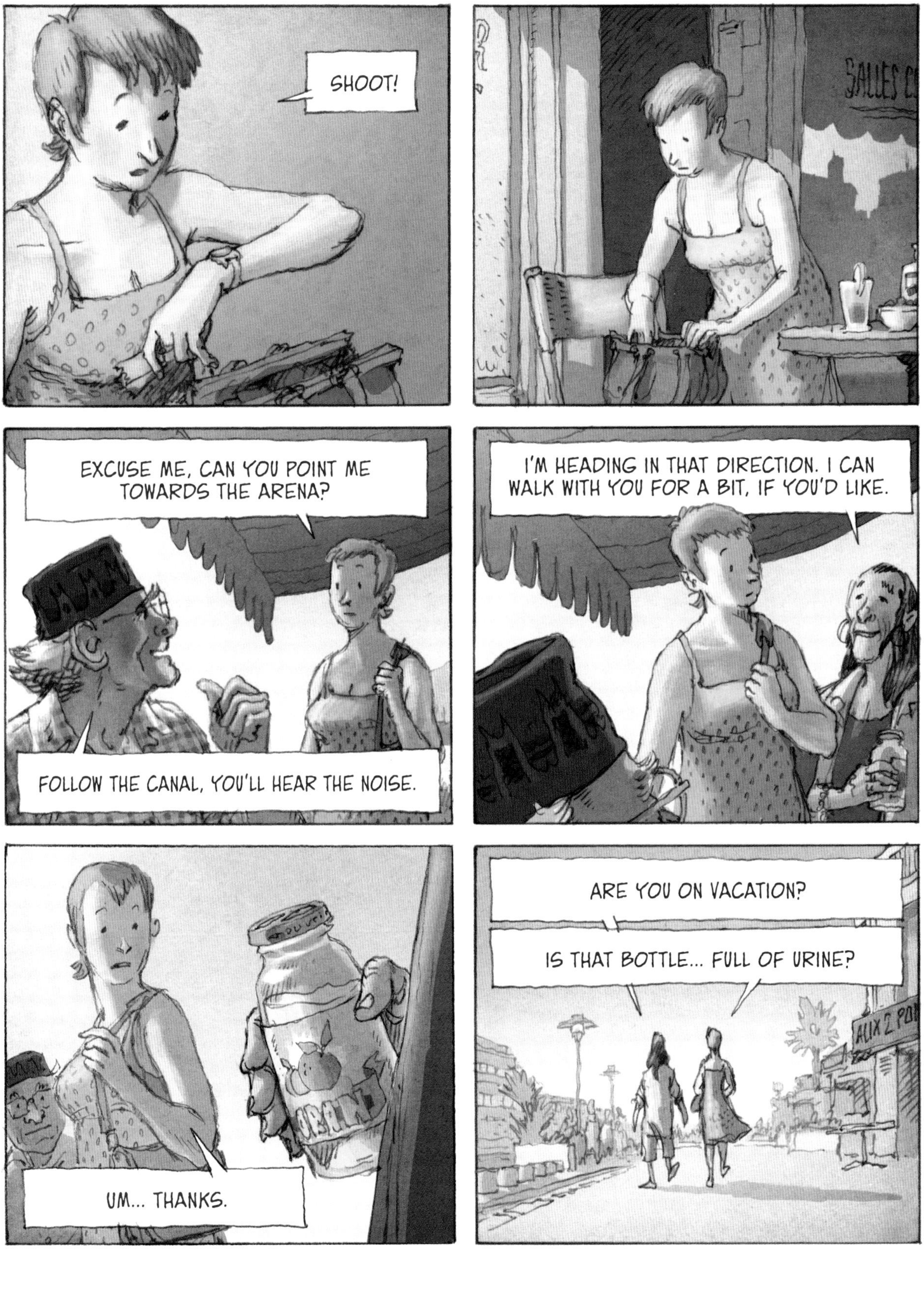
SHOOT!
SALLES
EXCUSE ME, CAN YOU POINT ME TOWARDS THE ARENA?
FOLLOW THE CANAL, YOU'LL HEAR THE NOISE.
I'M HEADING IN THAT DIRECTION. I CAN WALK WITH YOU FOR A BIT, IF YOU'D LIKE.
UM... THANKS.
ARE YOU ON VACATION?
IS THAT BOTTLE... FULL OF URINE?
AUX 2 PO

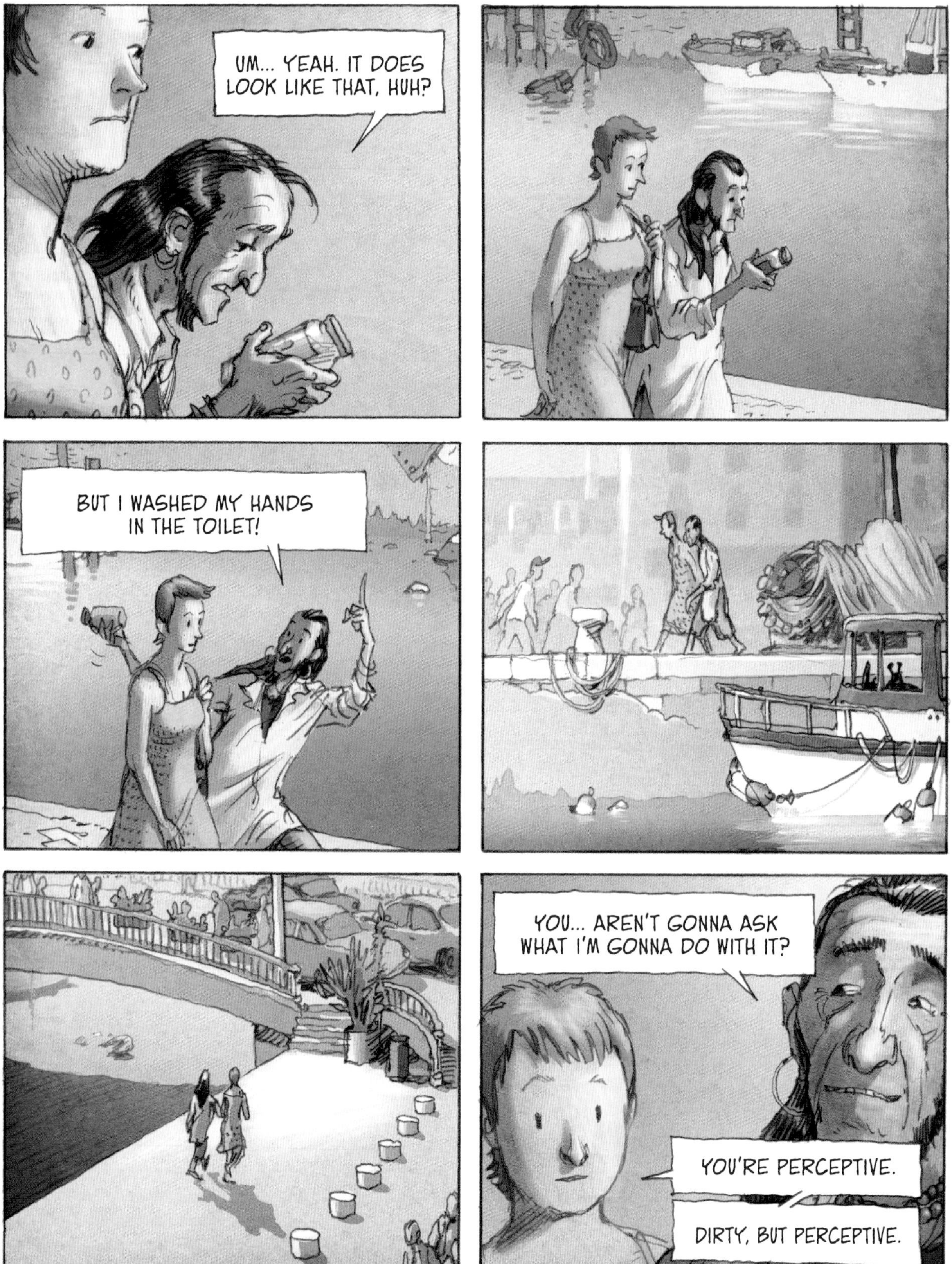
UM... YEAH. IT DOES LOOK LIKE THAT, HUH?
BUT I WASHED MY HANDS IN THE TOILET!
YOU... AREN'T GONNA ASK WHAT I'M GONNA DO WITH IT?
YOU'RE PERCEPTIVE.
DIRTY, BUT PERCEPTIVE.

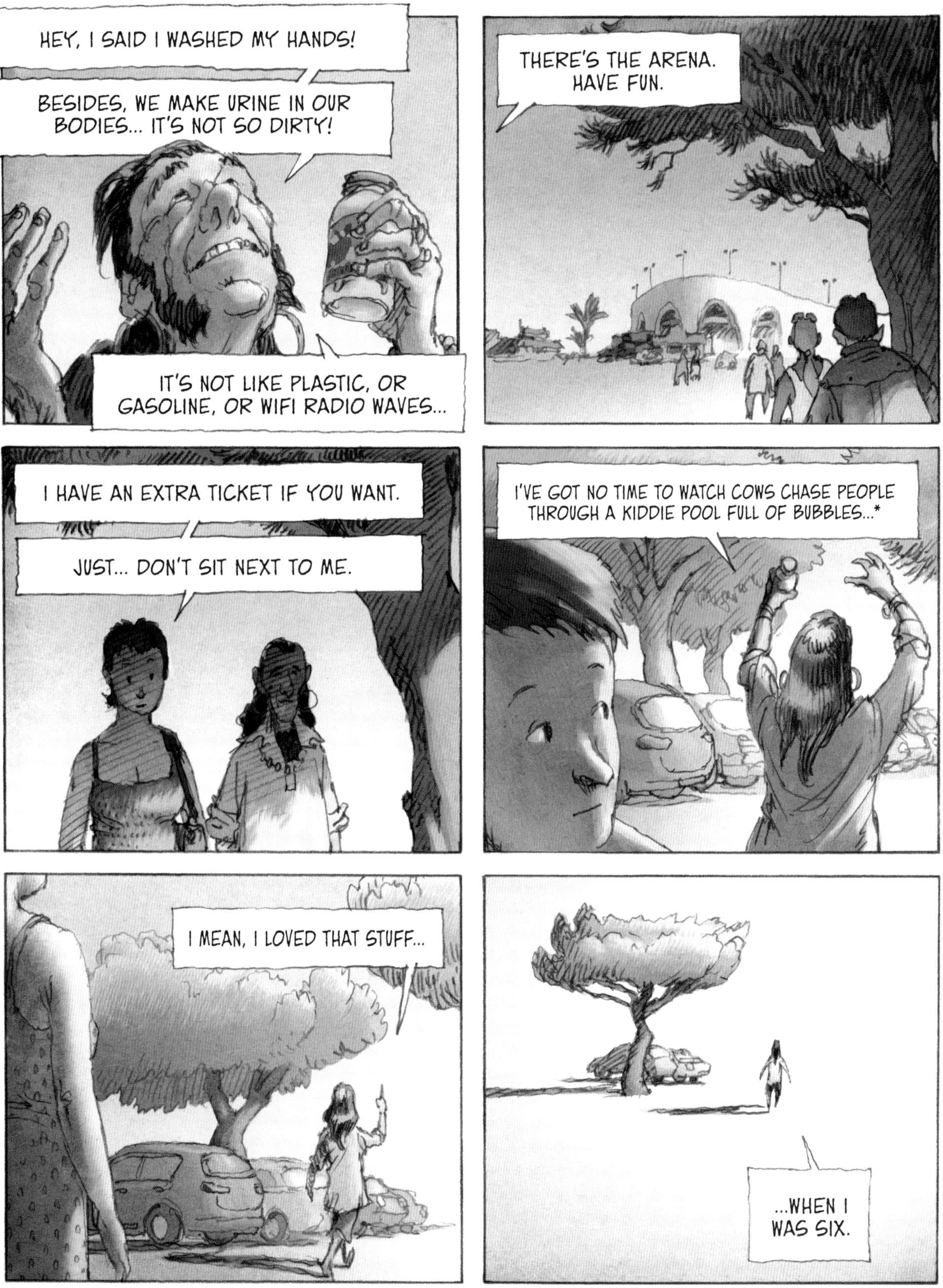
HEY, I SAID I WASHED MY HANDS!
BESIDES, WE MAKE URINE IN OUR BODIES... IT'S NOT SO DIRTY!
IT'S NOT LIKE PLASTIC, OR GASOLINE, OR WIFI RADIO WAVES...
THERE'S THE ARENA. HAVE FUN.
I HAVE AN EXTRA TICKET IF YOU WANT.
JUST... DON'T SIT NEXT TO ME.
I'VE GOT NO TIME TO WATCH COWS CHASE PEOPLE THROUGH A KIDDIE POOL FULL OF BUBBLES...*
I MEAN, I LOVED THAT STUFF...
...WHEN I WAS SIX.

* The **Taureau-Piscine** is a popular attraction in the South of France in which the audience is invited to run with cows around an arena with a pool of foamy water in the middle. The "winner" is whoever can lure or taunt the cow into the pool. It is a type of bullfight, but one where the cows are not hurt or put to death.

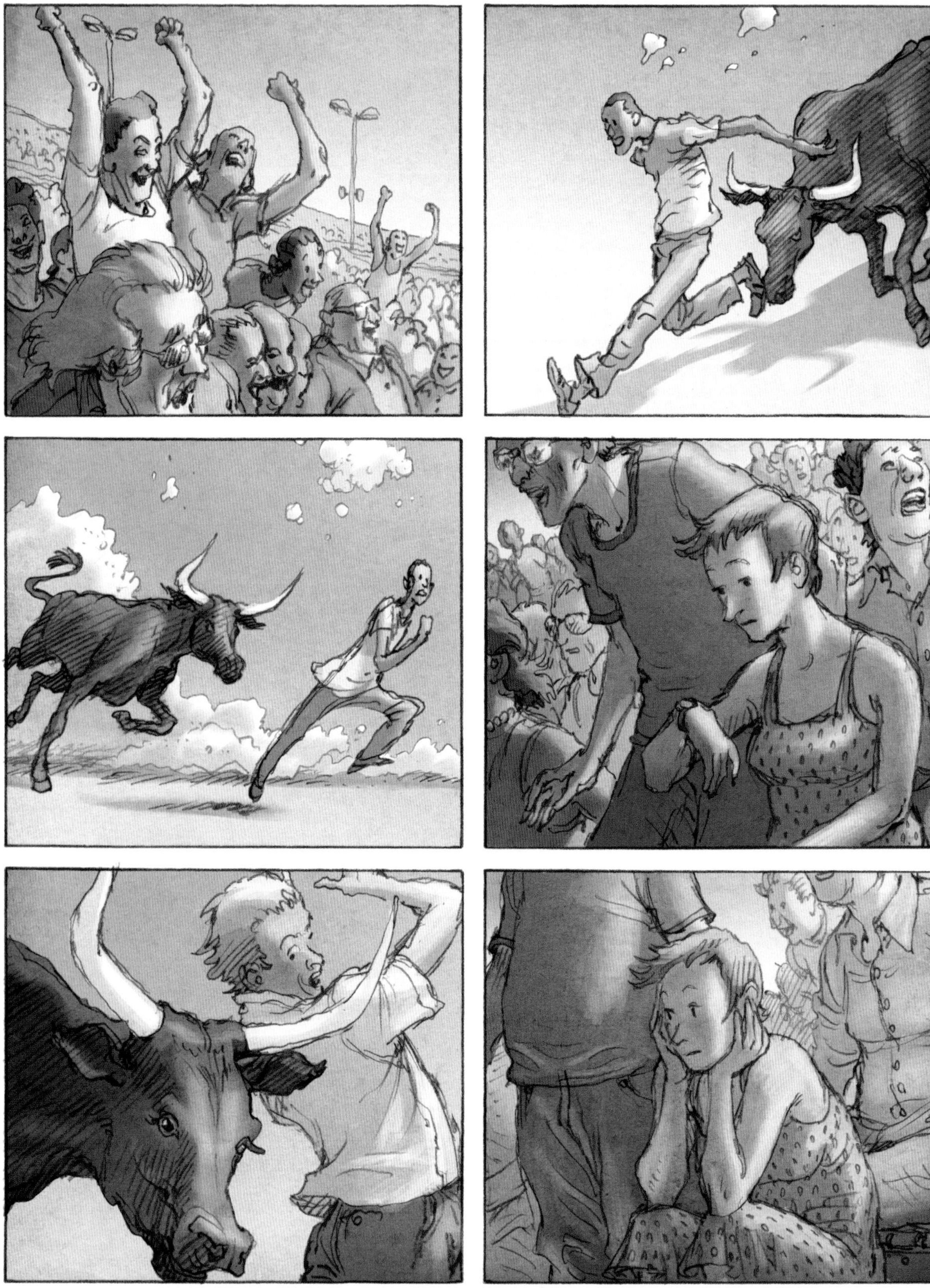

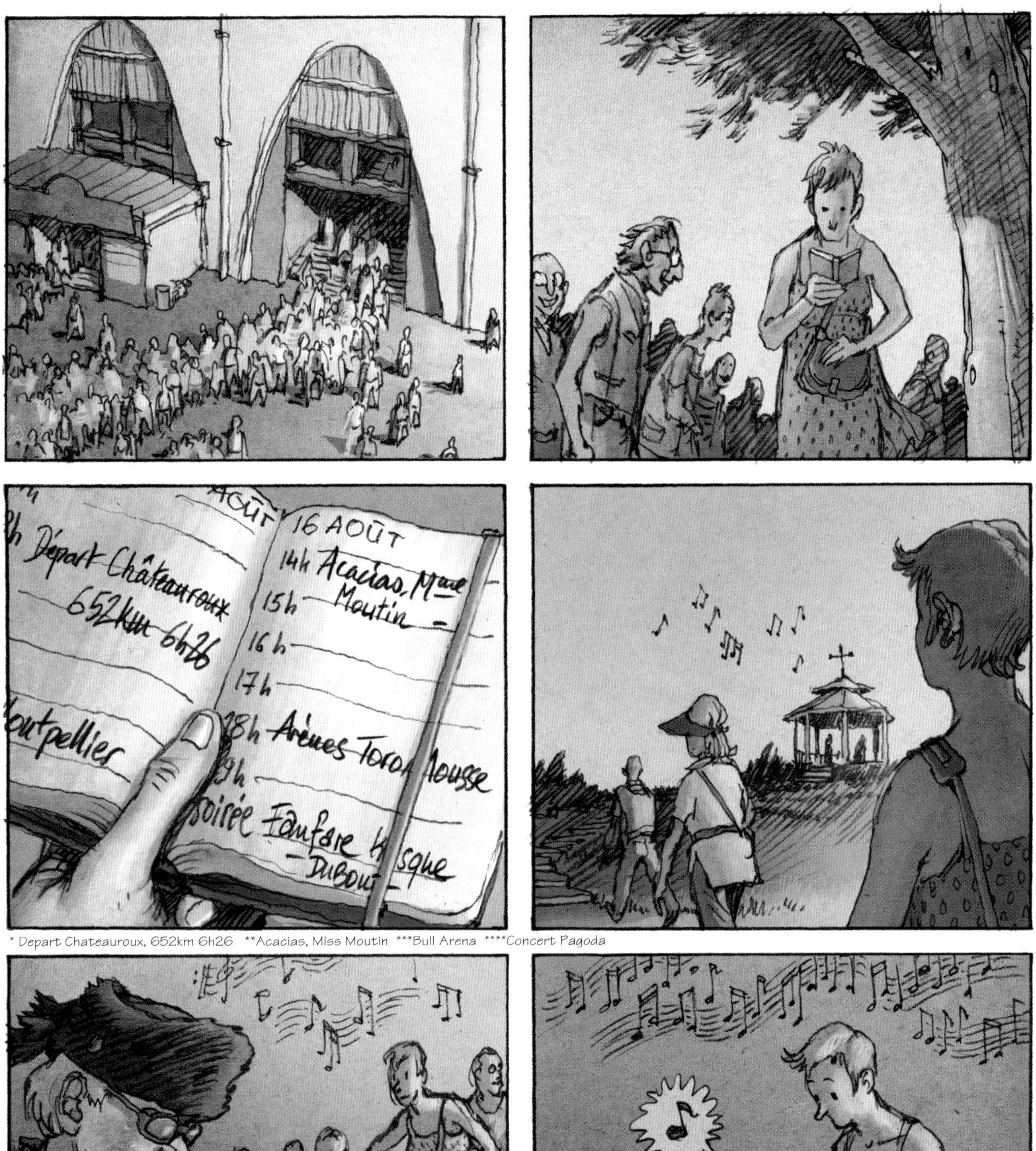
Départ Châteauroux
652km 6h26
16 AOÛT
14h Acacias, Mme Moutin
15h
16h
17h

* Depart Chateauroux, 652km 6h26 **Acacias, Miss Moutin ***Bull Arena ****Concert Pagoda

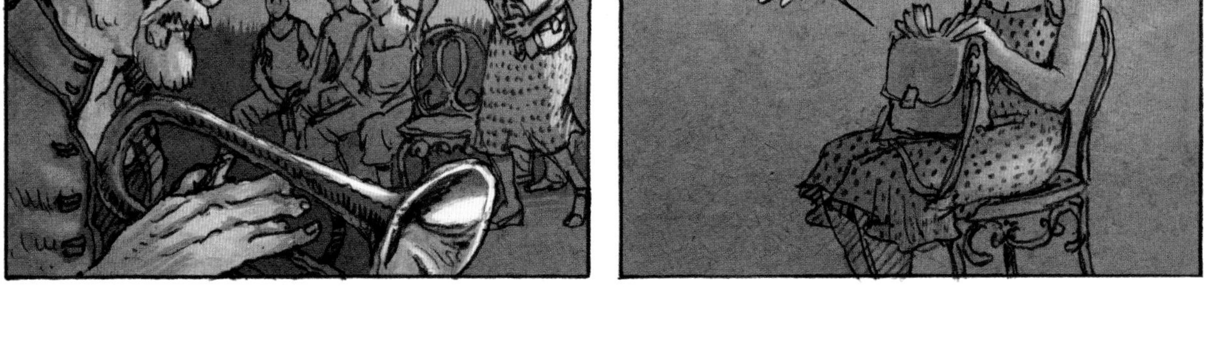

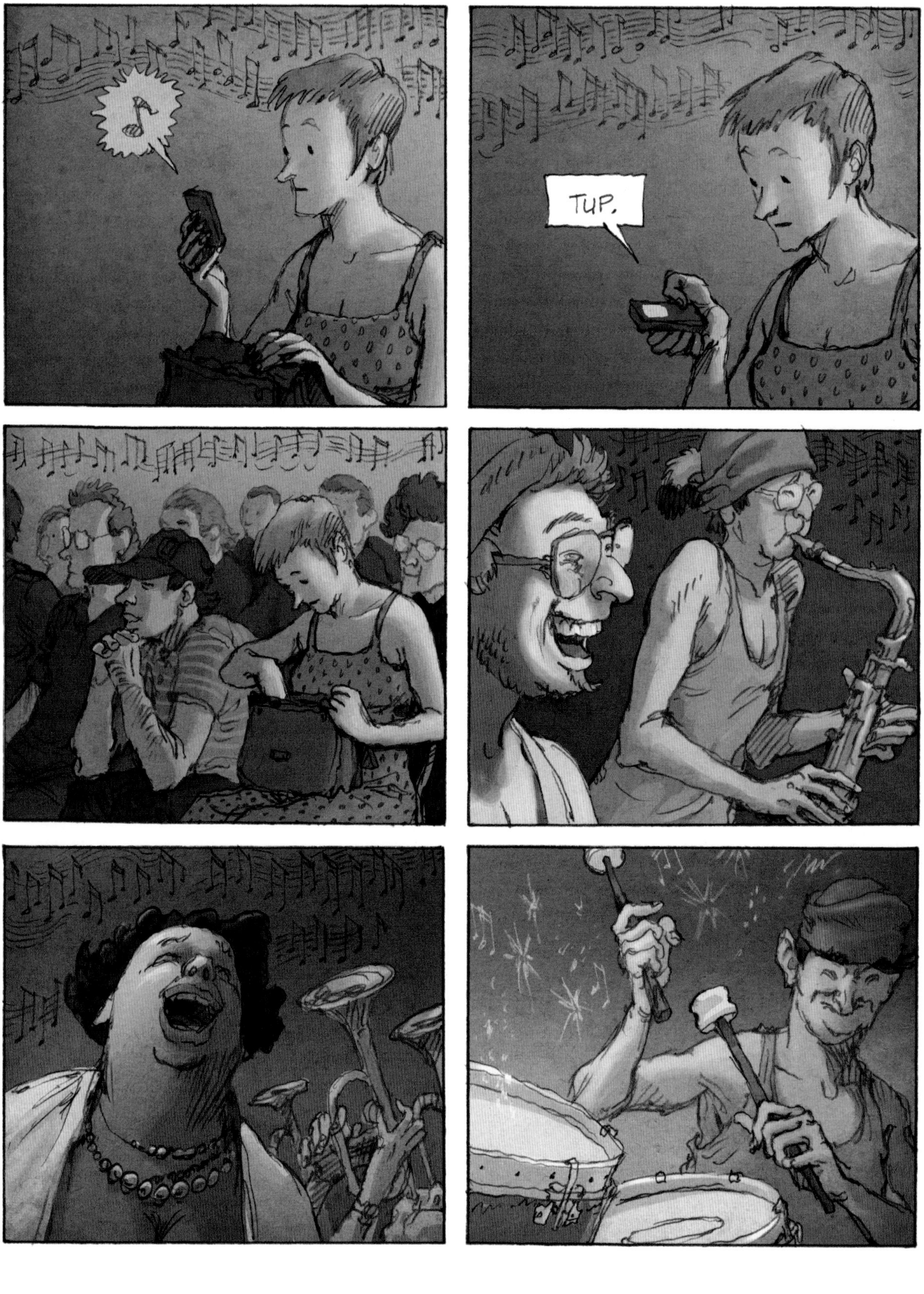
TUP.

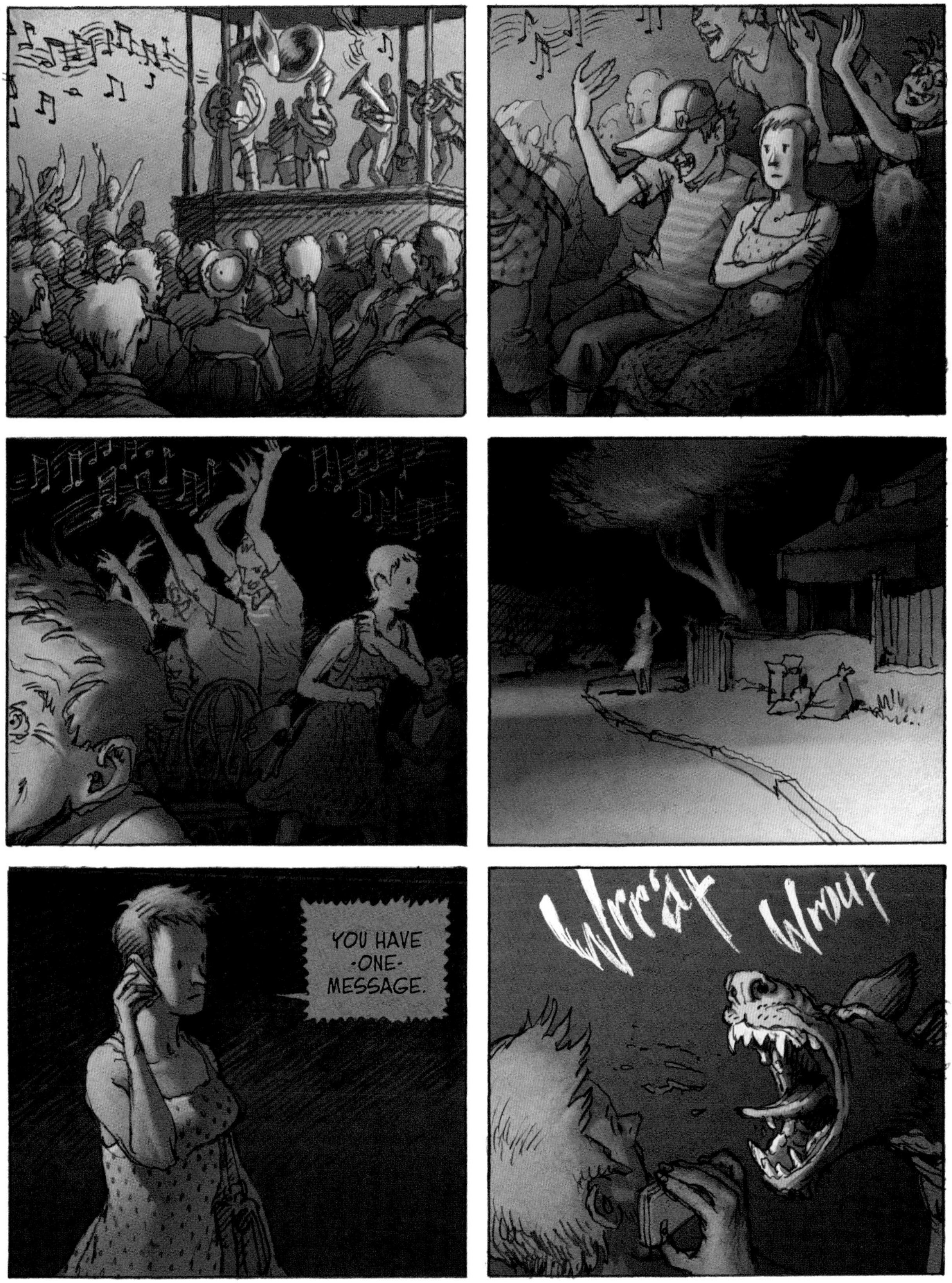
YOU HAVE -ONE- MESSAGE.
Wrr'af Wrouf

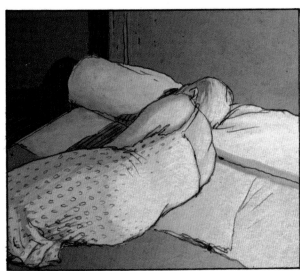
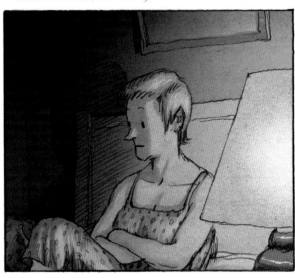

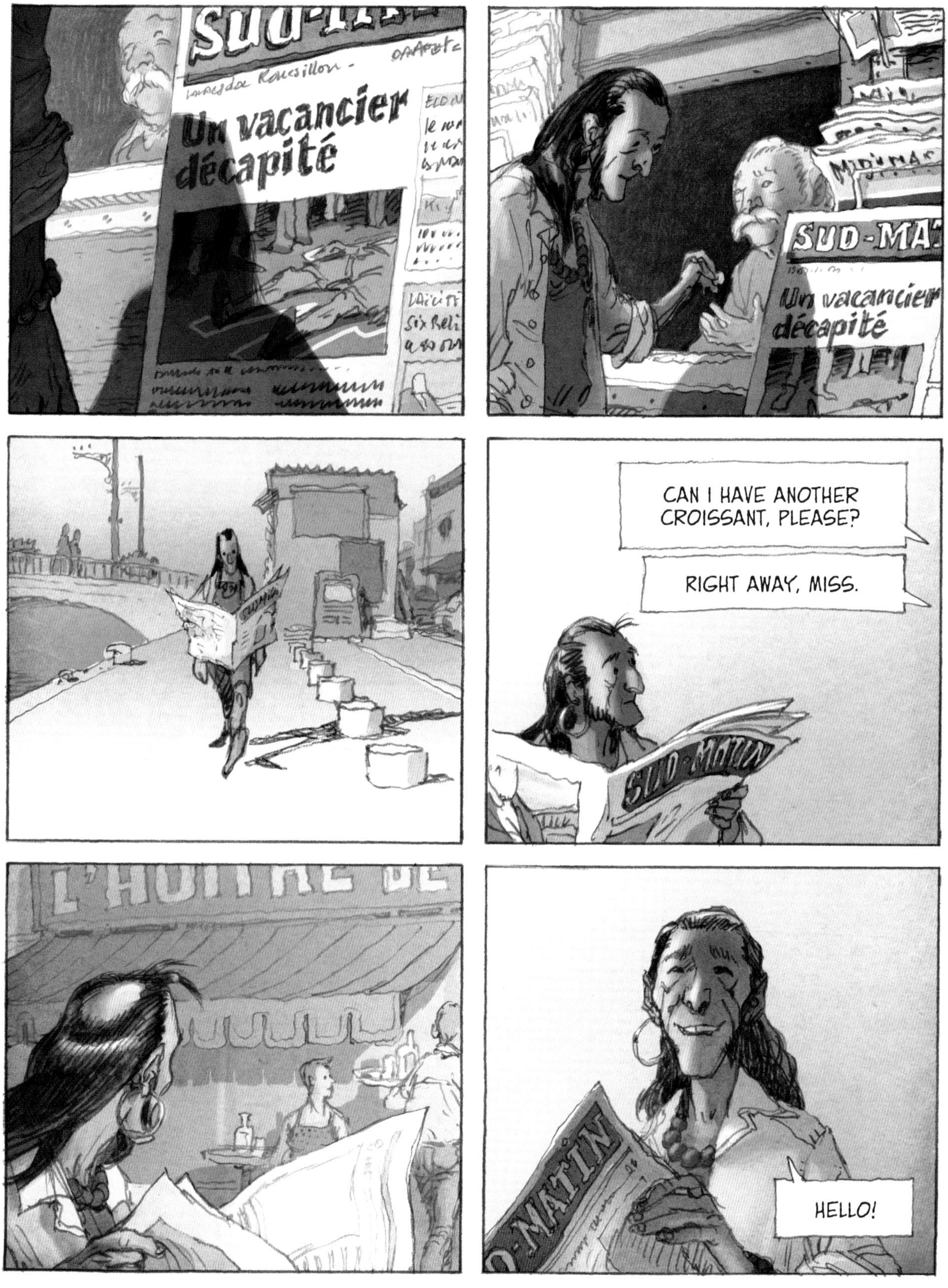
Un vacancier décapité
SUD-MAT
Un vacancier décapité
CAN I HAVE ANOTHER CROISSANT, PLEASE?
RIGHT AWAY, MISS.
SUD-MATIN
HELLO!

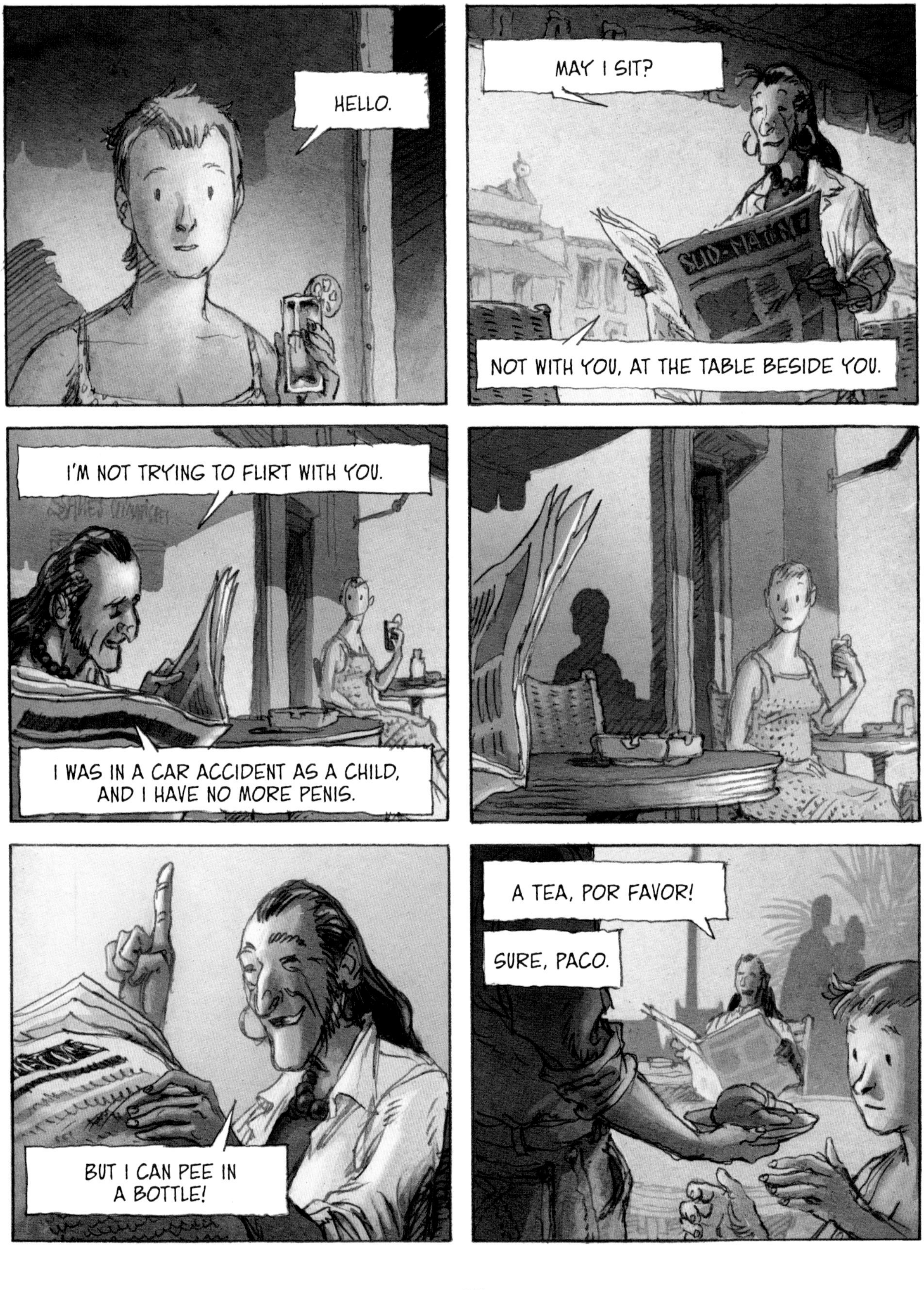
HELLO.
MAY I SIT?
SUD-MATIN
NOT WITH YOU, AT THE TABLE BESIDE YOU.
I'M NOT TRYING TO FLIRT WITH YOU.
I WAS IN A CAR ACCIDENT AS A CHILD, AND I HAVE NO MORE PENIS.
BUT I CAN PEE IN A BOTTLE!
A TEA, POR FAVOR!
SURE, PACO.

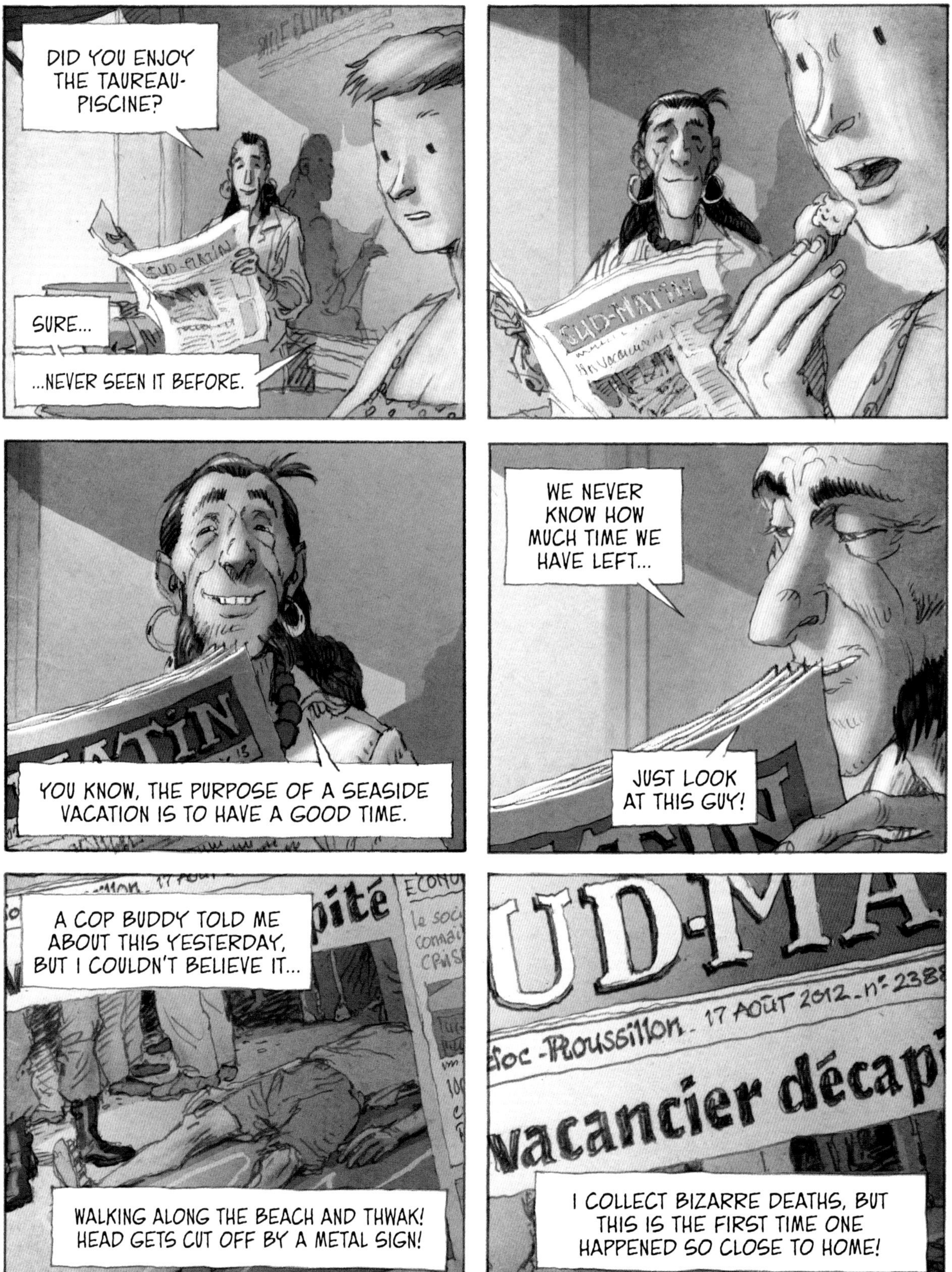

DID YOU ENJOY THE TAUREAU-PISCINE?
SURE...
...NEVER SEEN IT BEFORE.
YOU KNOW, THE PURPOSE OF A SEASIDE VACATION IS TO HAVE A GOOD TIME.
WE NEVER KNOW HOW MUCH TIME WE HAVE LEFT...
JUST LOOK AT THIS GUY!
A COP BUDDY TOLD ME ABOUT THIS YESTERDAY, BUT I COULDN'T BELIEVE IT...
WALKING ALONG THE BEACH AND THWAK! HEAD GETS CUT OFF BY A METAL SIGN!
I COLLECT BIZARRE DEATHS, BUT THIS IS THE FIRST TIME ONE HAPPENED SO CLOSE TO HOME!

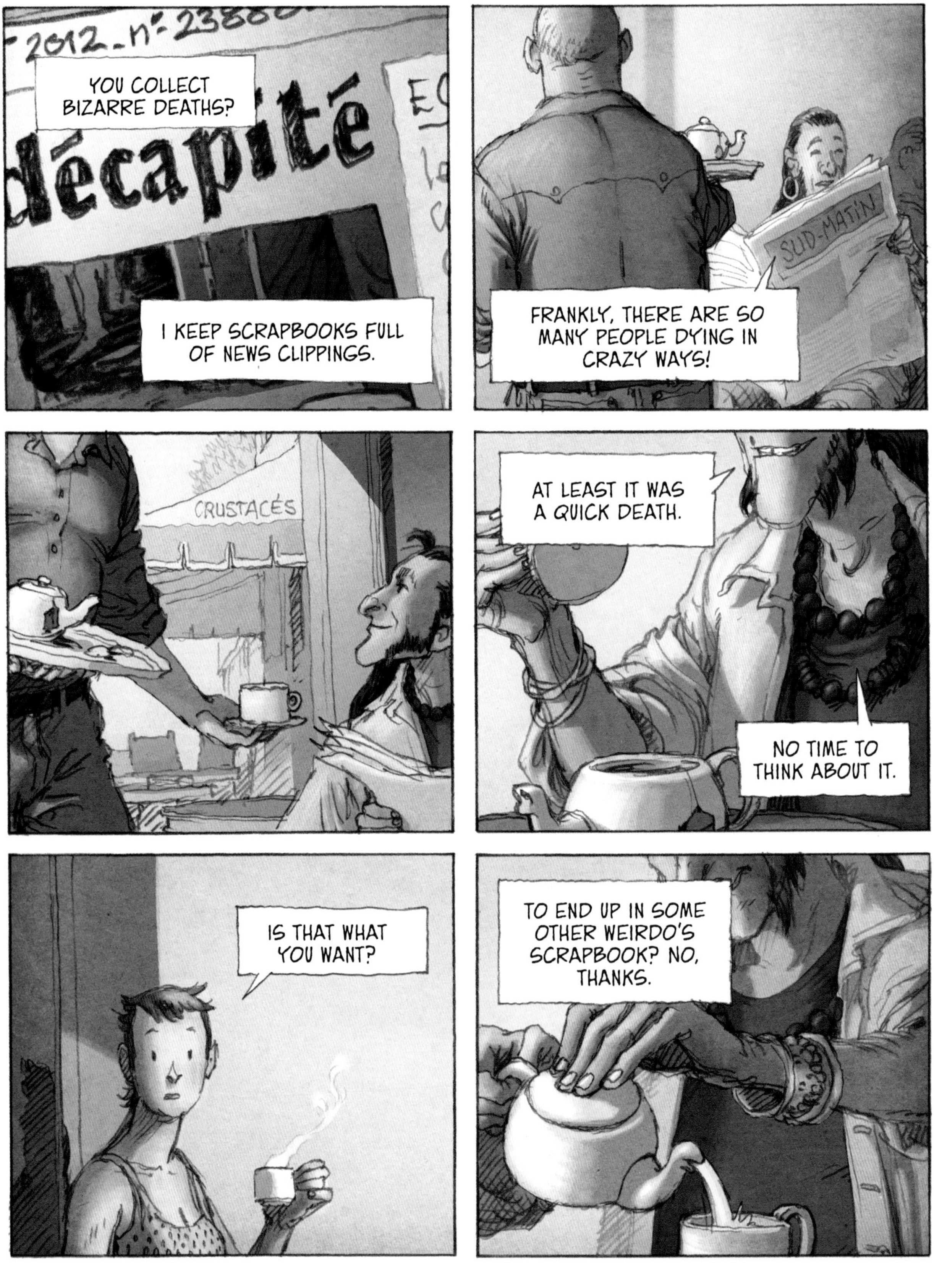
2012_n° 2388
décapité
YOU COLLECT BIZARRE DEATHS?
I KEEP SCRAPBOOKS FULL OF NEWS CLIPPINGS.
SUD-MATIN
FRANKLY, THERE ARE SO MANY PEOPLE DYING IN CRAZY WAYS!
CRUSTACÉS
AT LEAST IT WAS A QUICK DEATH.
NO TIME TO THINK ABOUT IT.
IS THAT WHAT YOU WANT?
TO END UP IN SOME OTHER WEIRDO'S SCRAPBOOK? NO, THANKS.

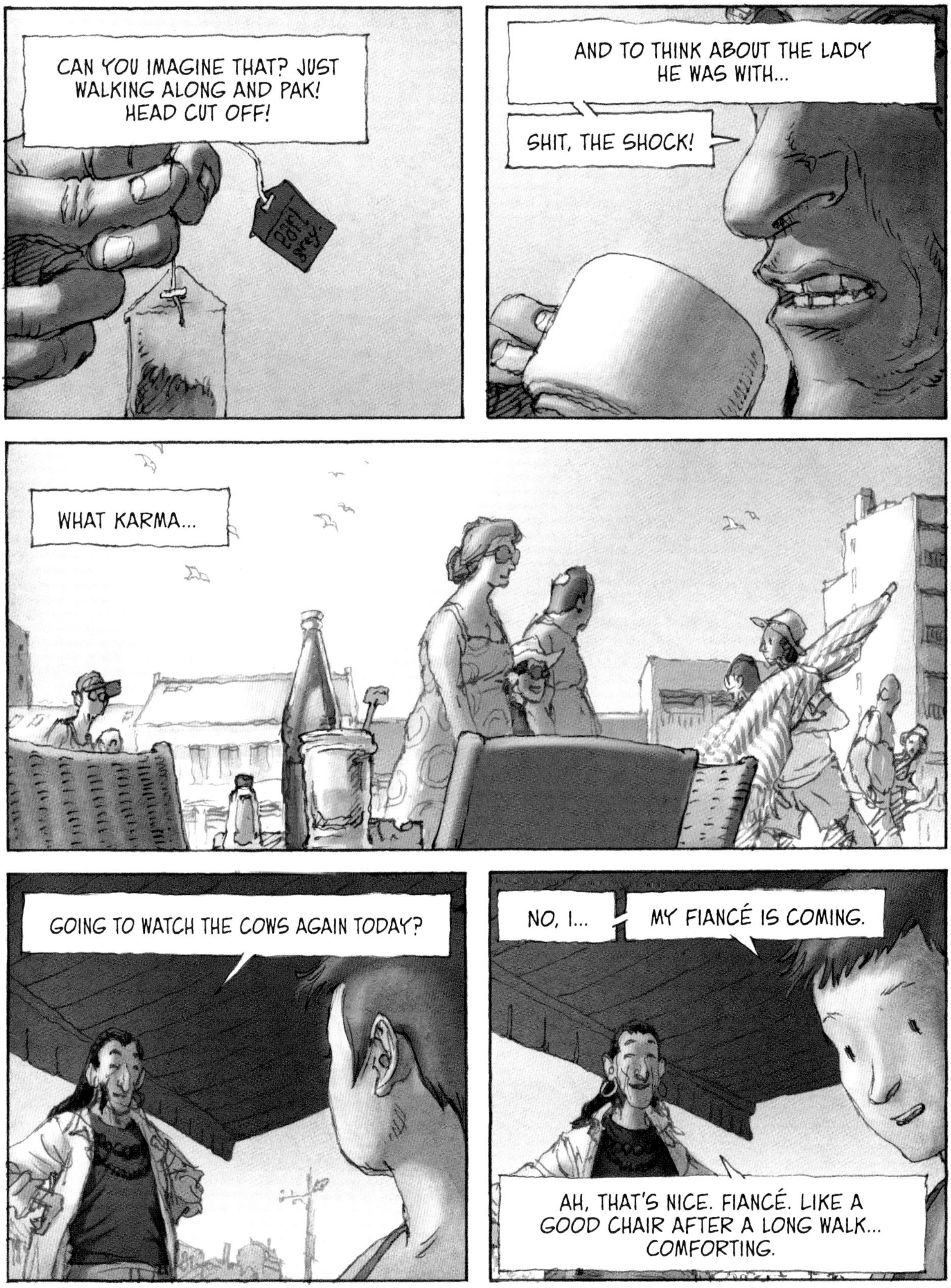
CAN YOU IMAGINE THAT? JUST WALKING ALONG AND PAK! HEAD CUT OFF!
AND TO THINK ABOUT THE LADY HE WAS WITH...
SHIT, THE SHOCK!
WHAT KARMA...
GOING TO WATCH THE COWS AGAIN TODAY?
NO, I...
MY FIANCÉ IS COMING.
AH, THAT'S NICE. FIANCÉ. LIKE A GOOD CHAIR AFTER A LONG WALK... COMFORTING.

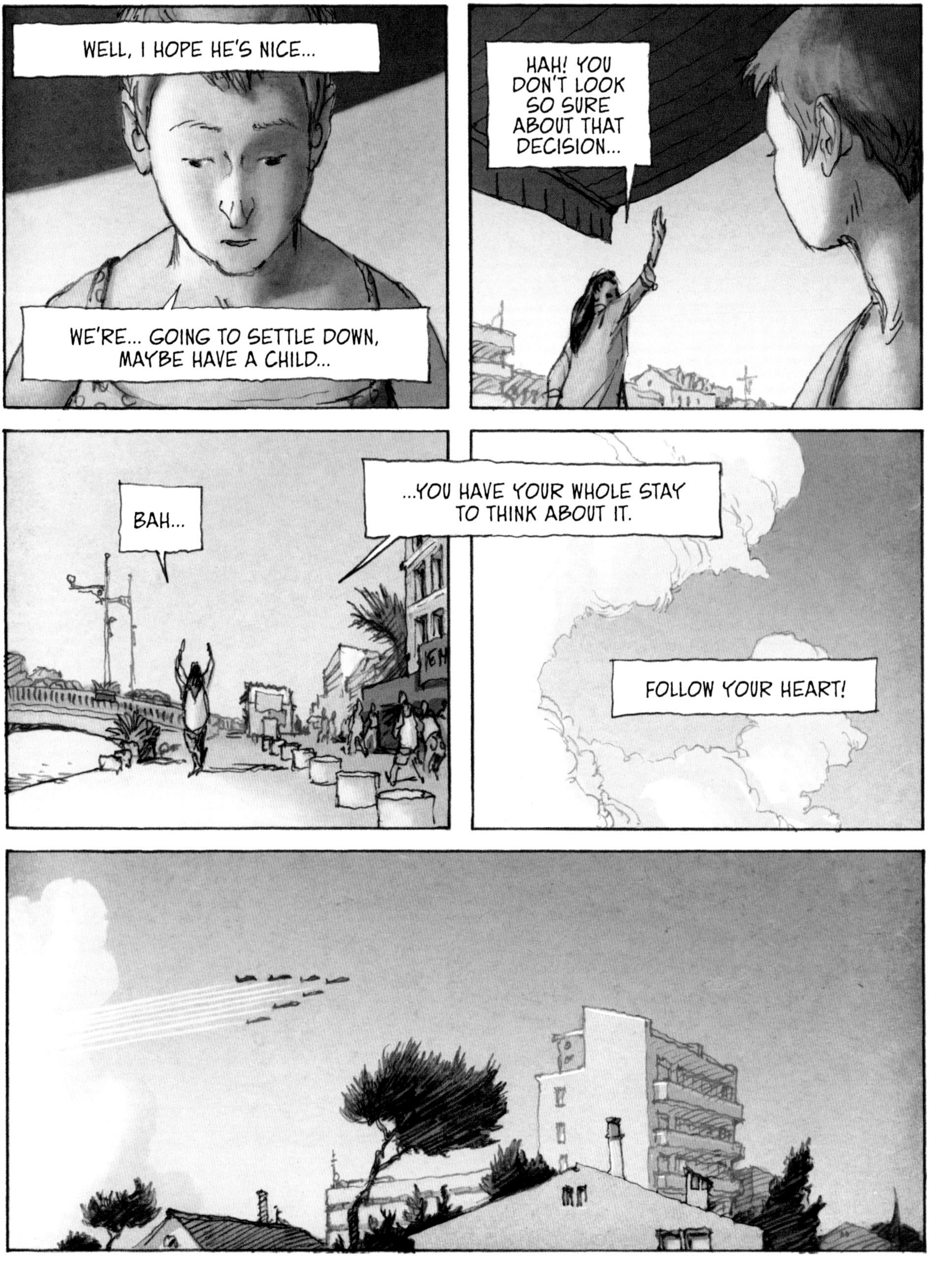
WELL, I HOPE HE'S NICE...
WE'RE... GOING TO SETTLE DOWN, MAYBE HAVE A CHILD...
HAH! YOU DON'T LOOK SO SURE ABOUT THAT DECISION...
BAH...
...YOU HAVE YOUR WHOLE STAY TO THINK ABOUT IT.
FOLLOW YOUR HEART!

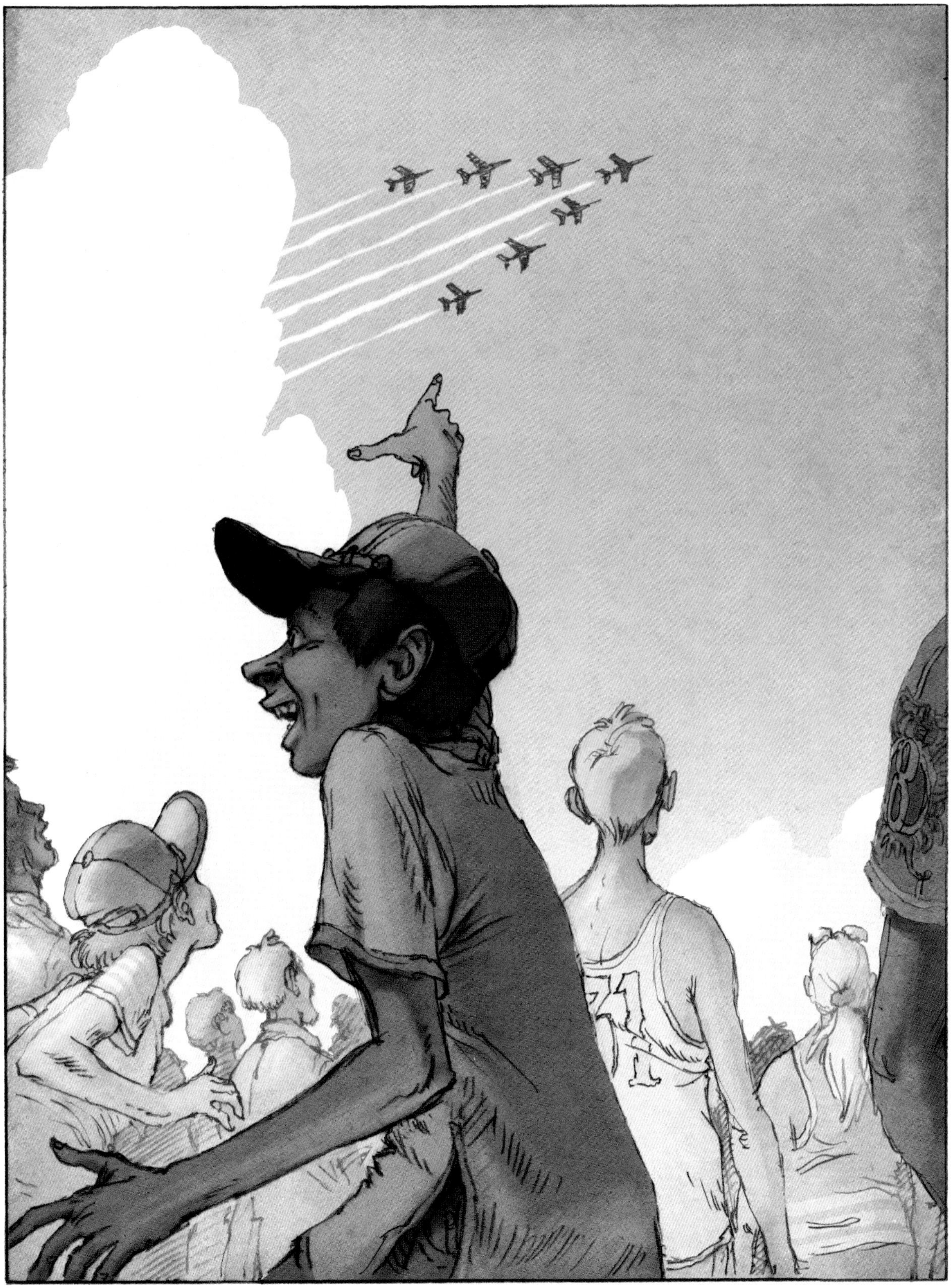

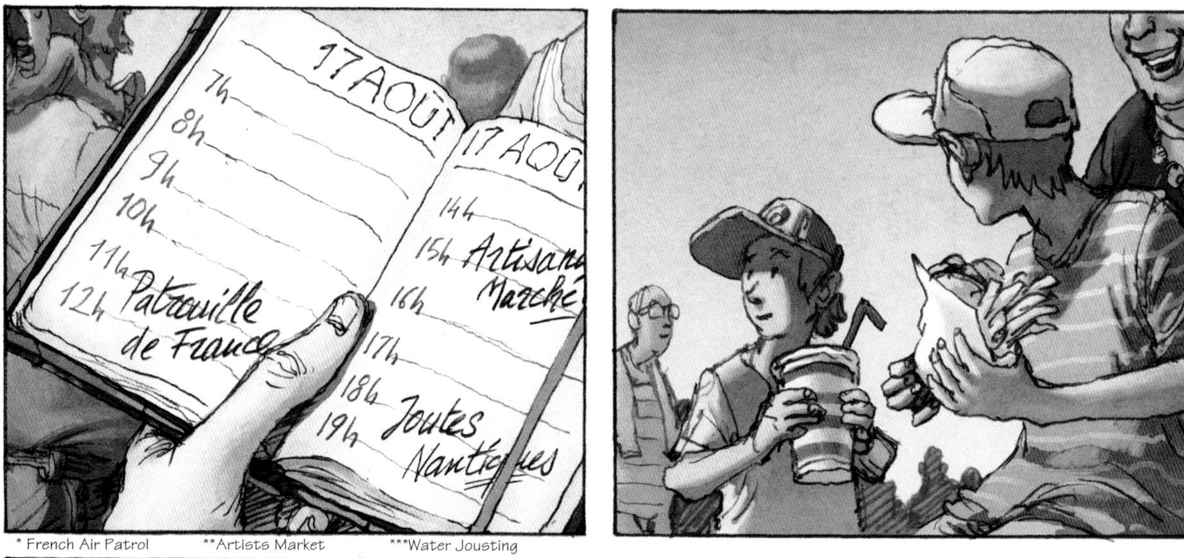

17 AOUT
7h
8h
9h
10h
11h
12h Patrouille de France
17 AOUT
14h
15h Artisans Marché
16h
17h
18h
19h Joutes Nautiques

* French Air Patrol **Artists Market ***Water Jousting

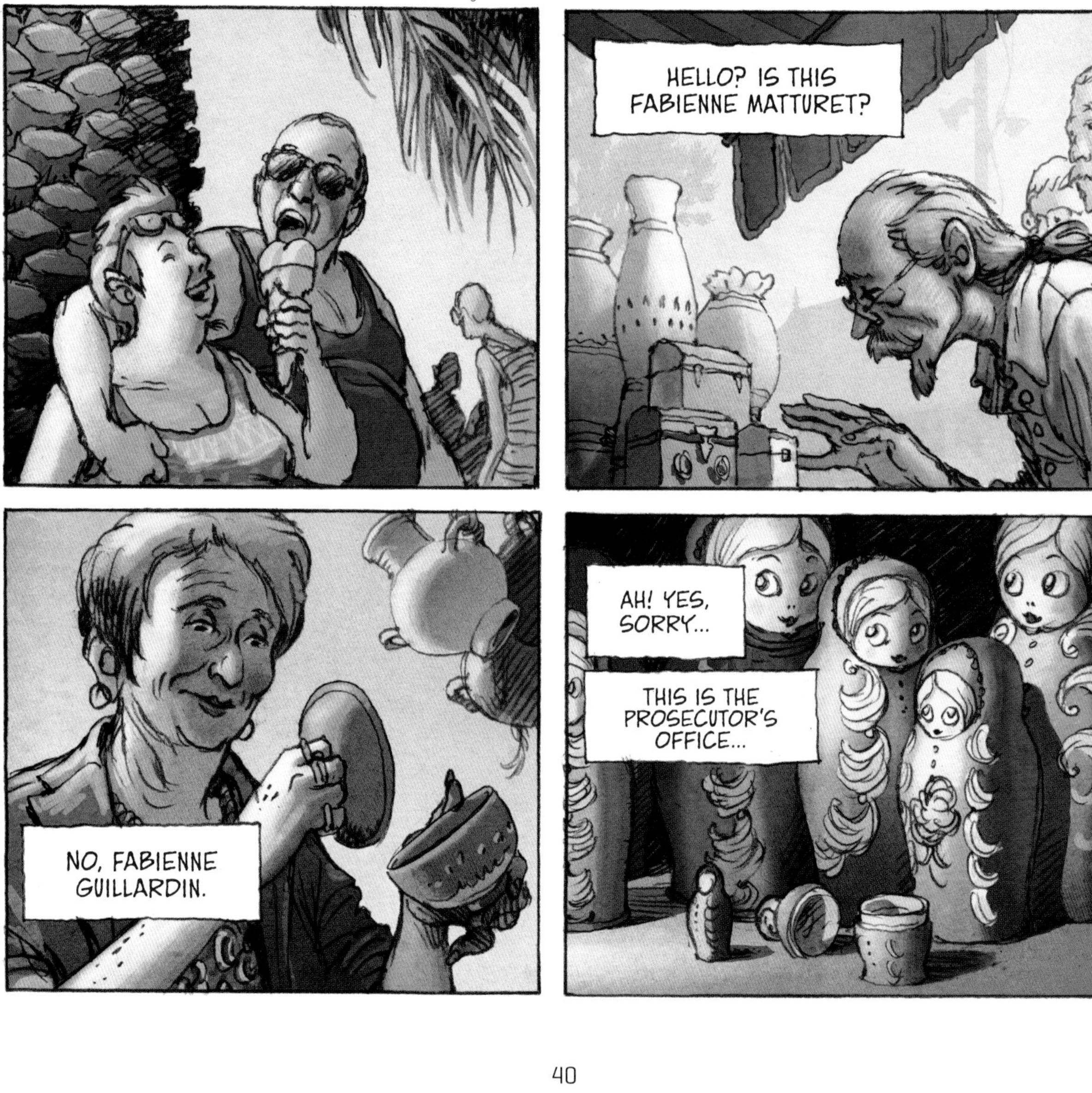

HELLO? IS THIS FABIENNE MATTURET?
NO, FABIENNE GUILLARDIN.
AH! YES, SORRY...
THIS IS THE PROSECUTOR'S OFFICE...

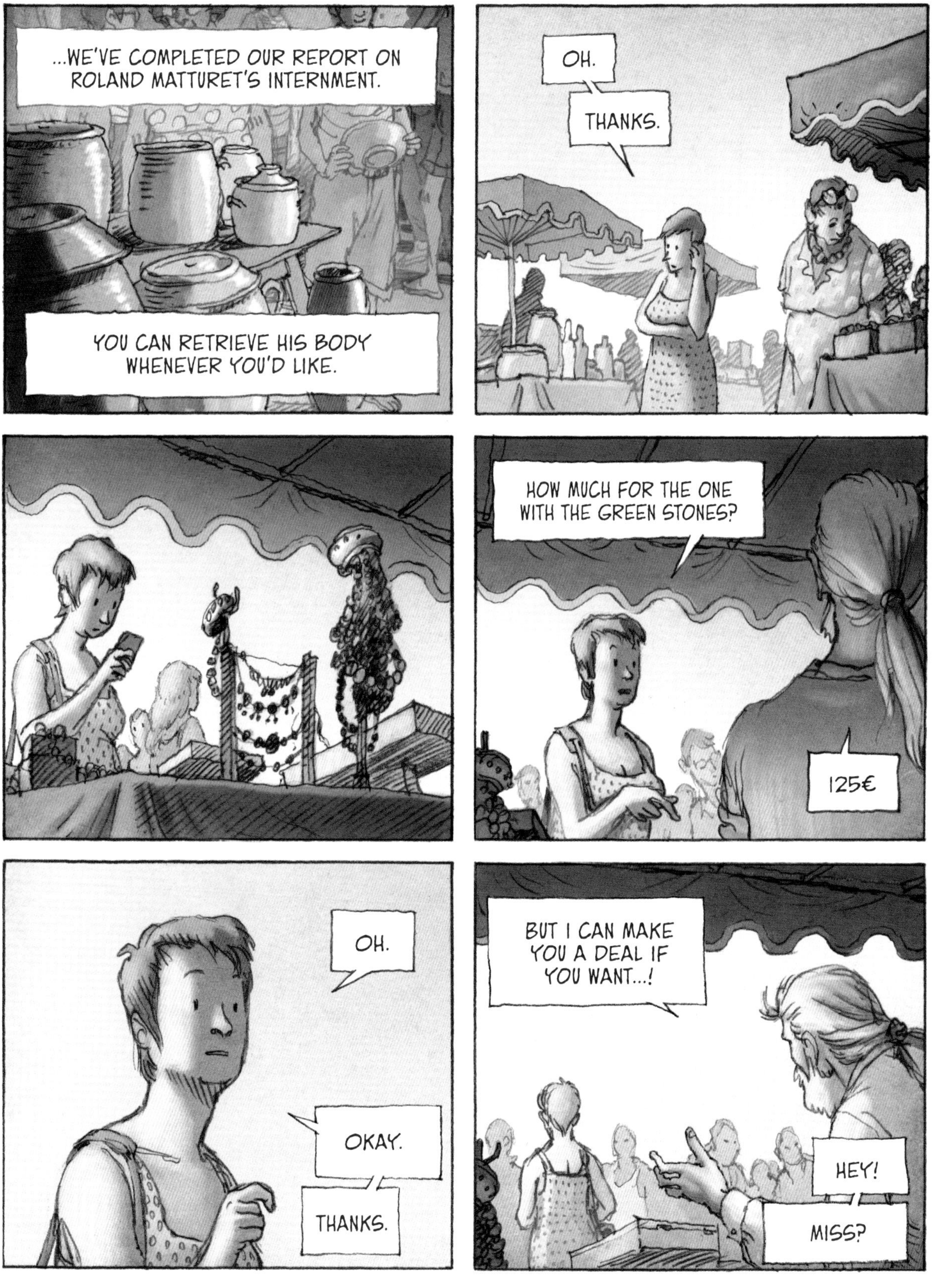
...WE'VE COMPLETED OUR REPORT ON ROLAND MATTURET'S INTERNMENT.
YOU CAN RETRIEVE HIS BODY WHENEVER YOU'D LIKE.
OH.
THANKS.
HOW MUCH FOR THE ONE WITH THE GREEN STONES?
125€
OH.
OKAY.
THANKS.
BUT I CAN MAKE YOU A DEAL IF YOU WANT...!
HEY!
MISS?

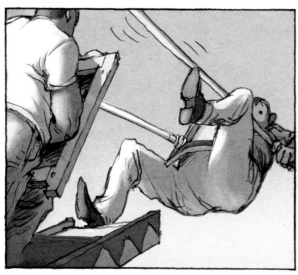

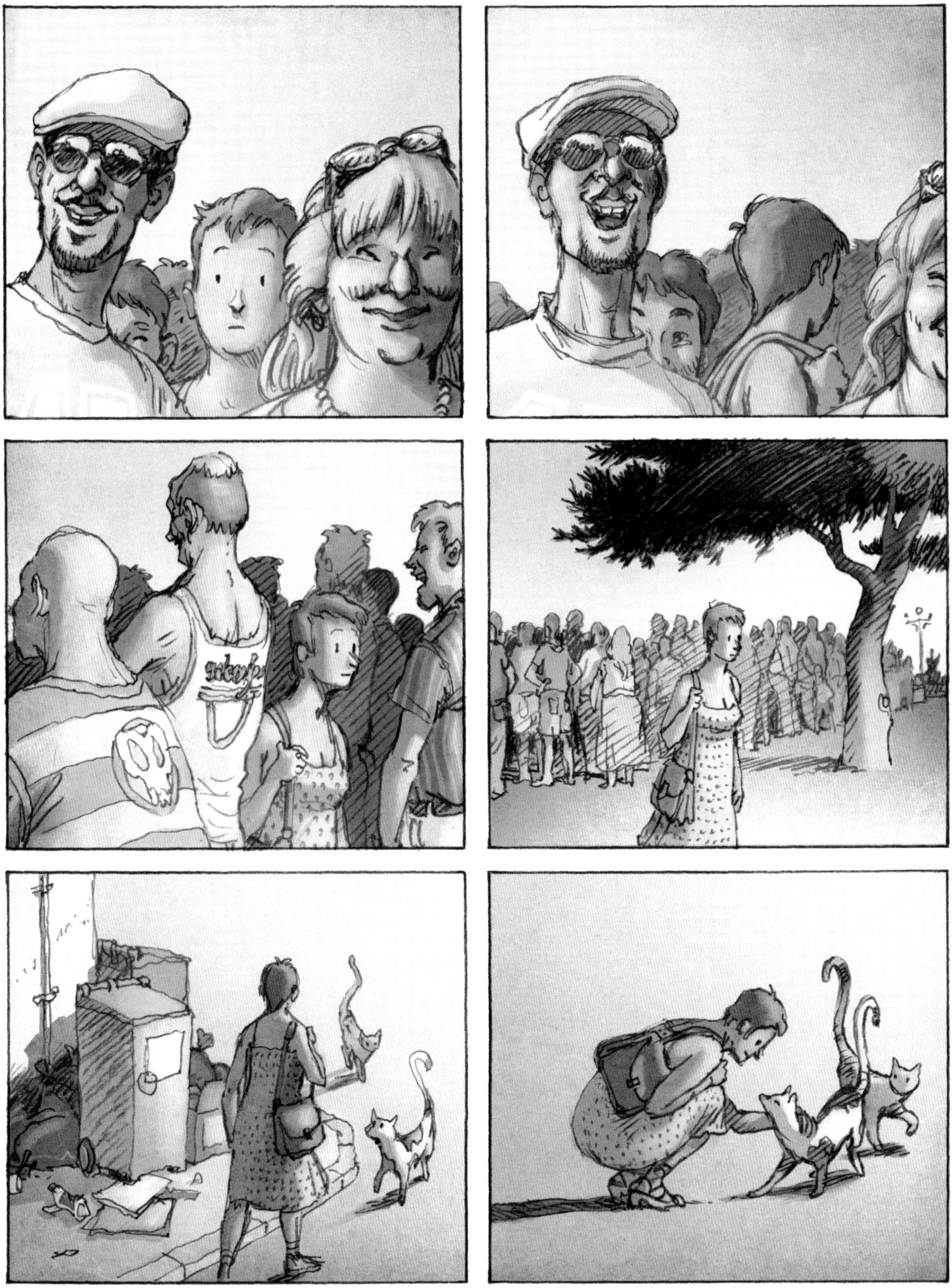

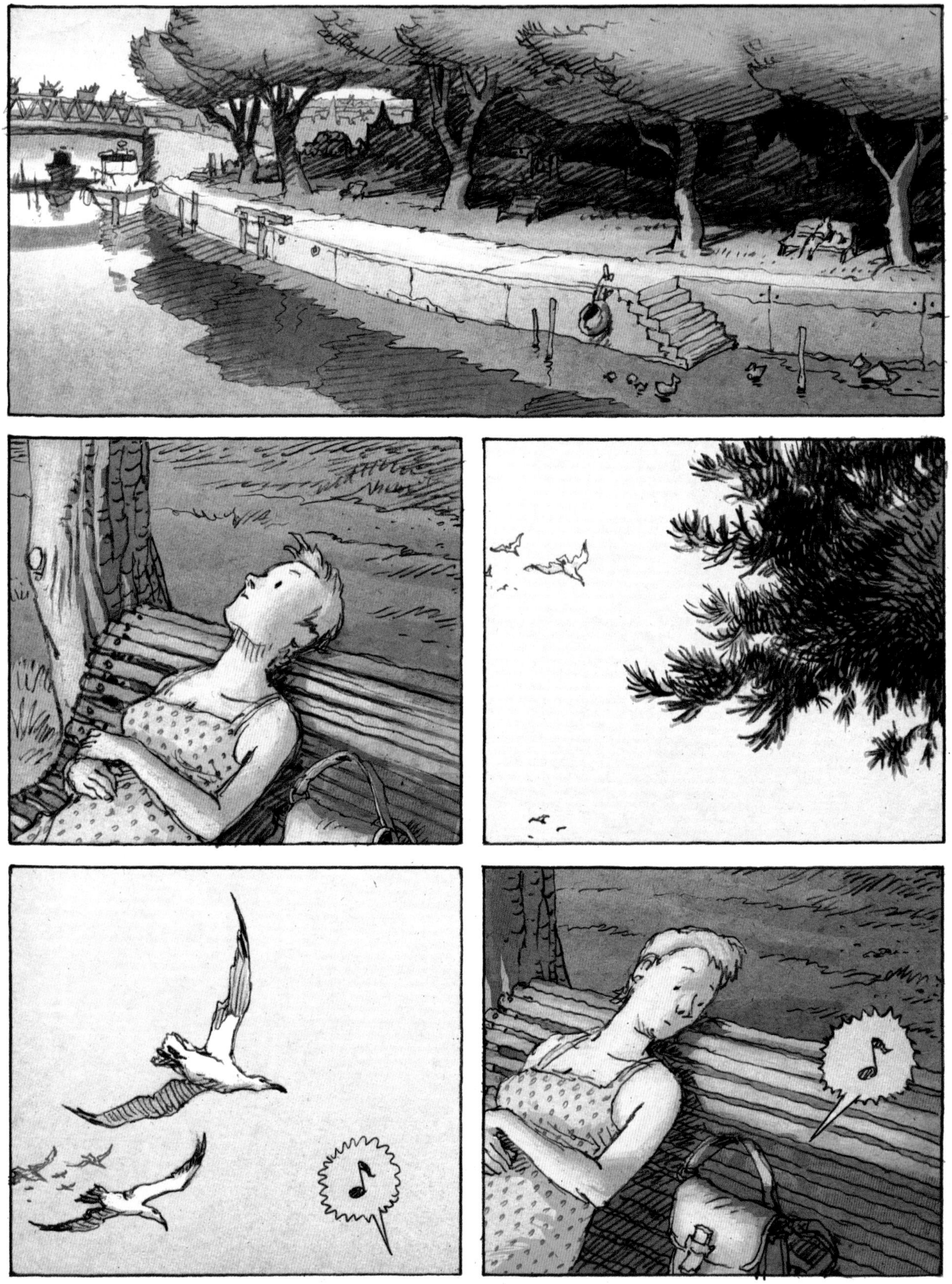

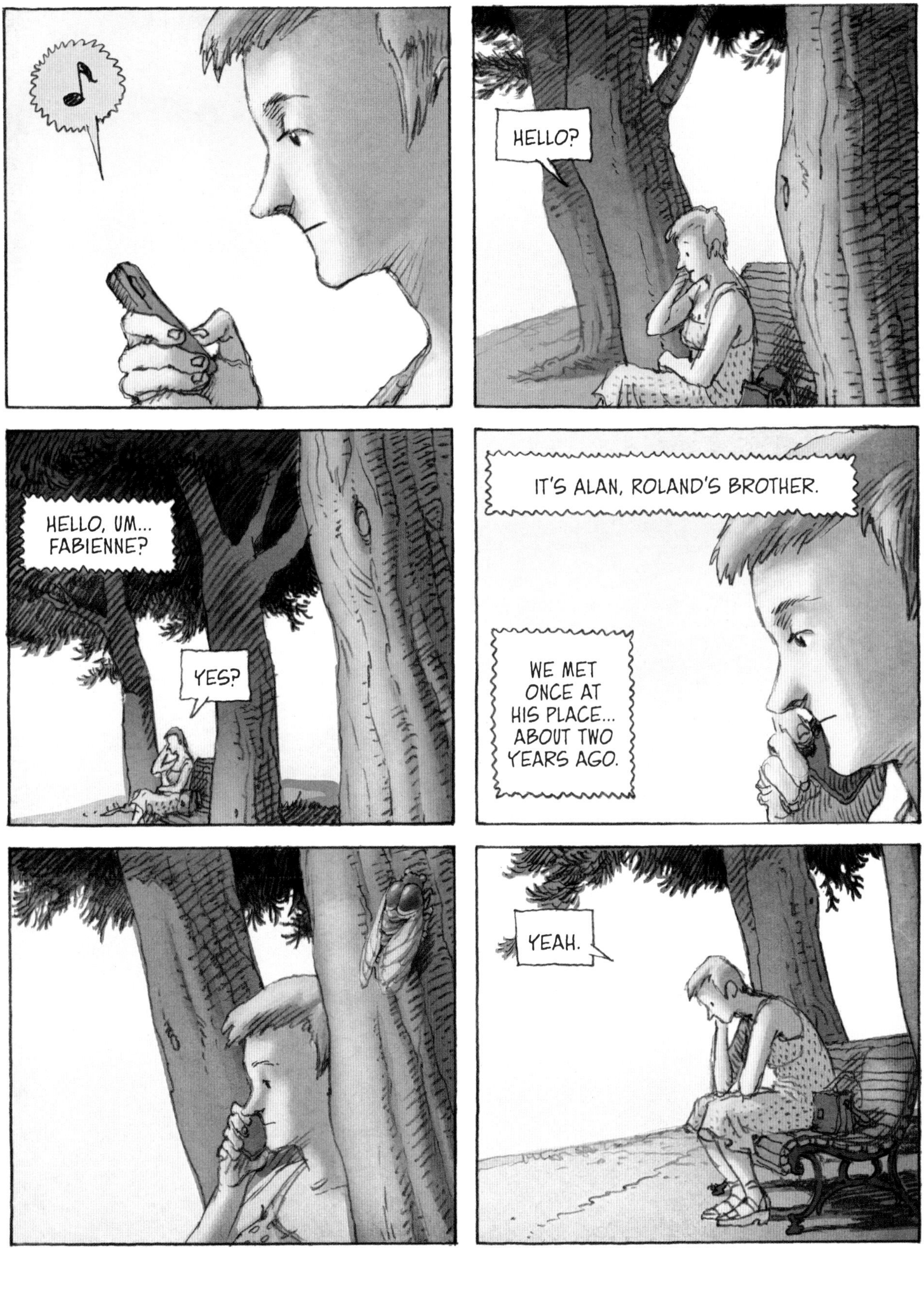
HELLO?
HELLO, UM... FABIENNE?
YES?
IT'S ALAN, ROLAND'S BROTHER.
WE MET ONCE AT HIS PLACE... ABOUT TWO YEARS AGO.
YEAH.

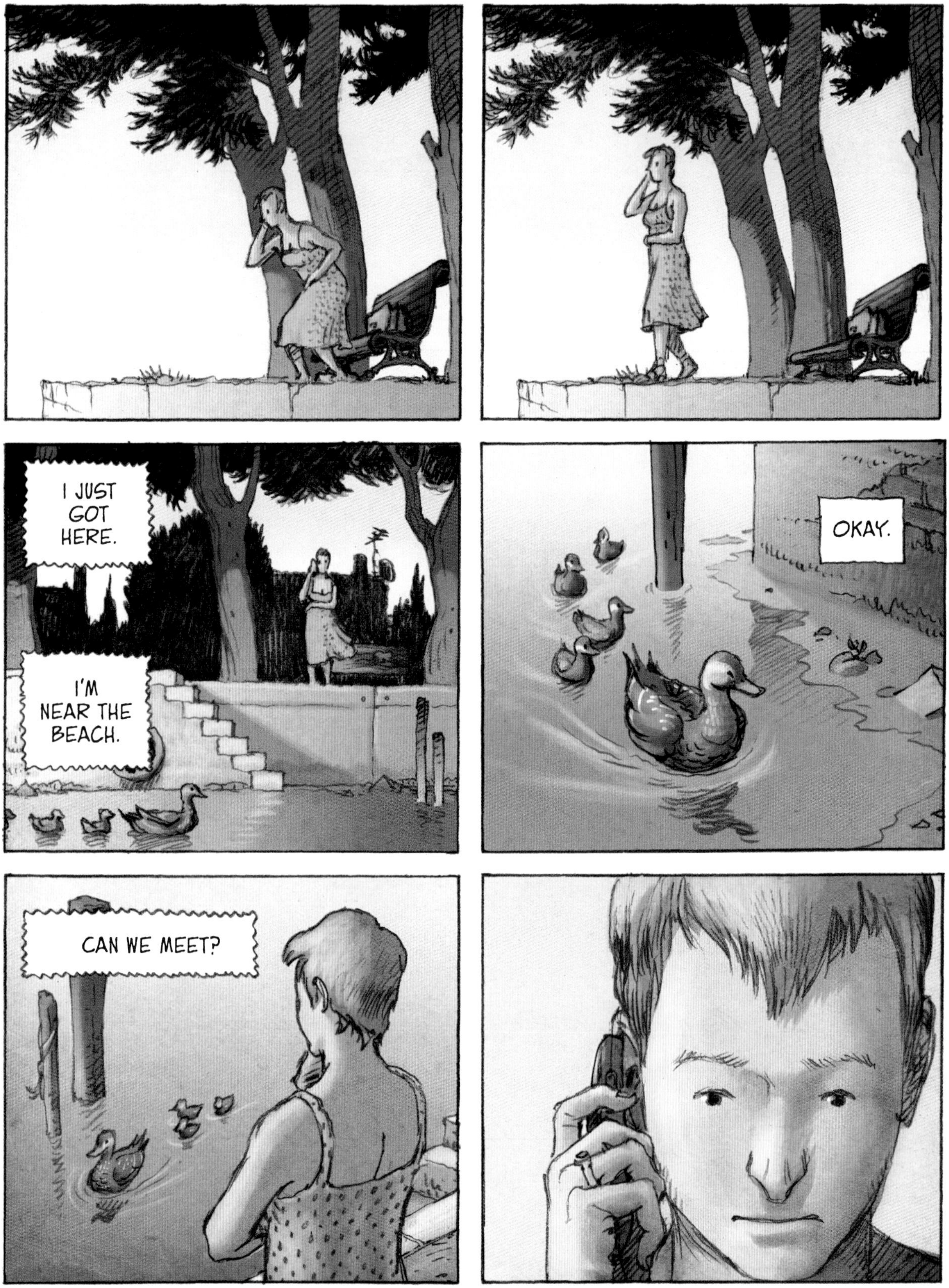
I JUST GOT HERE.
I'M NEAR THE BEACH.
OKAY.
CAN WE MEET?

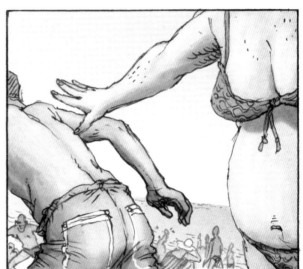

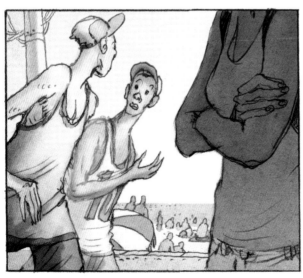

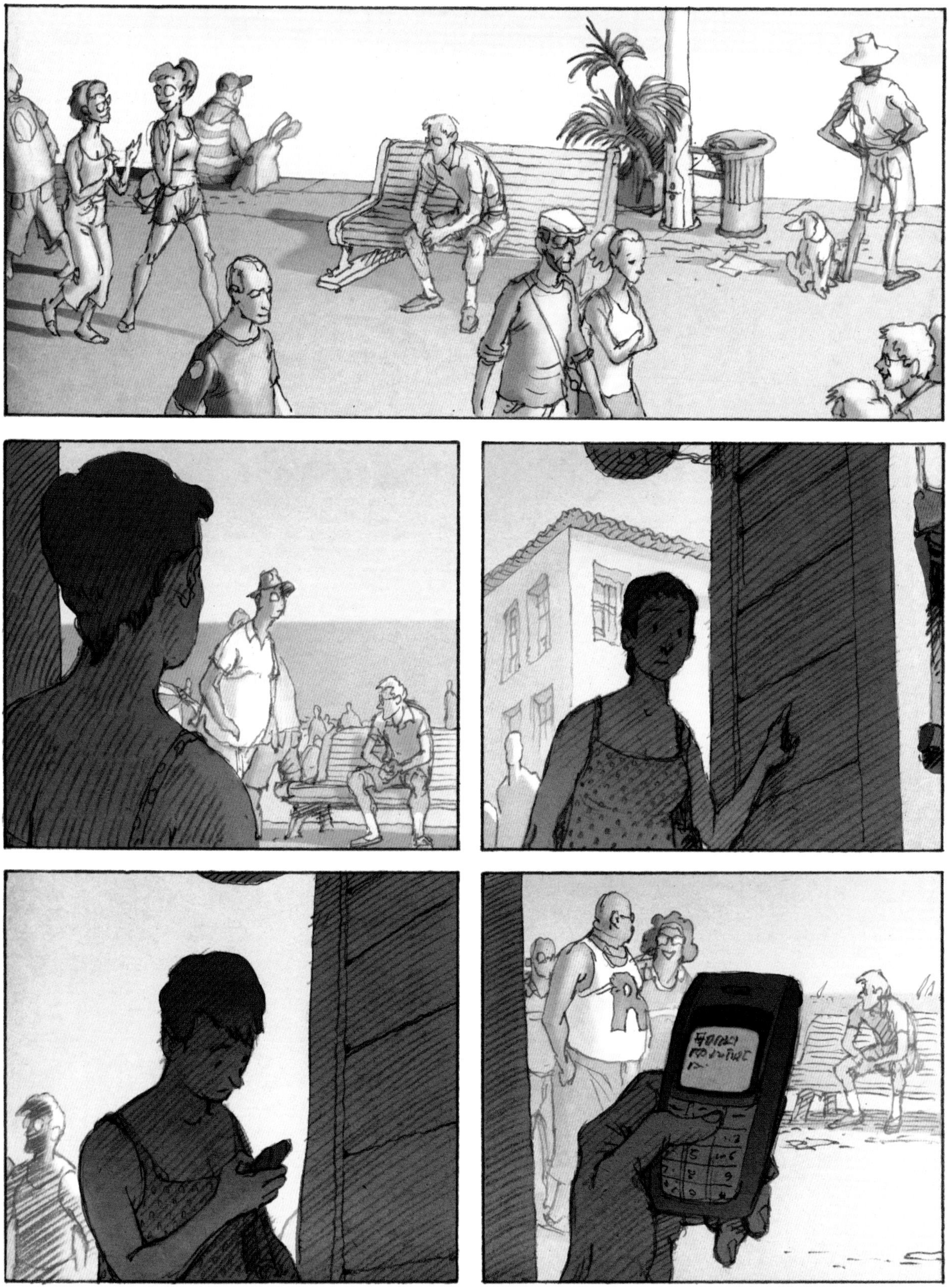

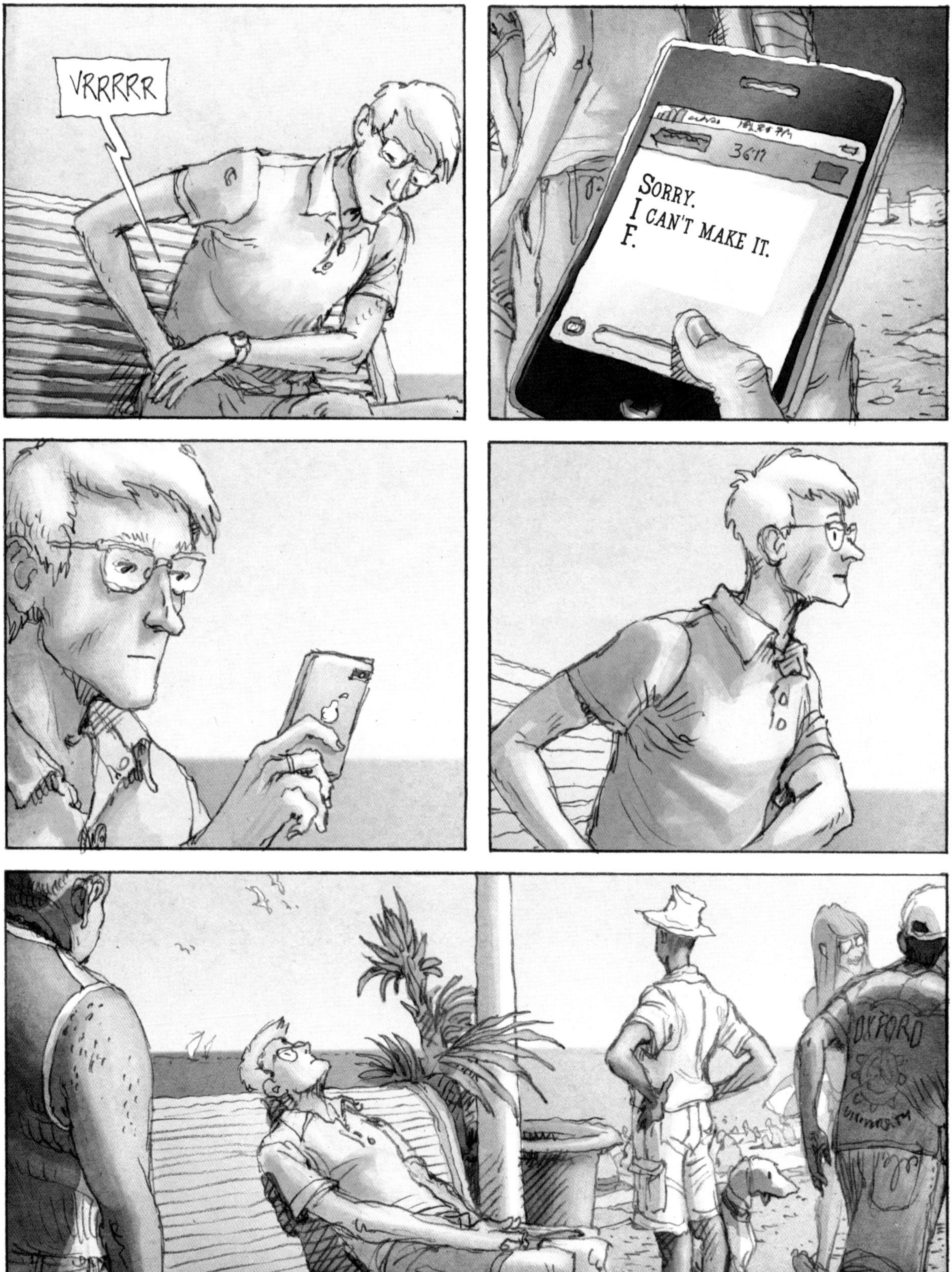
VRRRRR
SORRY.
I CAN'T MAKE IT.
F.
OXFORD

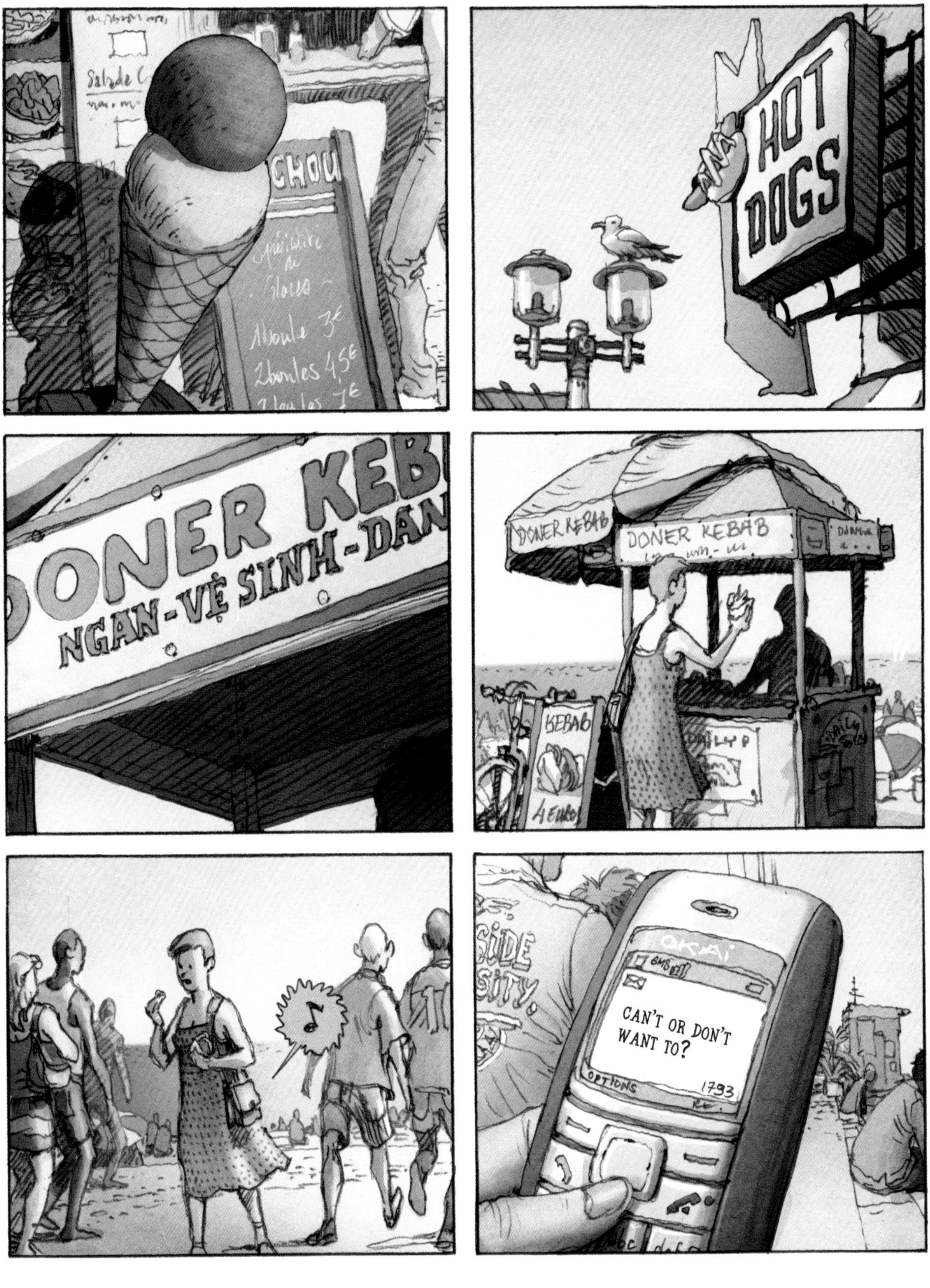
CHOU
HOT DOGS
DONER KEB
NGAN-VỆ SINH-DAN
DONER KEBAB
KEBAB
CAN'T OR DON'T WANT TO?
OPTIONS
1793

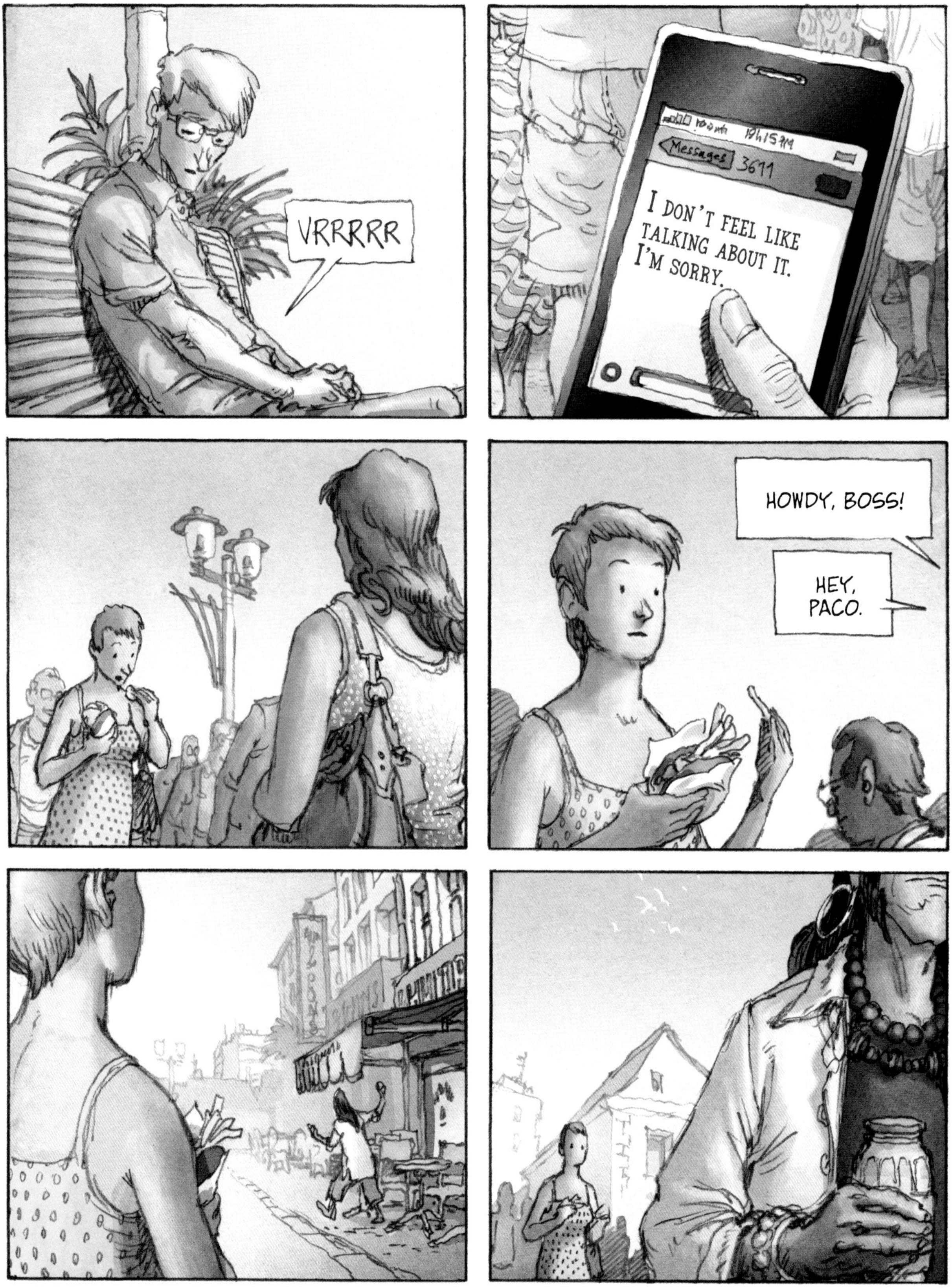
VRRRRR
I DON'T FEEL LIKE TALKING ABOUT IT. I'M SORRY.
HOWDY, BOSS!
HEY, PACO.

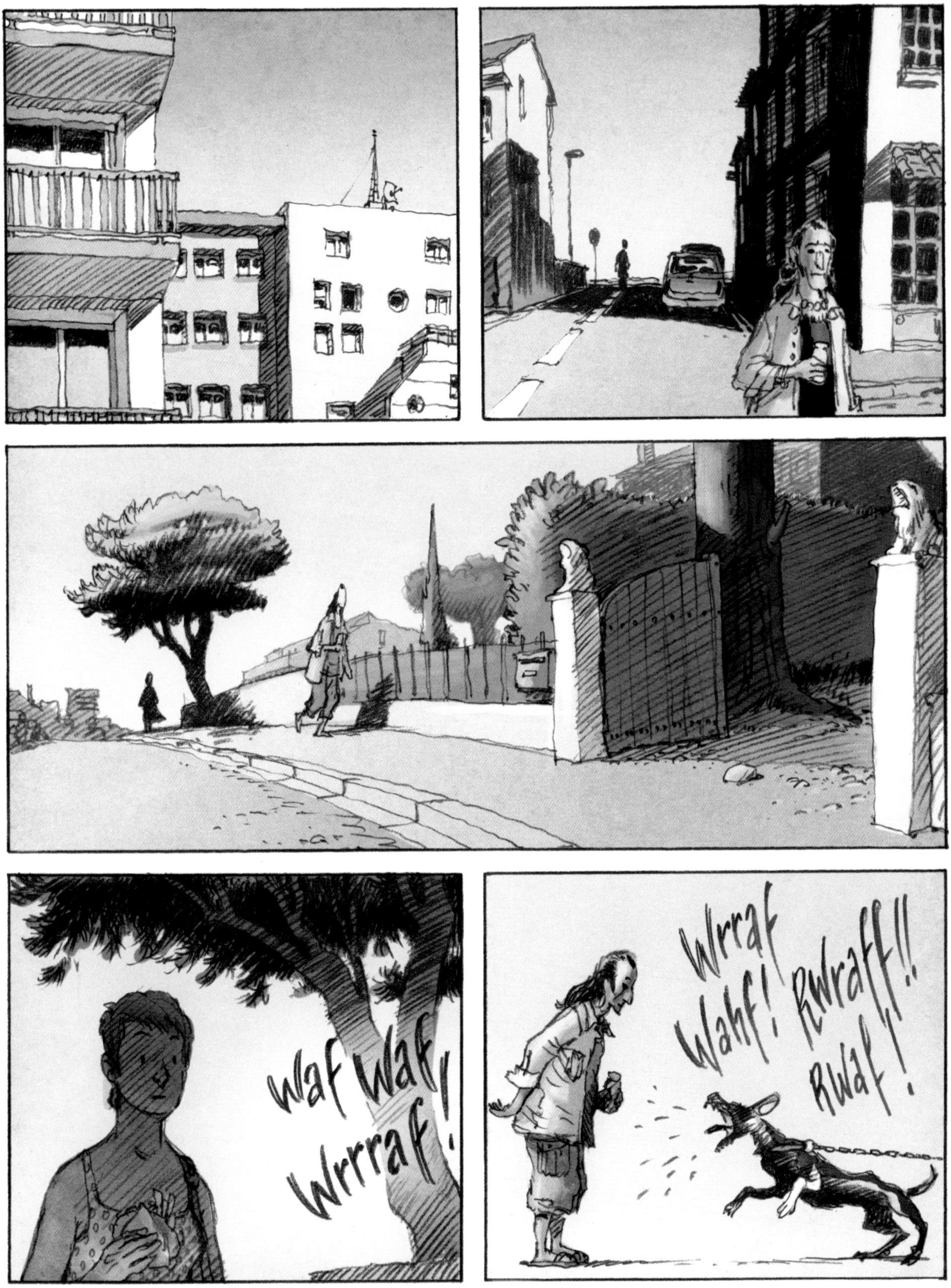
Waf Waf!
Wrrraf!
Wrraf
Wahf! Rwraff!!
Rwaf!

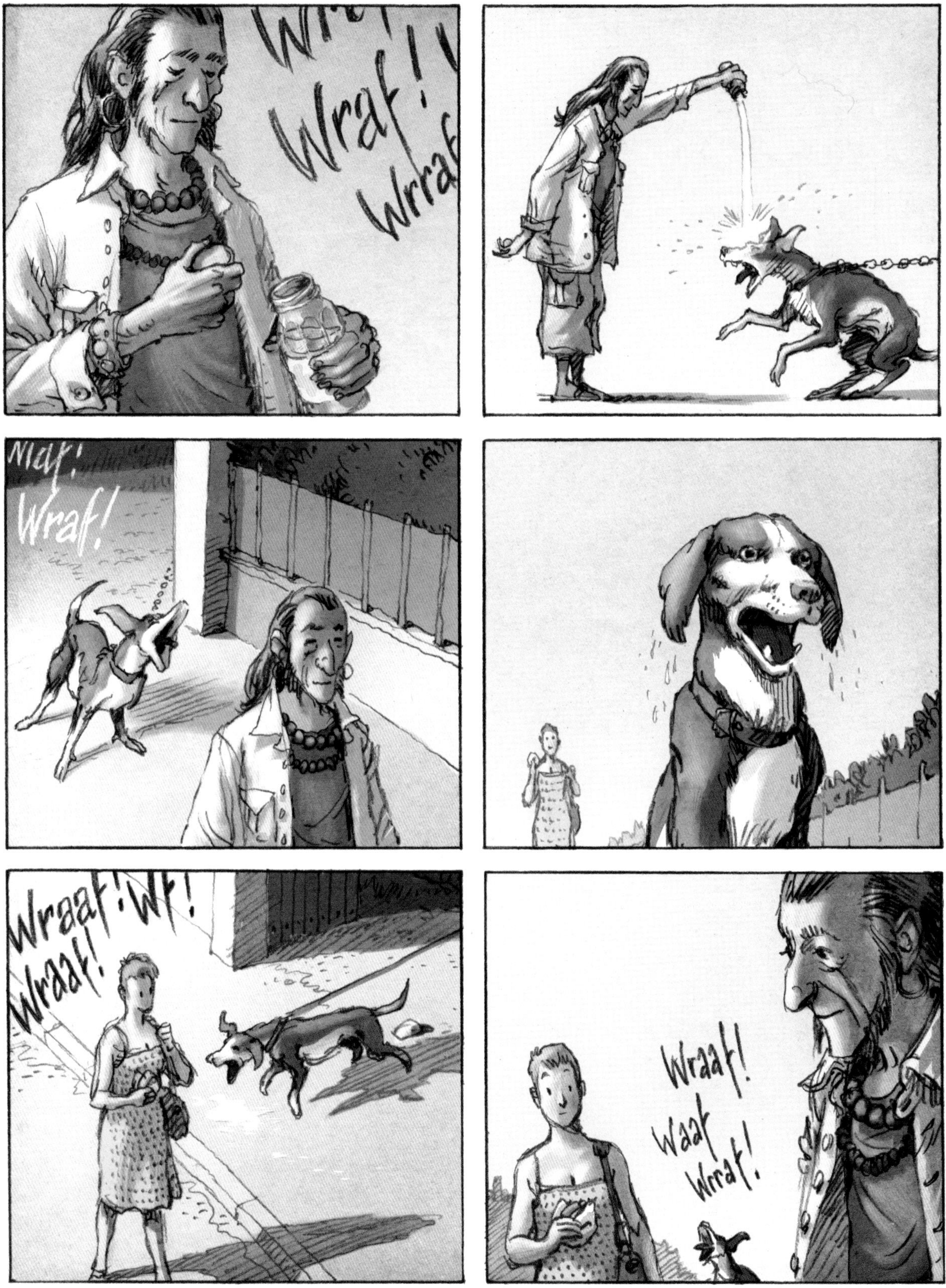
Wraf!
Wraf!
Wraaf! Wf!
Wraaf!
Wraaf!
Waaf
Wraf!

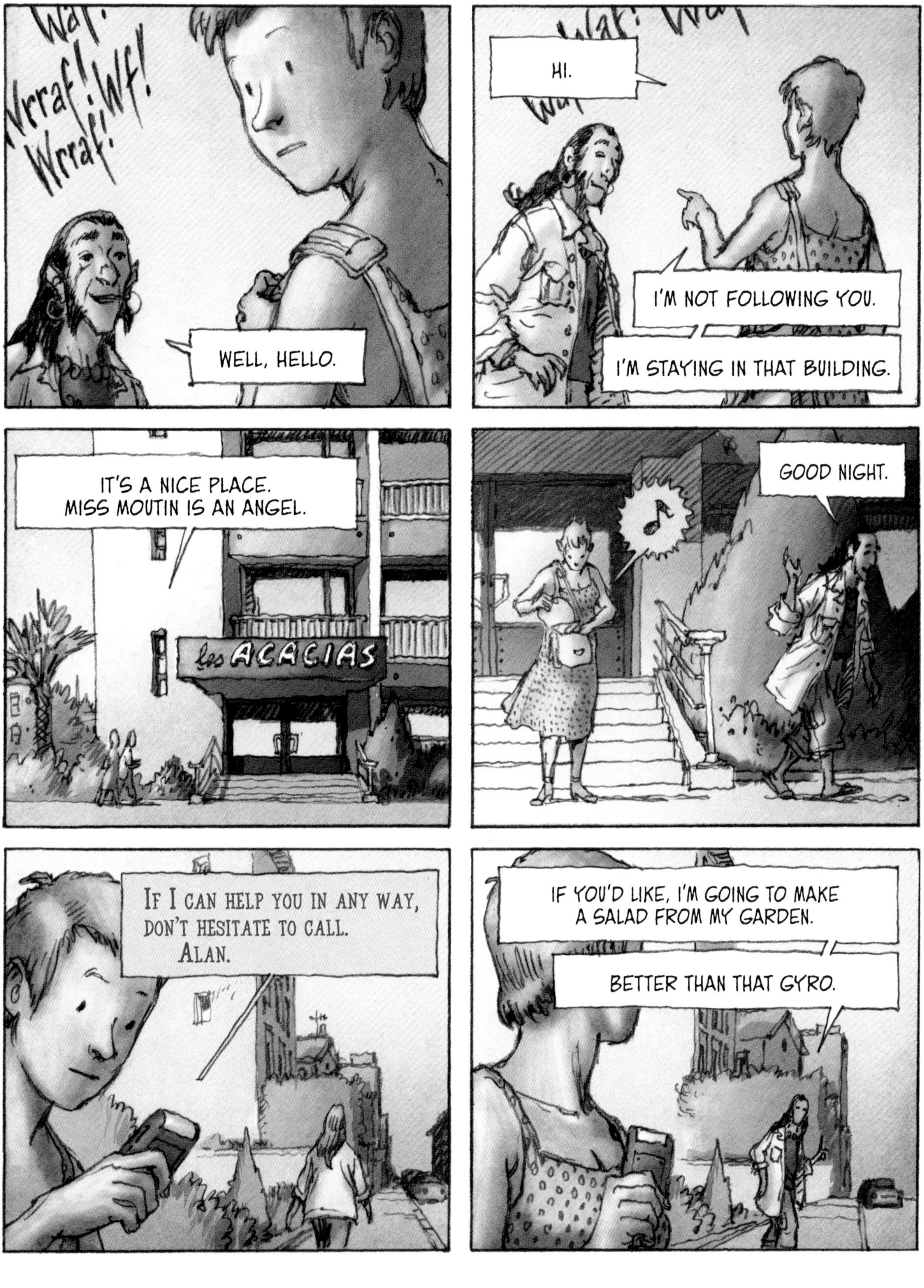
Wrraf!
Wf!
Wrraf!
WELL, HELLO.
HI.
I'M NOT FOLLOWING YOU.
I'M STAYING IN THAT BUILDING.
IT'S A NICE PLACE.
MISS MOUTIN IS AN ANGEL.
les ACACIAS
♪
GOOD NIGHT.
IF I CAN HELP YOU IN ANY WAY,
DON'T HESITATE TO CALL.
ALAN.
IF YOU'D LIKE, I'M GOING TO MAKE
A SALAD FROM MY GARDEN.
BETTER THAN THAT GYRO.

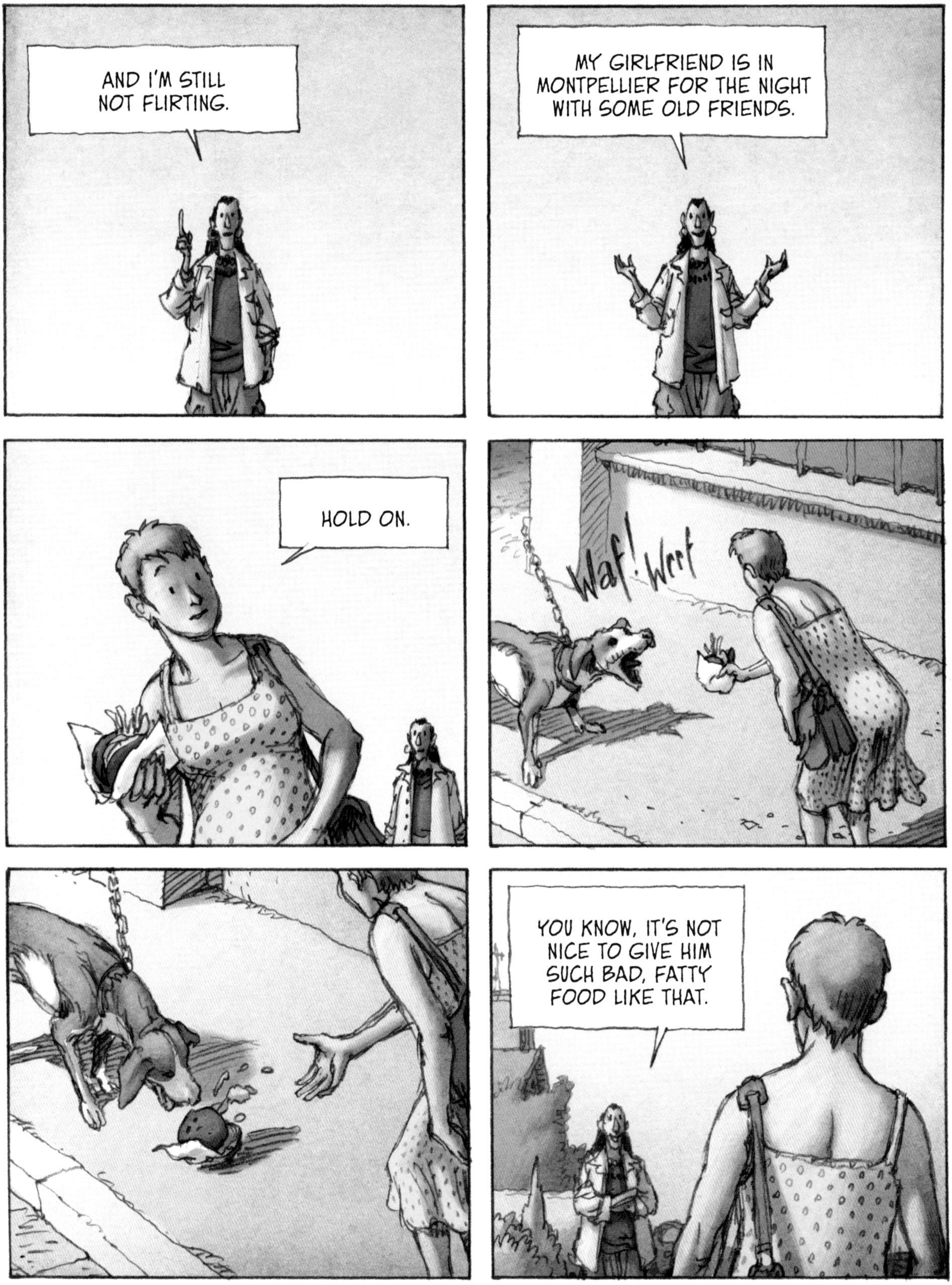
AND I'M STILL NOT FLIRTING.
MY GIRLFRIEND IS IN MONTPELLIER FOR THE NIGHT WITH SOME OLD FRIENDS.
HOLD ON.
Waf! Wrrf
YOU KNOW, IT'S NOT NICE TO GIVE HIM SUCH BAD, FATTY FOOD LIKE THAT.

WE ALL HAVE OUR WAYS.

HMM...

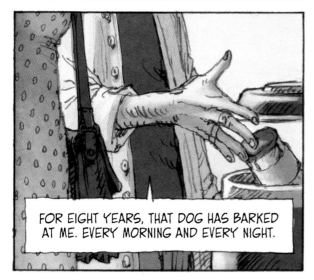

FOR EIGHT YEARS, THAT DOG HAS BARKED AT ME. EVERY MORNING AND EVERY NIGHT.

HE'S A DOG.

HE WAS MADE TO BARK.

I'M A MAN. WHAT WAS I MADE FOR?

UM...

HM...

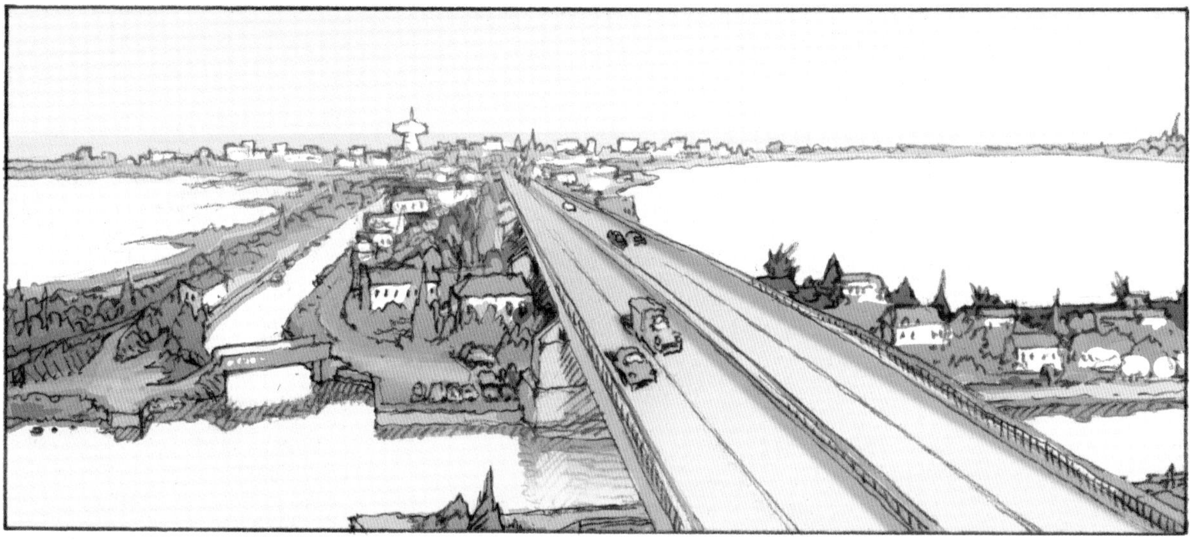

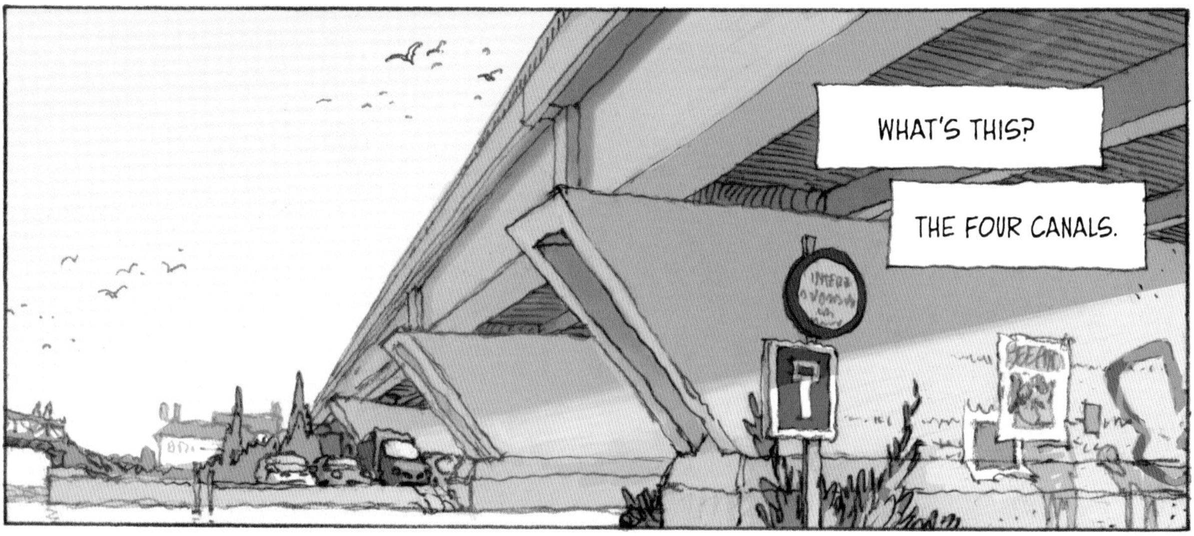
WHAT'S THIS?
THE FOUR CANALS.

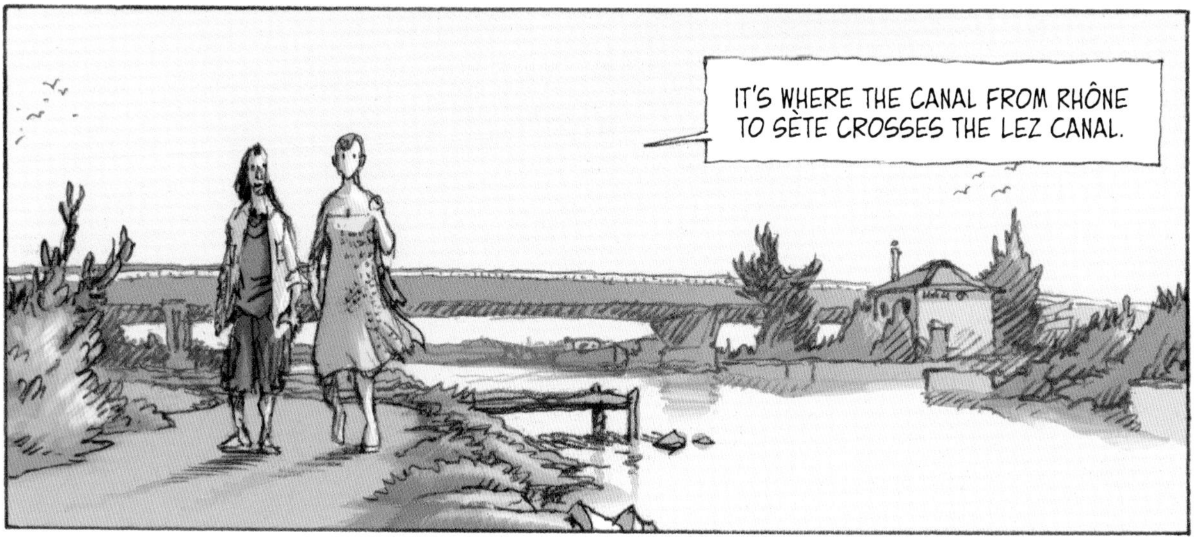
IT'S WHERE THE CANAL FROM RHÔNE TO SÈTE CROSSES THE LEZ CANAL.

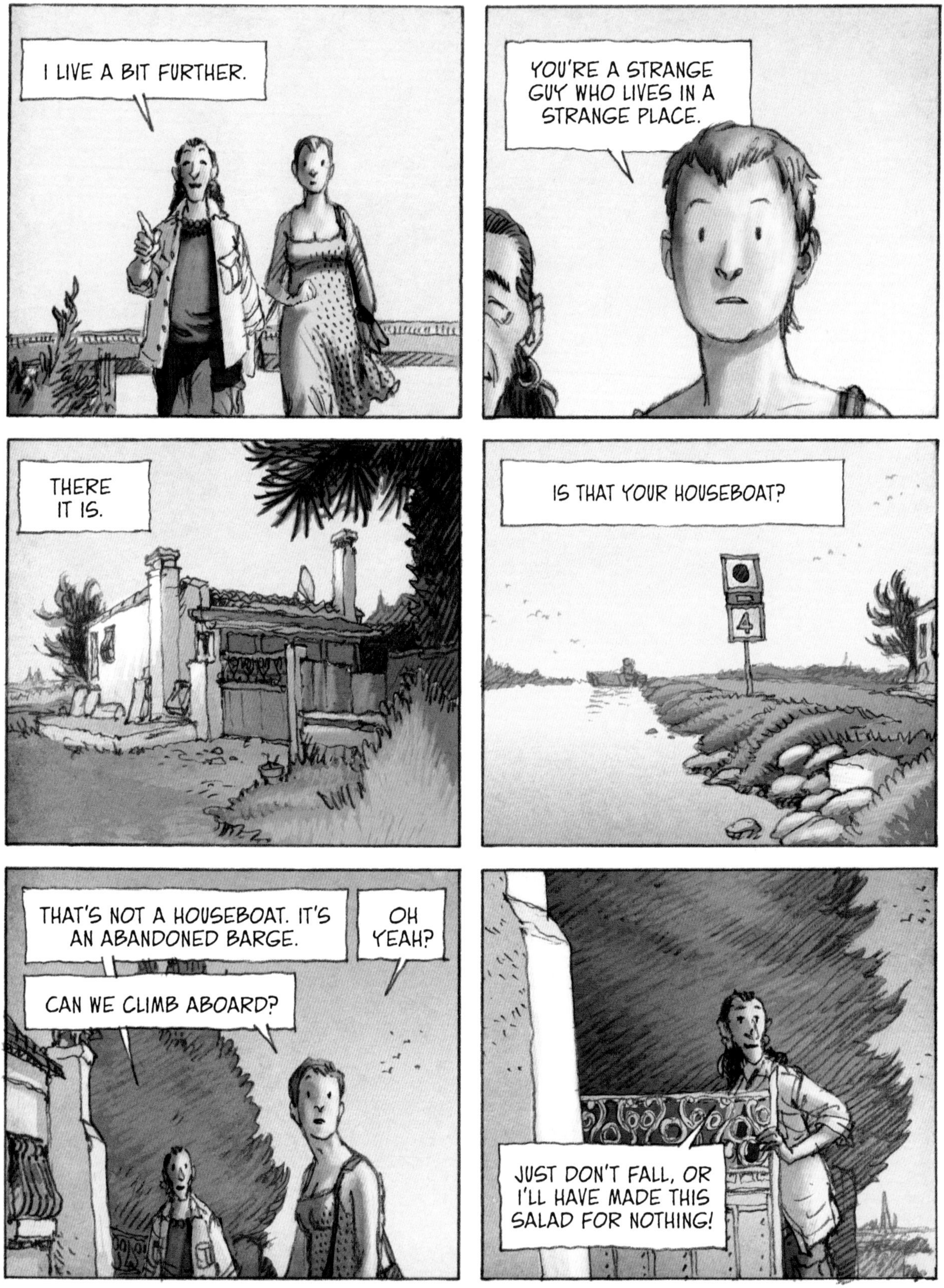
I LIVE A BIT FURTHER.
YOU'RE A STRANGE GUY WHO LIVES IN A STRANGE PLACE.
THERE IT IS.
IS THAT YOUR HOUSEBOAT?
4
THAT'S NOT A HOUSEBOAT. IT'S AN ABANDONED BARGE.
OH YEAH?
CAN WE CLIMB ABOARD?
JUST DON'T FALL, OR I'LL HAVE MADE THIS SALAD FOR NOTHING!

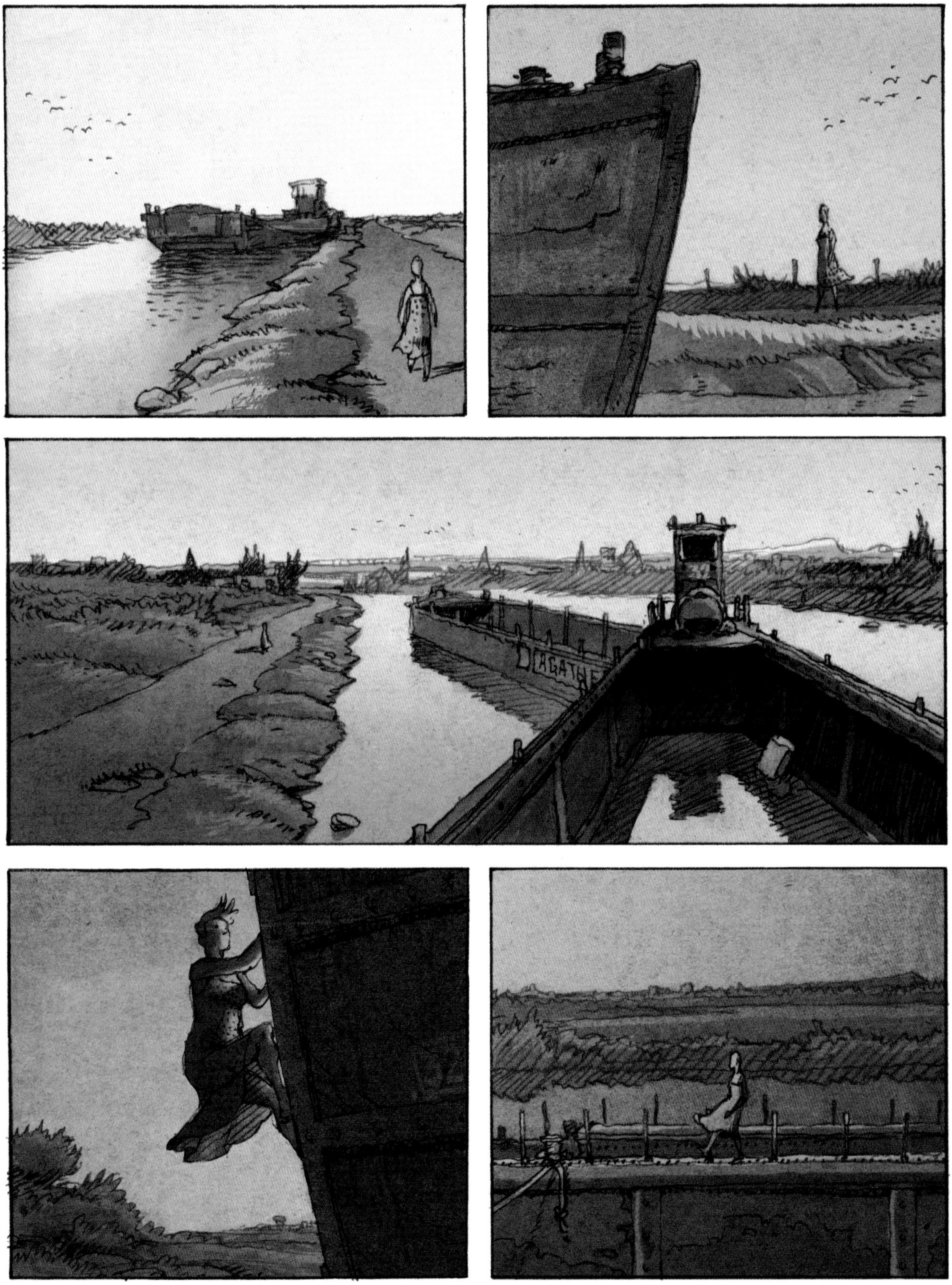
AGATHE

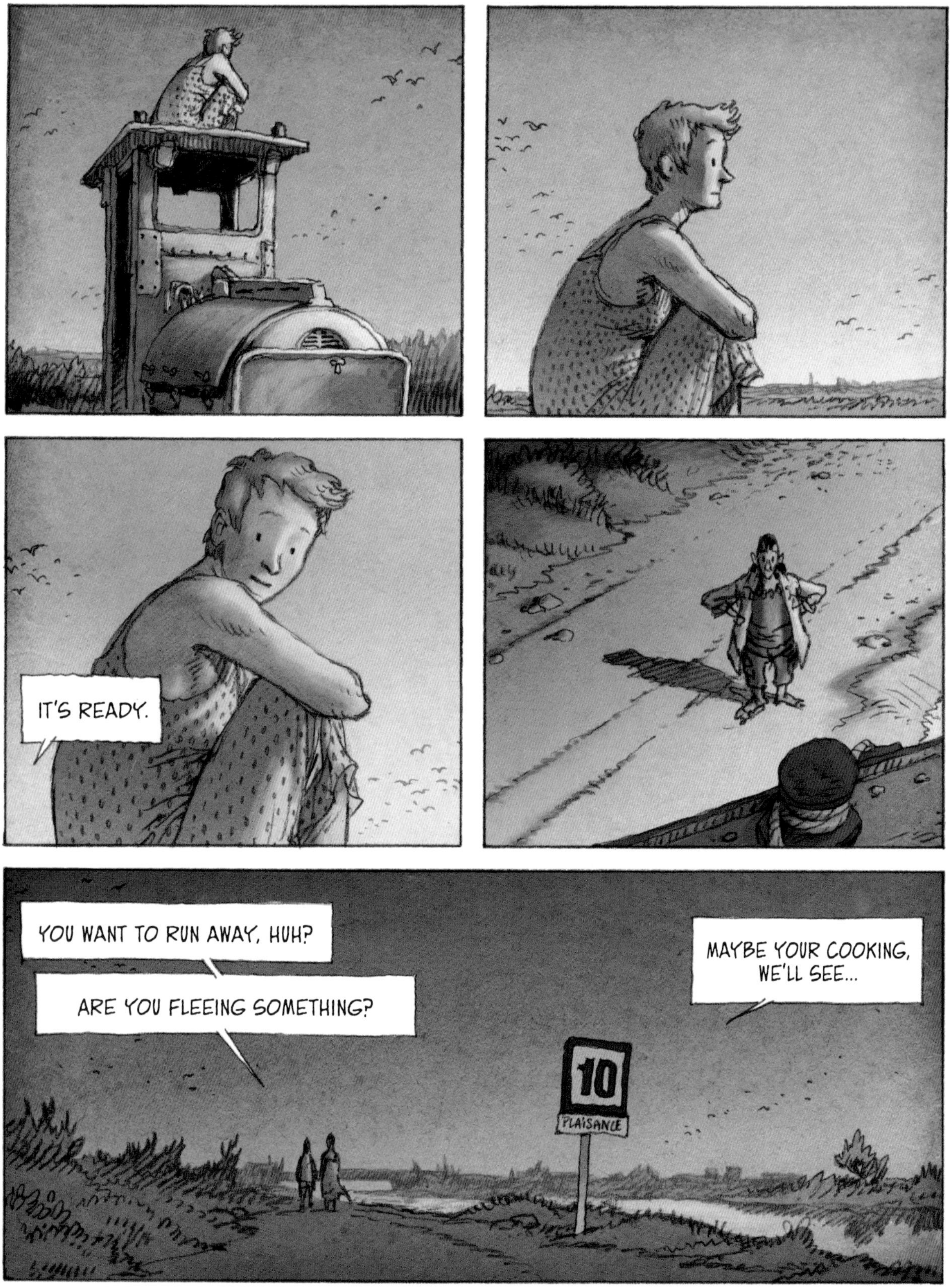
IT'S READY.
YOU WANT TO RUN AWAY, HUH?
ARE YOU FLEEING SOMETHING?
MAYBE YOUR COOKING, WE'LL SEE...
10
PLAISANCE

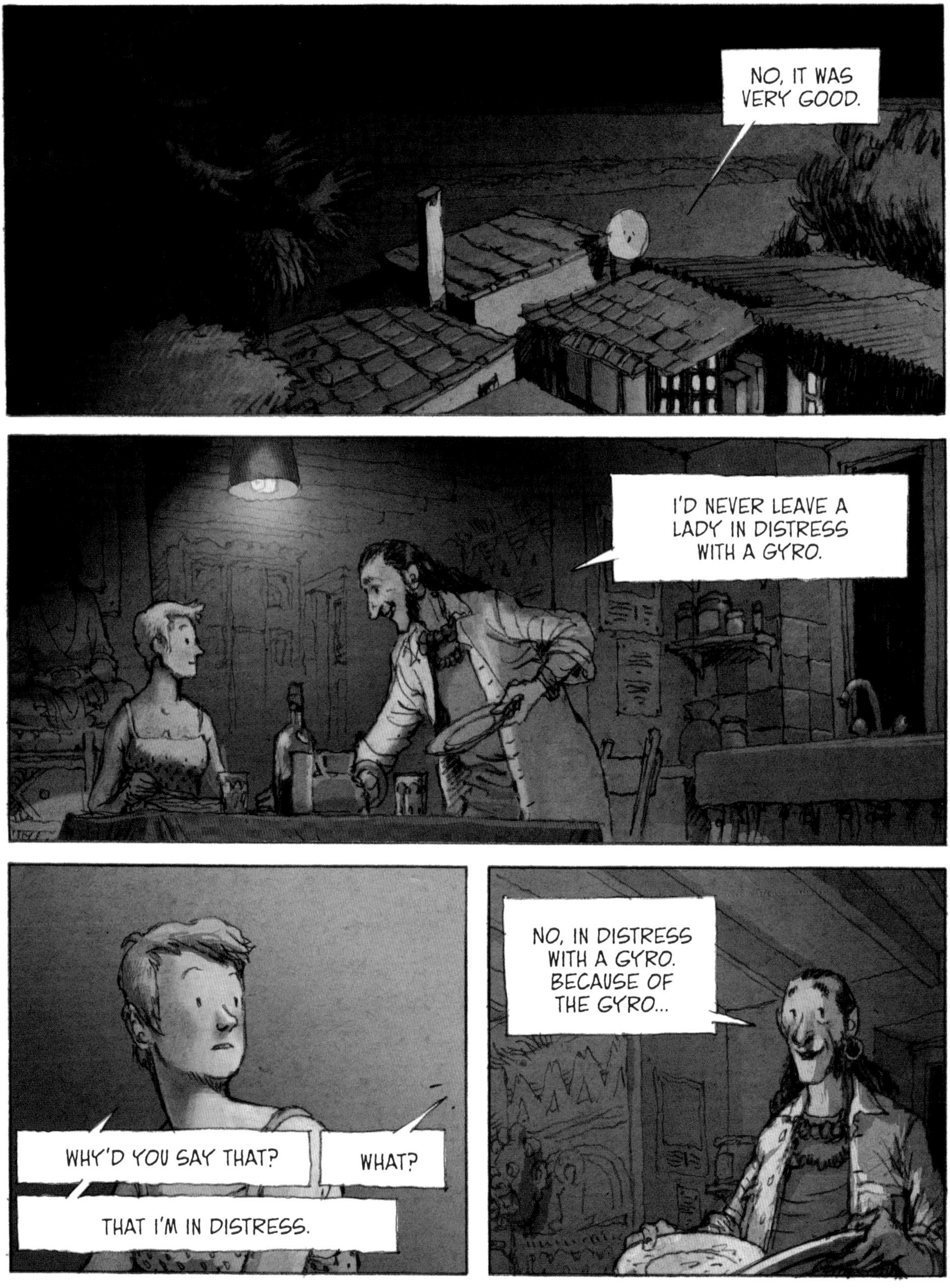
NO, IT WAS VERY GOOD.
I'D NEVER LEAVE A LADY IN DISTRESS WITH A GYRO.
WHY'D YOU SAY THAT?
WHAT?
THAT I'M IN DISTRESS.
NO, IN DISTRESS WITH A GYRO. BECAUSE OF THE GYRO...

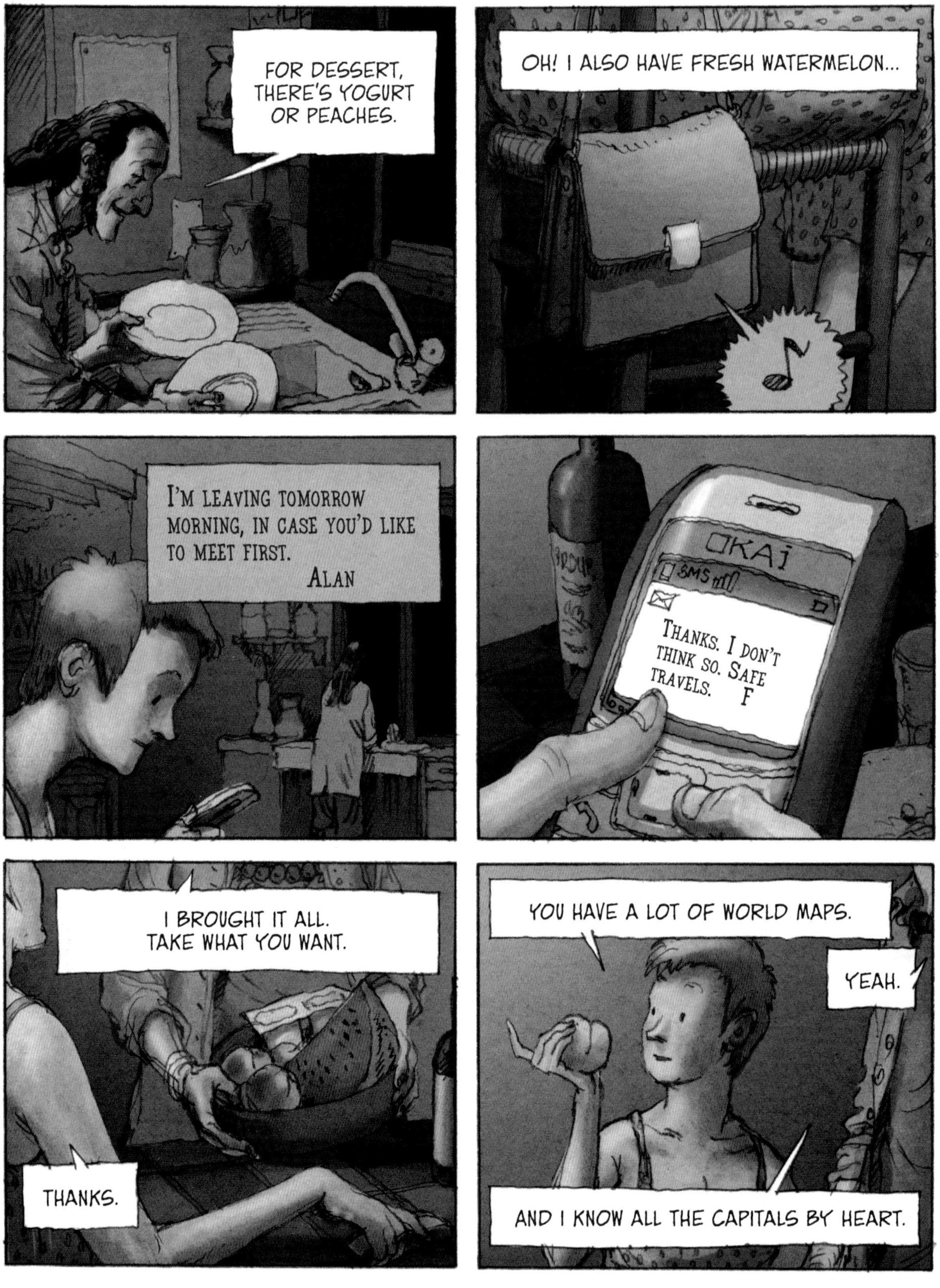
FOR DESSERT, THERE'S YOGURT OR PEACHES.
OH! I ALSO HAVE FRESH WATERMELON...
I'M LEAVING TOMORROW MORNING, IN CASE YOU'D LIKE TO MEET FIRST. ALAN
OKAI
SMS
THANKS. I DON'T THINK SO. SAFE TRAVELS. F
I BROUGHT IT ALL. TAKE WHAT YOU WANT.
THANKS.
YOU HAVE A LOT OF WORLD MAPS.
YEAH.
AND I KNOW ALL THE CAPITALS BY HEART.

YOU'VE DONE A LOT OF TRAVELING...

NO, THOSE ARE PLACES WHERE A STUPID DEATH OCCURRED.

I HAVE TWENTY-SEVEN NOTEBOOKS FULL OF SAD STORIES.

LOOK.

HERE -- 1990, COLMAR...

...A PILOT PUSHES THE WRONG BUTTON AND EJECTS WHILE STILL ON THE GROUND. HE DIED.

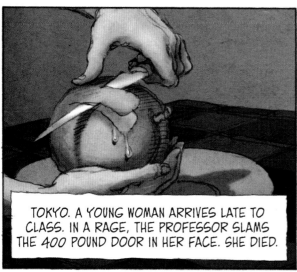

TOKYO. A YOUNG WOMAN ARRIVES LATE TO CLASS. IN A RAGE, THE PROFESSOR SLAMS THE 400 POUND DOOR IN HER FACE. SHE DIED.

TARN-ET-GARONNE. A FARMER DIES OF ASPHYXIATION CLEANING HIS MANURE PIT. HIS WIFE AND FRIEND COME TO HELP HIM. THEY DIE TOO.

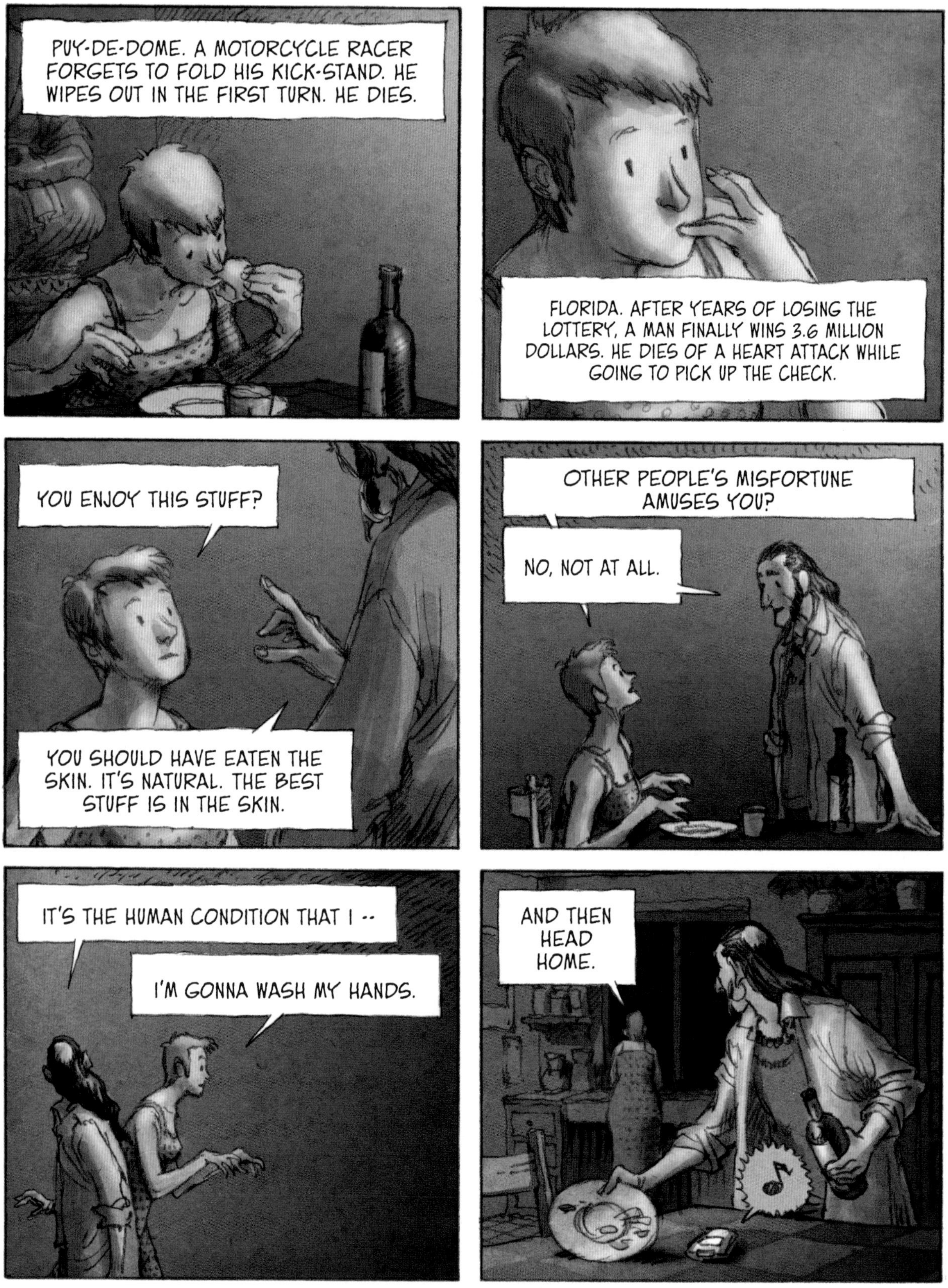
PUY-DE-DOME. A MOTORCYCLE RACER FORGETS TO FOLD HIS KICK-STAND. HE WIPES OUT IN THE FIRST TURN. HE DIES.
FLORIDA. AFTER YEARS OF LOSING THE LOTTERY, A MAN FINALLY WINS 3.6 MILLION DOLLARS. HE DIES OF A HEART ATTACK WHILE GOING TO PICK UP THE CHECK.
YOU ENJOY THIS STUFF?
YOU SHOULD HAVE EATEN THE SKIN. IT'S NATURAL. THE BEST STUFF IS IN THE SKIN.
OTHER PEOPLE'S MISFORTUNE AMUSES YOU?
NO, NOT AT ALL.
IT'S THE HUMAN CONDITION THAT I --
I'M GONNA WASH MY HANDS.
AND THEN HEAD HOME.

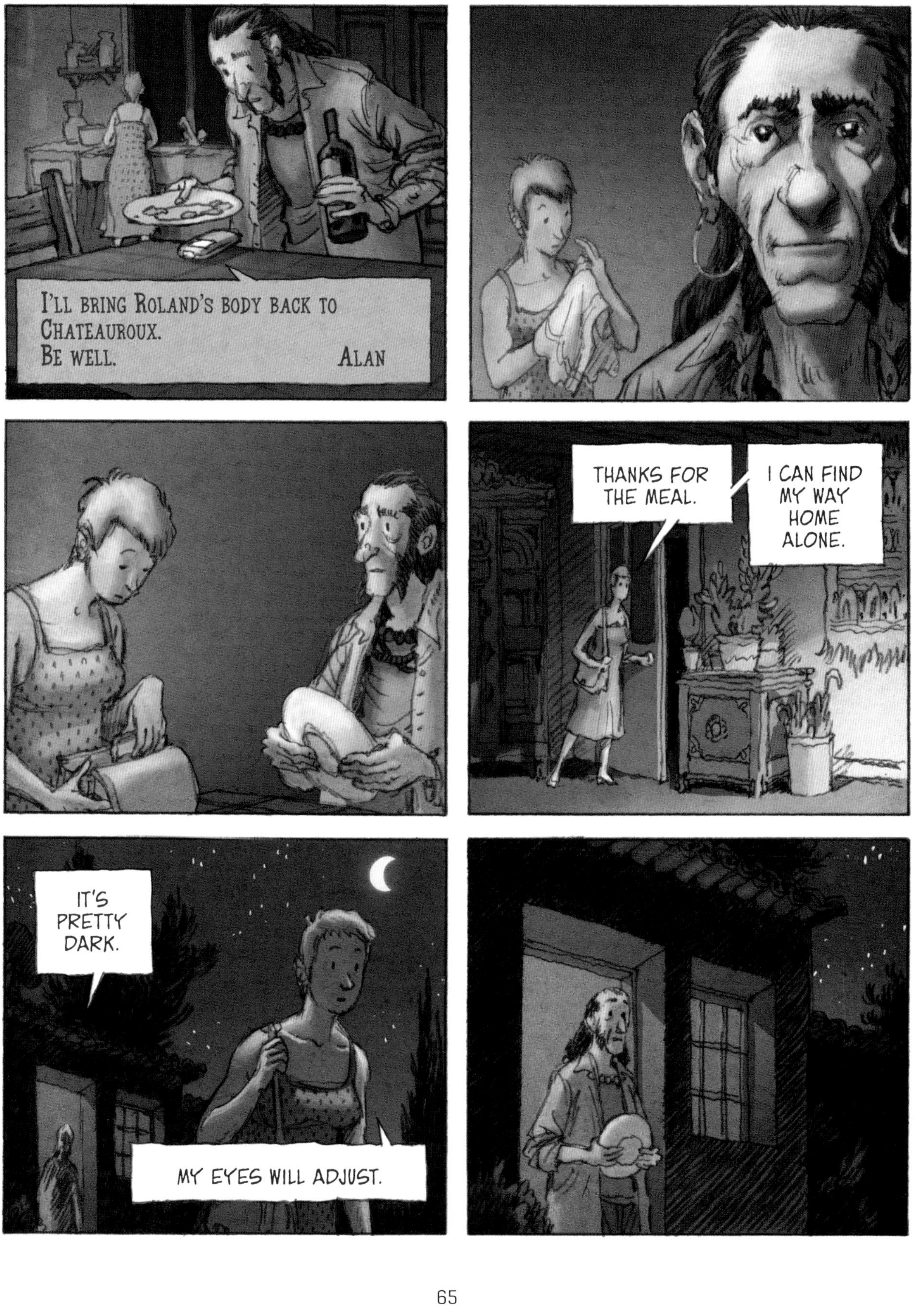
I'll bring Roland's body back to
Chateauroux.
Be well. Alan
Thanks for the meal.
I can find my way home alone.
It's pretty dark.
My eyes will adjust.

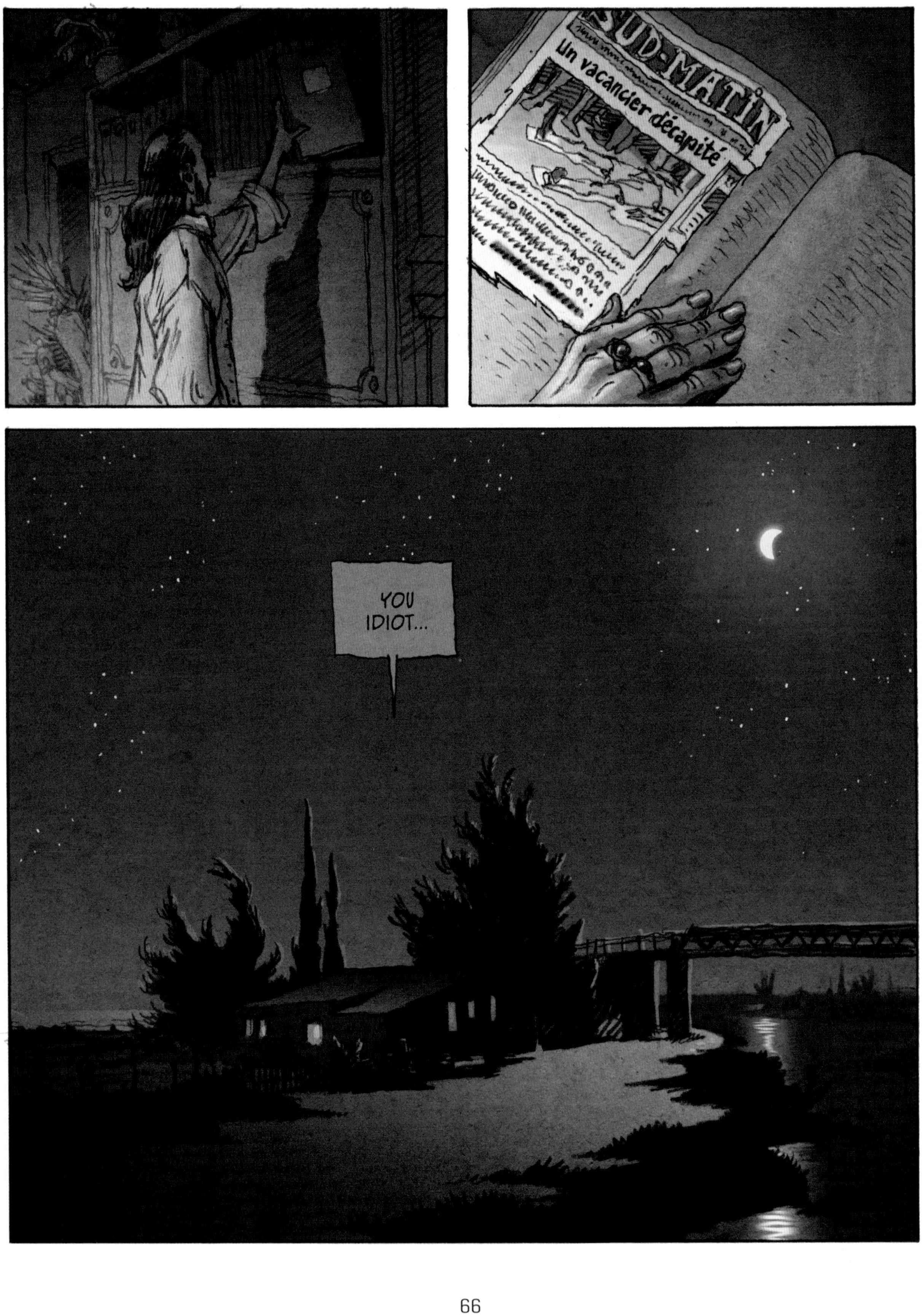
SUD-MATIN
Un vacancier décapité
YOU IDIOT...

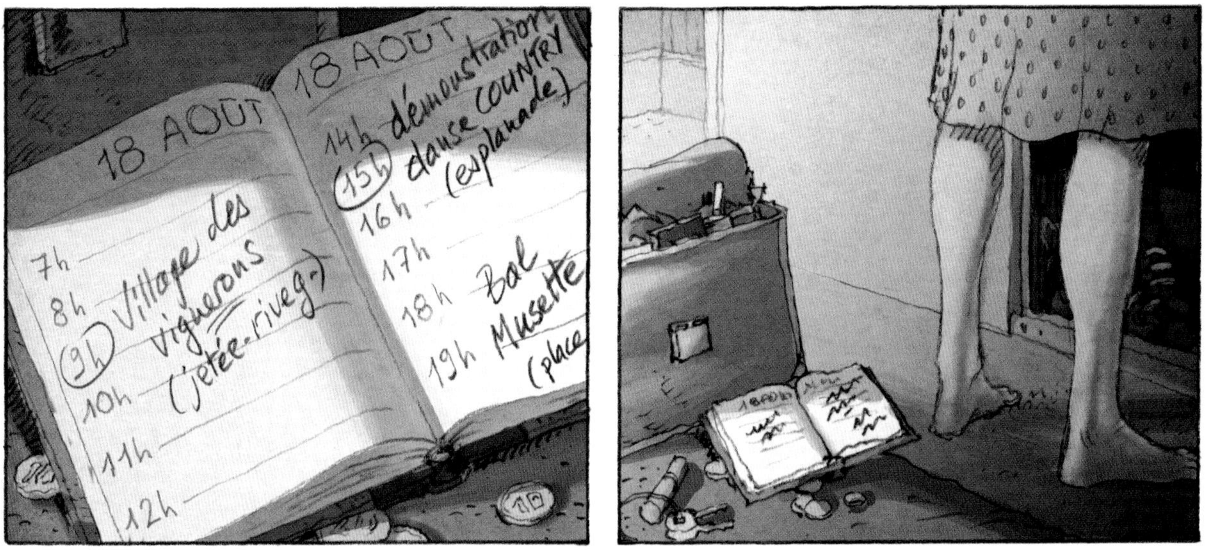
18 AOÛT
7h
8h
9h Village des vignerons
10h (jetée-riveg.)
11h
12h
18 AOÛT
14h démonstration
15h danse COUNTRY
16h (esplanade)
17h
18h Bal
19h Musette
(place

* Village of winemakers (pier shore) **Country dance demonstration ***Folk music

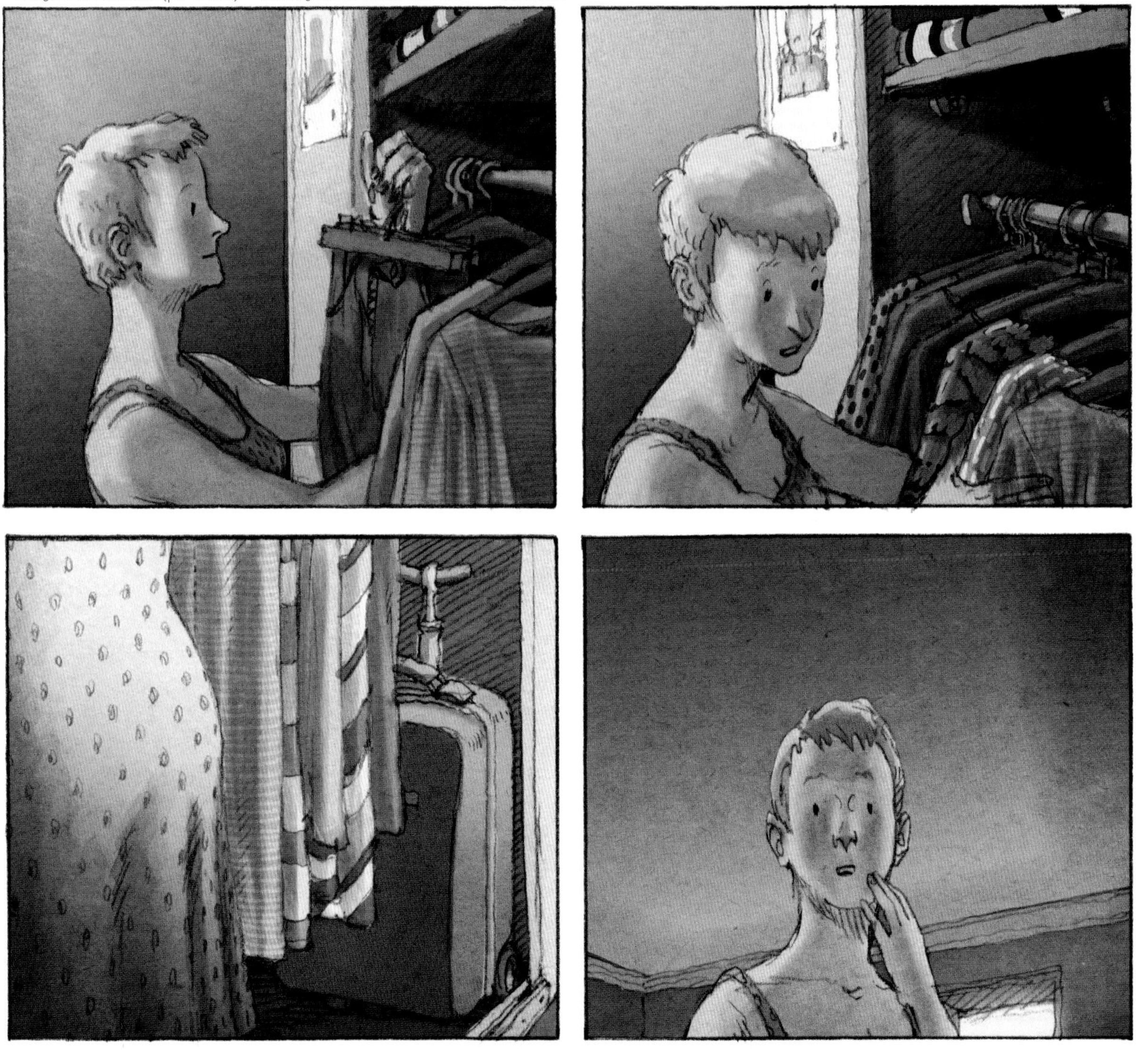

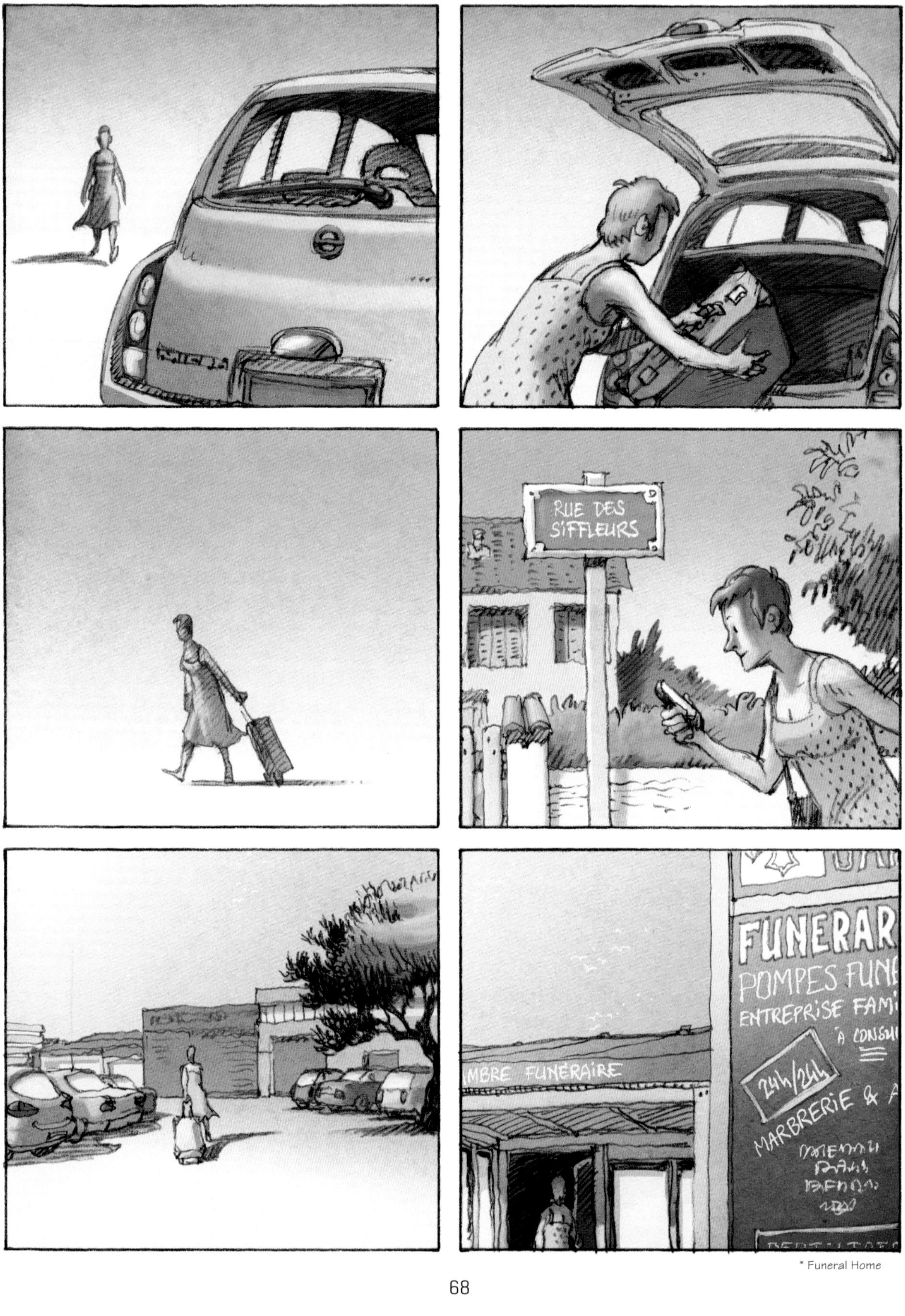
RUE DES SIFFLEURS
FUNERAR
POMPES FUNE
ENTREPRISE FAMI
À CONSU
24h/24h
MARBRERIE & A
MBRE FUNÉRAIRE

* Funeral Home

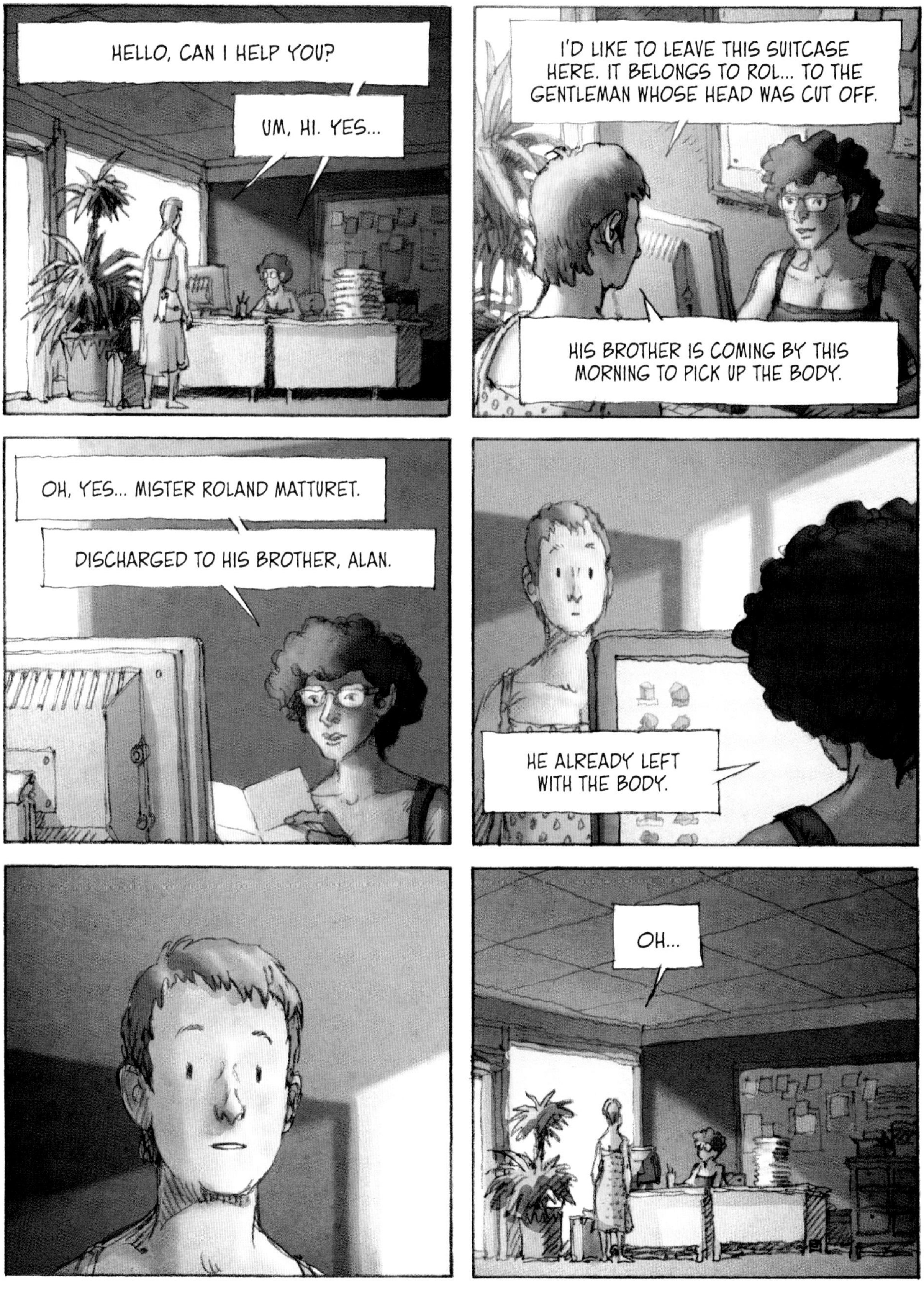
HELLO, CAN I HELP YOU?
UM, HI. YES...
I'D LIKE TO LEAVE THIS SUITCASE HERE. IT BELONGS TO ROL... TO THE GENTLEMAN WHOSE HEAD WAS CUT OFF.
HIS BROTHER IS COMING BY THIS MORNING TO PICK UP THE BODY.
OH, YES... MISTER ROLAND MATTURET.
DISCHARGED TO HIS BROTHER, ALAN.
HE ALREADY LEFT WITH THE BODY.
OH...

1UP
COPAGAB

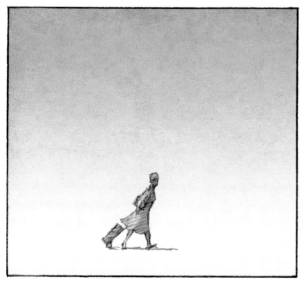

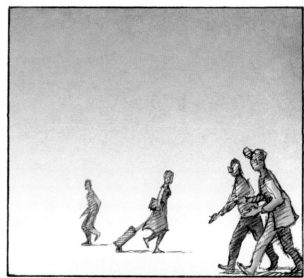

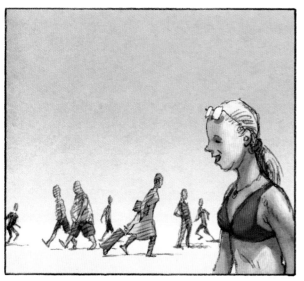

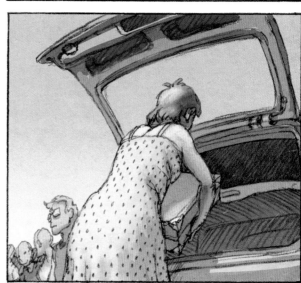

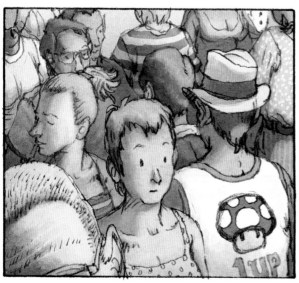

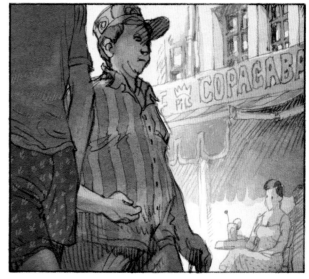

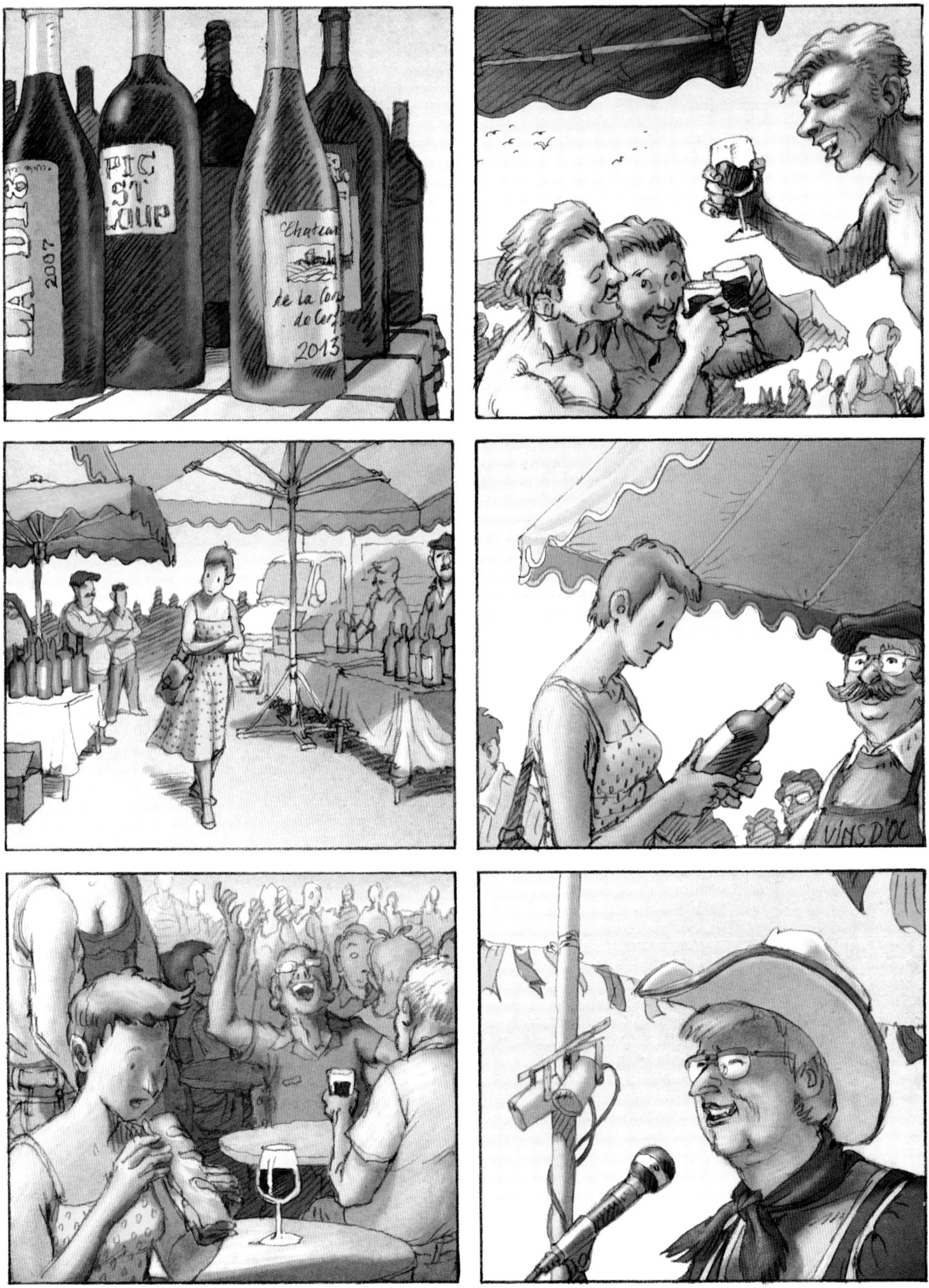

PIC ST LOUP
2007
Chateau
2013
VINS D'OC

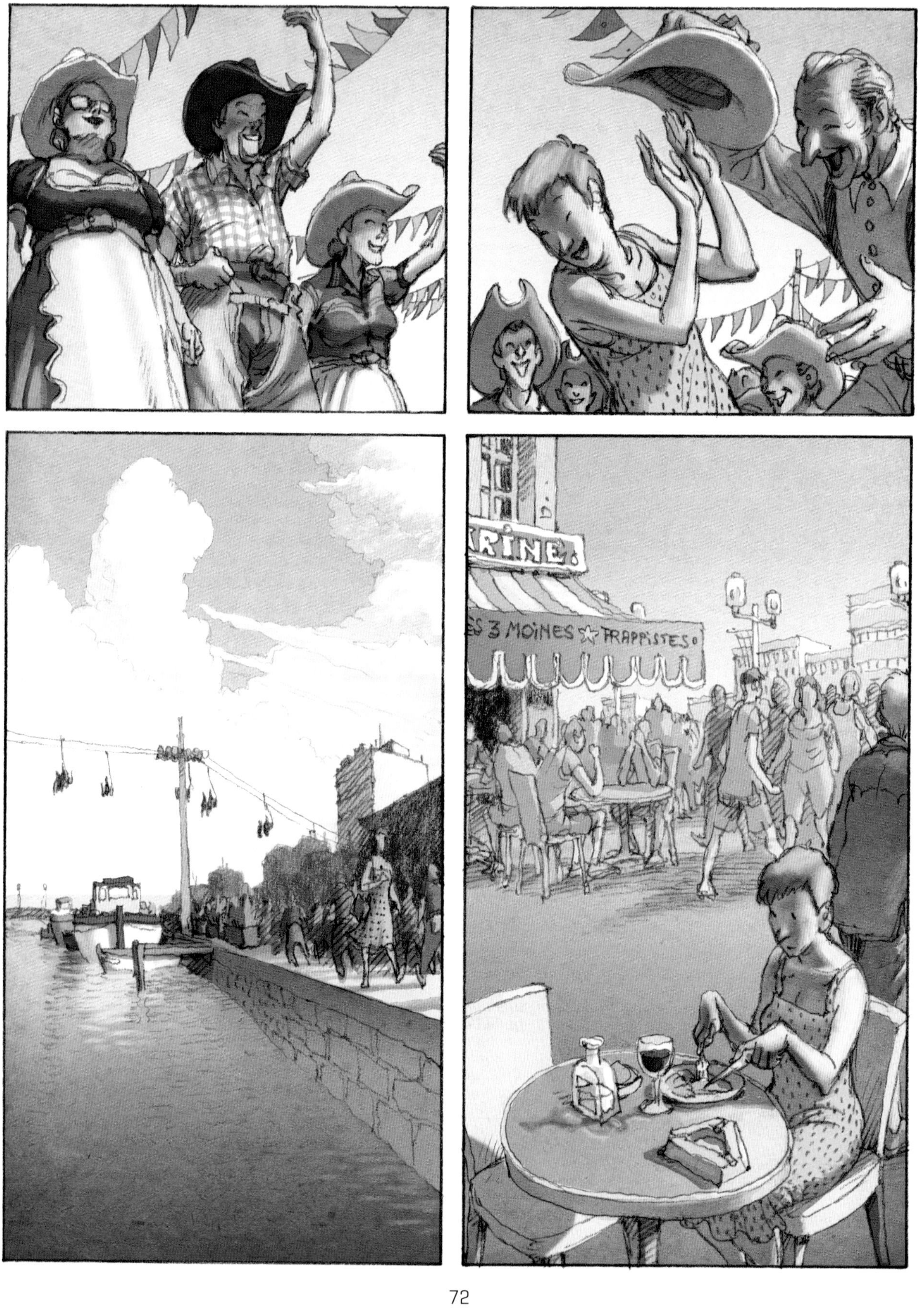
RINE
ES 3 MOINES ★ TRAPPISTES

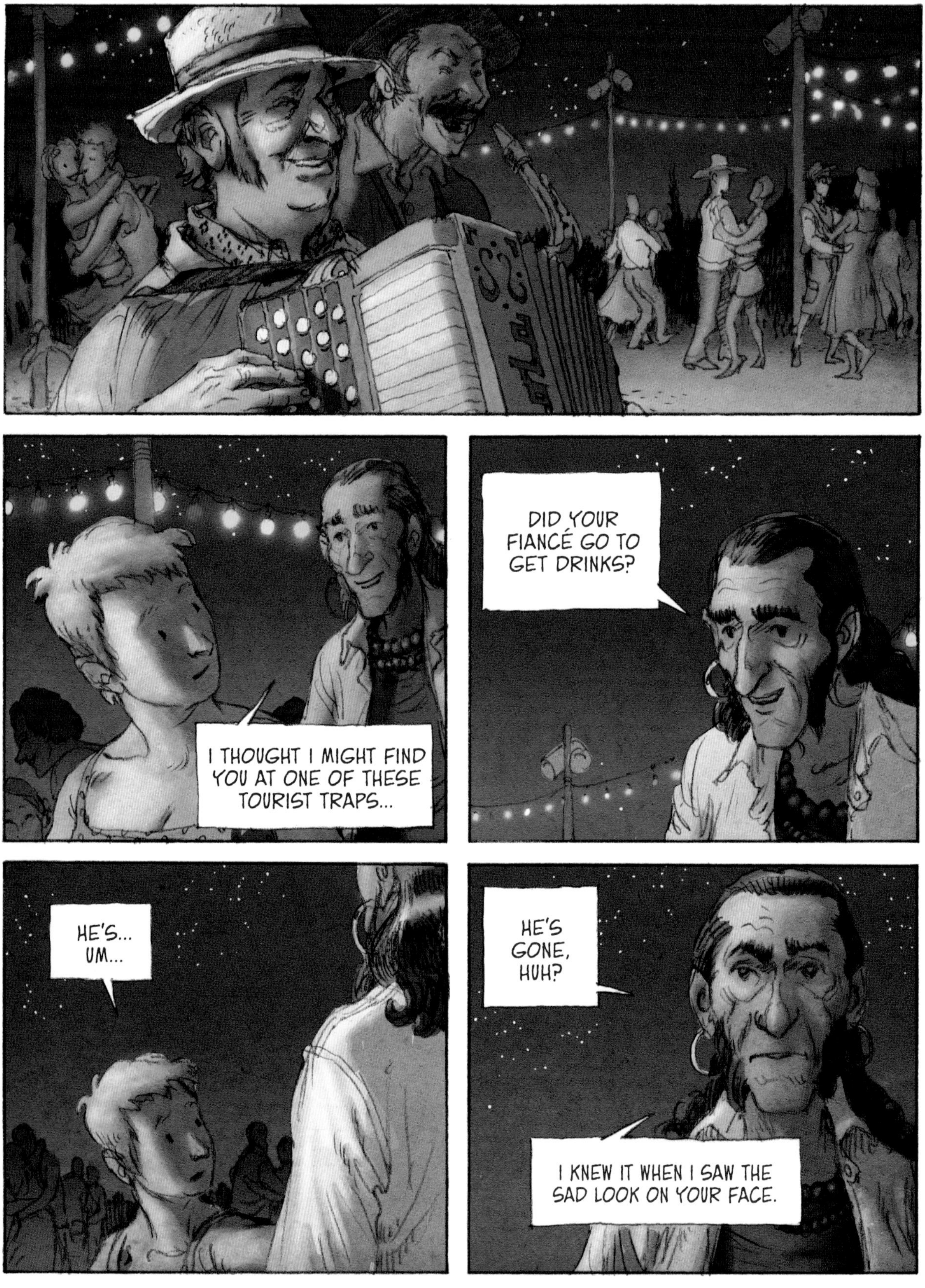
I THOUGHT I MIGHT FIND YOU AT ONE OF THESE TOURIST TRAPS...
DID YOUR FIANCÉ GO TO GET DRINKS?
HE'S... UM...
HE'S GONE, HUH?
I KNEW IT WHEN I SAW THE SAD LOOK ON YOUR FACE.

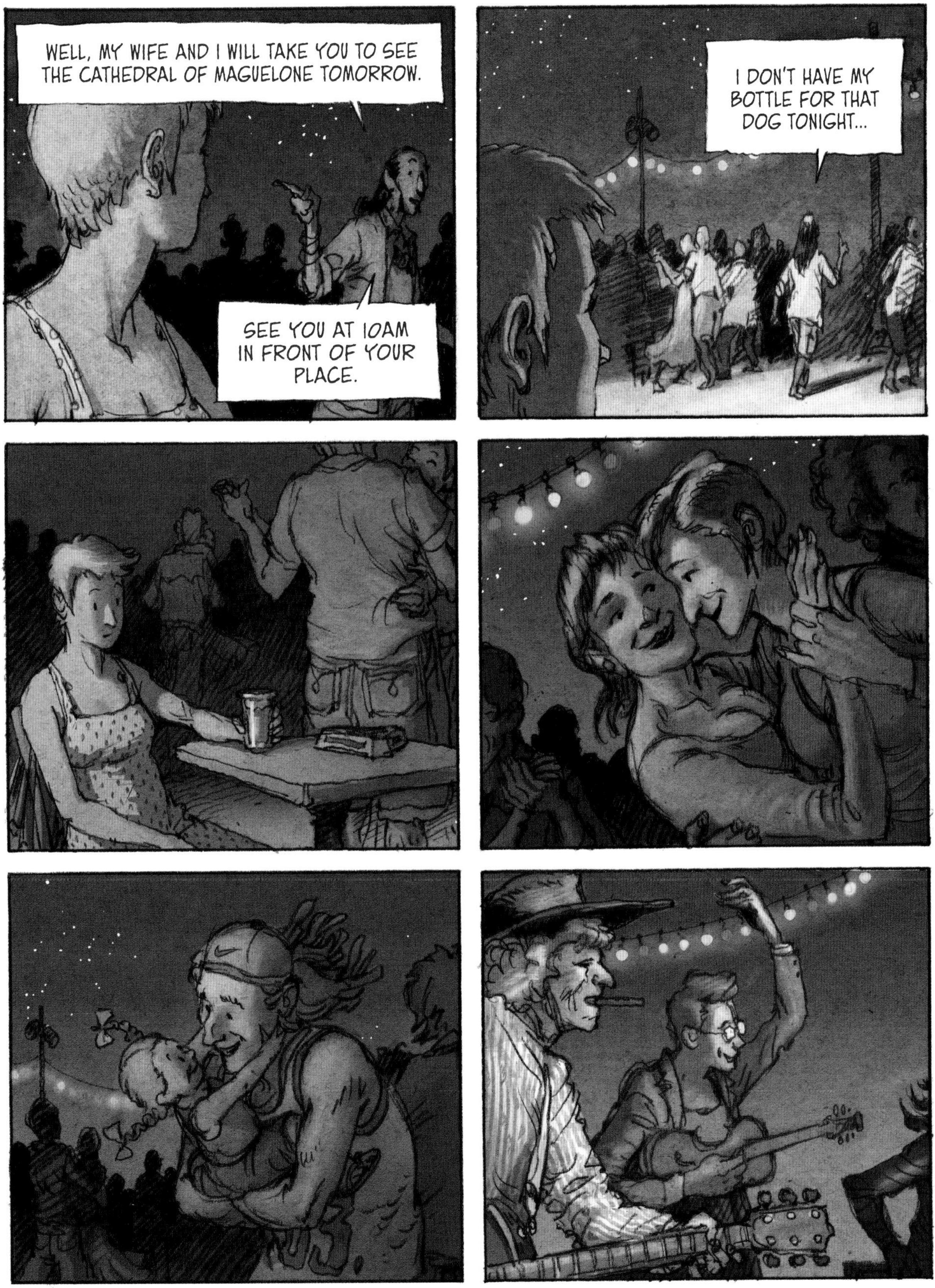
WELL, MY WIFE AND I WILL TAKE YOU TO SEE THE CATHEDRAL OF MAGUELONE TOMORROW.
SEE YOU AT 10AM IN FRONT OF YOUR PLACE.
I DON'T HAVE MY BOTTLE FOR THAT DOG TONIGHT...

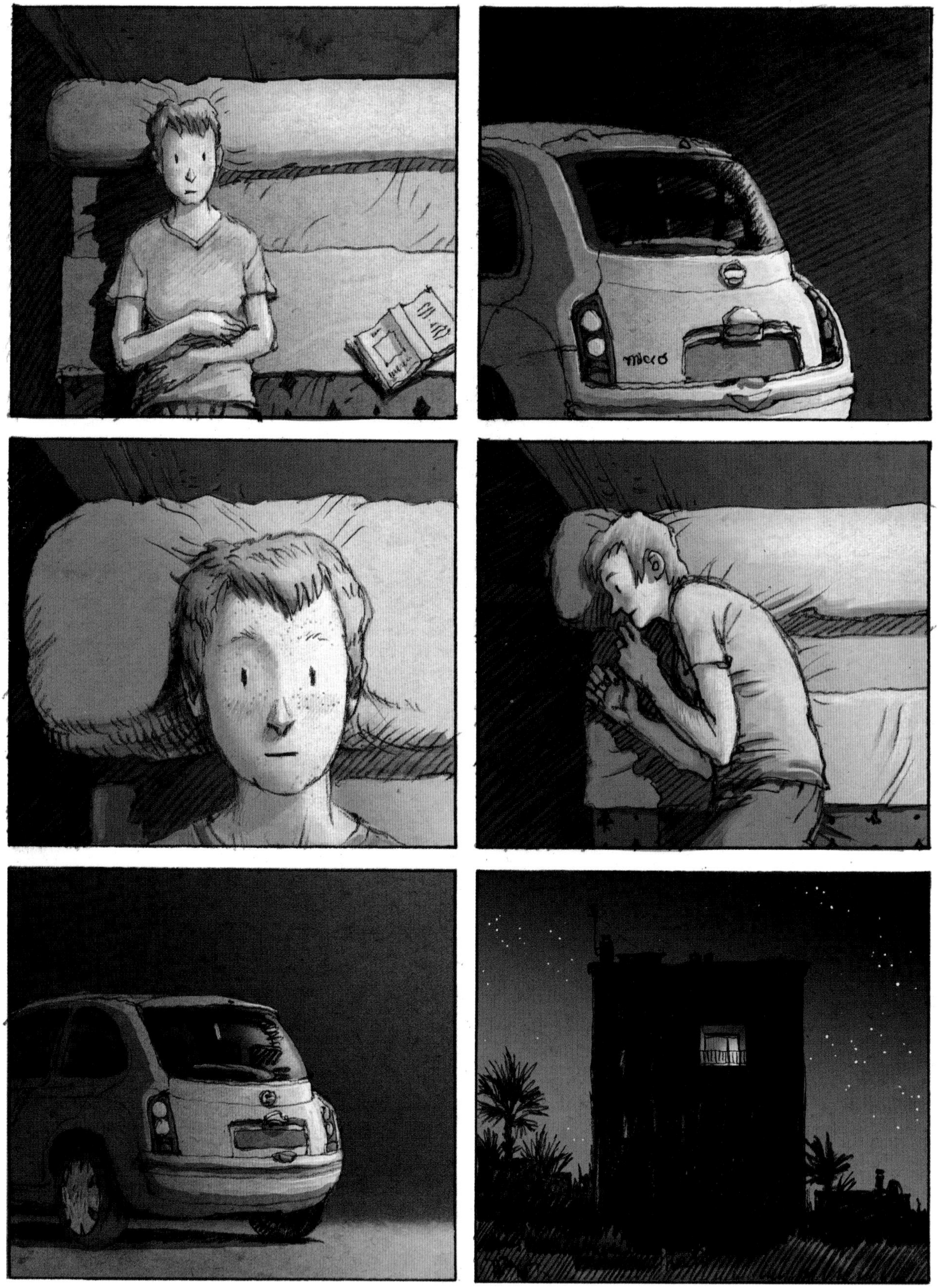
Micra

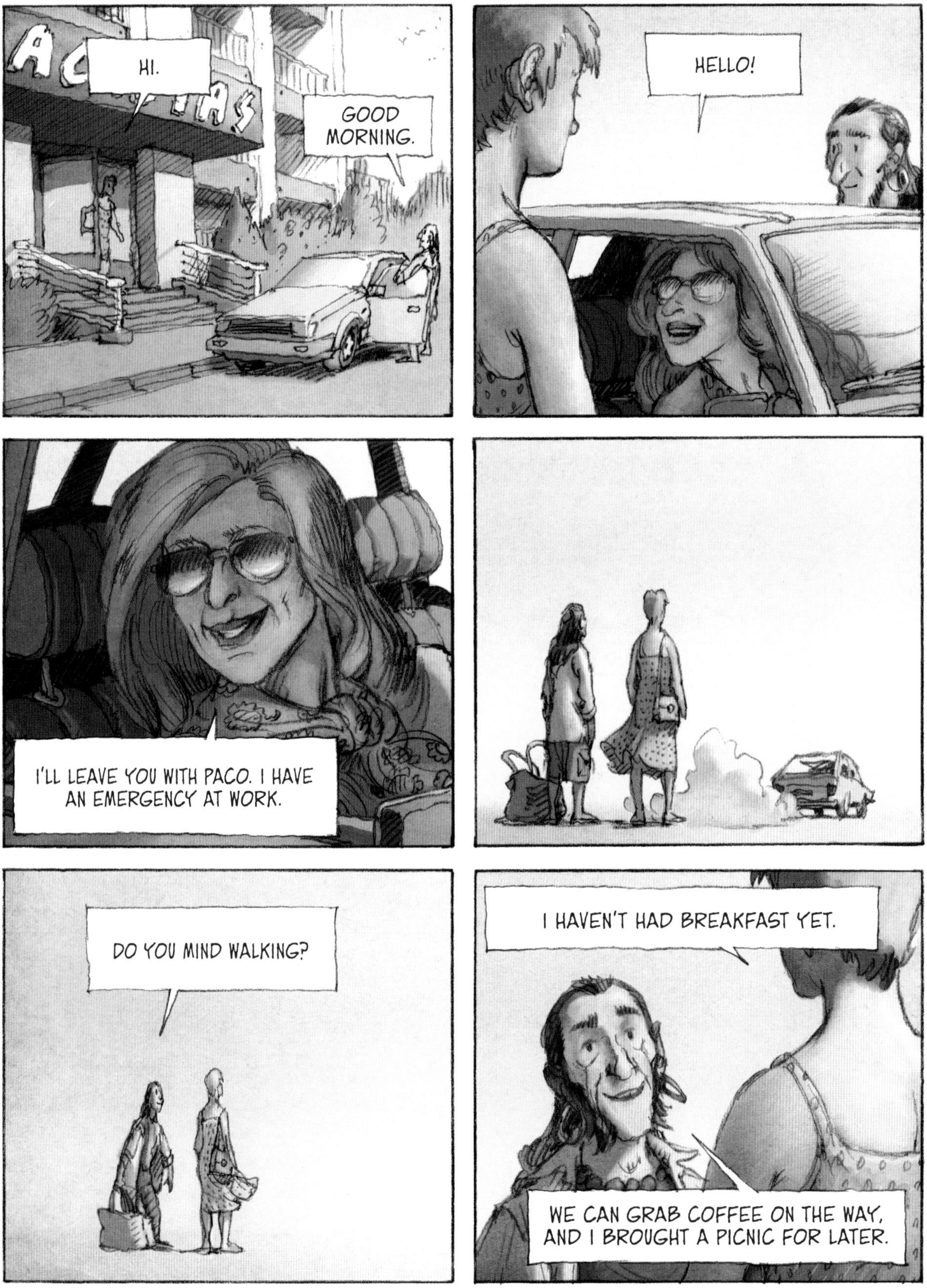
HI.
GOOD MORNING.
HELLO!
I'LL LEAVE YOU WITH PACO. I HAVE AN EMERGENCY AT WORK.
DO YOU MIND WALKING?
I HAVEN'T HAD BREAKFAST YET.
WE CAN GRAB COFFEE ON THE WAY, AND I BROUGHT A PICNIC FOR LATER.

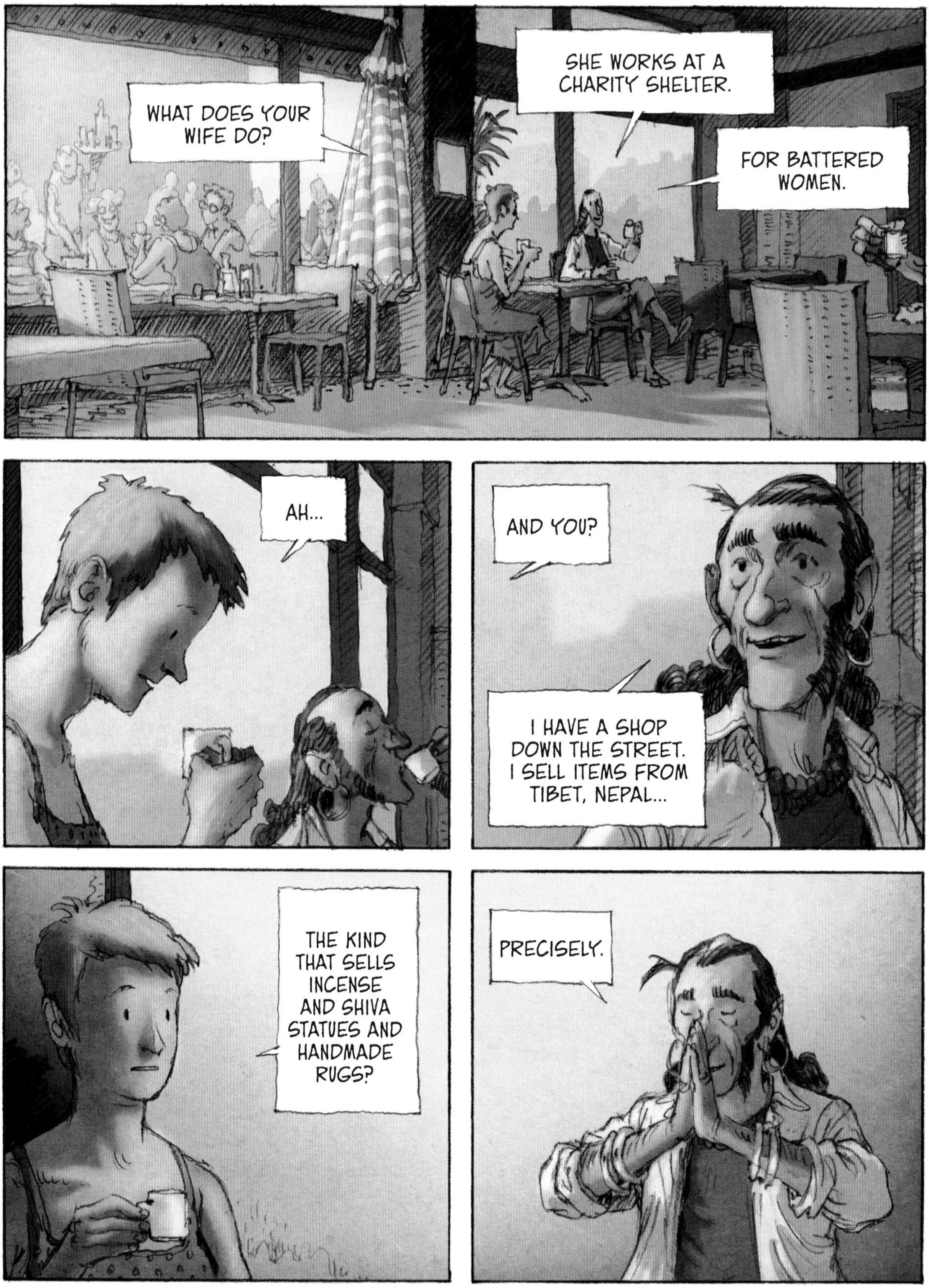
WHAT DOES YOUR WIFE DO?
SHE WORKS AT A CHARITY SHELTER.
FOR BATTERED WOMEN.
AH...
AND YOU?
I HAVE A SHOP DOWN THE STREET. I SELL ITEMS FROM TIBET, NEPAL...
THE KIND THAT SELLS INCENSE AND SHIVA STATUES AND HANDMADE RUGS?
PRECISELY.

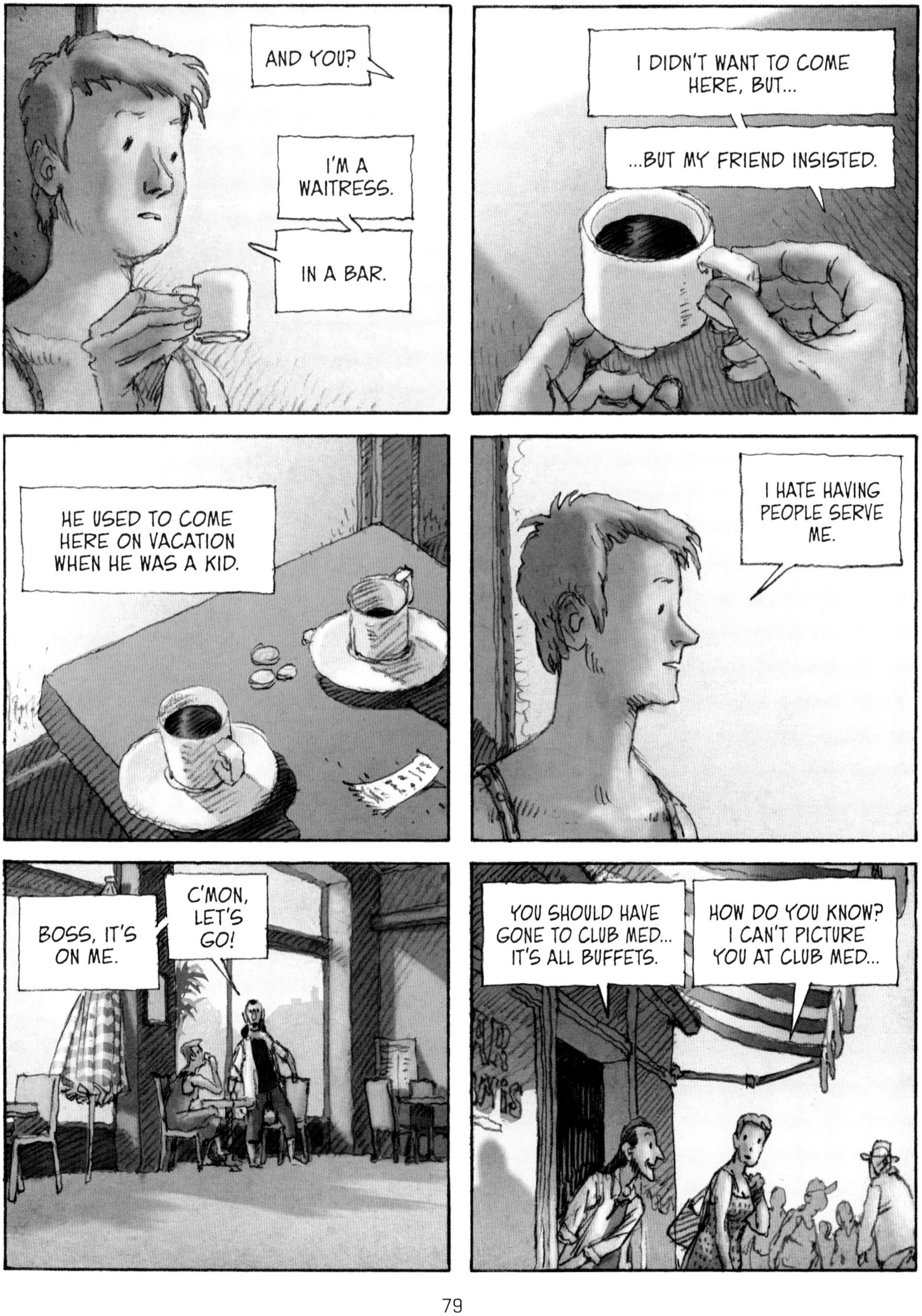
AND YOU?
I'M A WAITRESS.
IN A BAR.
I DIDN'T WANT TO COME HERE, BUT...
...BUT MY FRIEND INSISTED.
HE USED TO COME HERE ON VACATION WHEN HE WAS A KID.
I HATE HAVING PEOPLE SERVE ME.
C'MON, LET'S GO!
BOSS, IT'S ON ME.
YOU SHOULD HAVE GONE TO CLUB MED... IT'S ALL BUFFETS.
HOW DO YOU KNOW? I CAN'T PICTURE YOU AT CLUB MED...

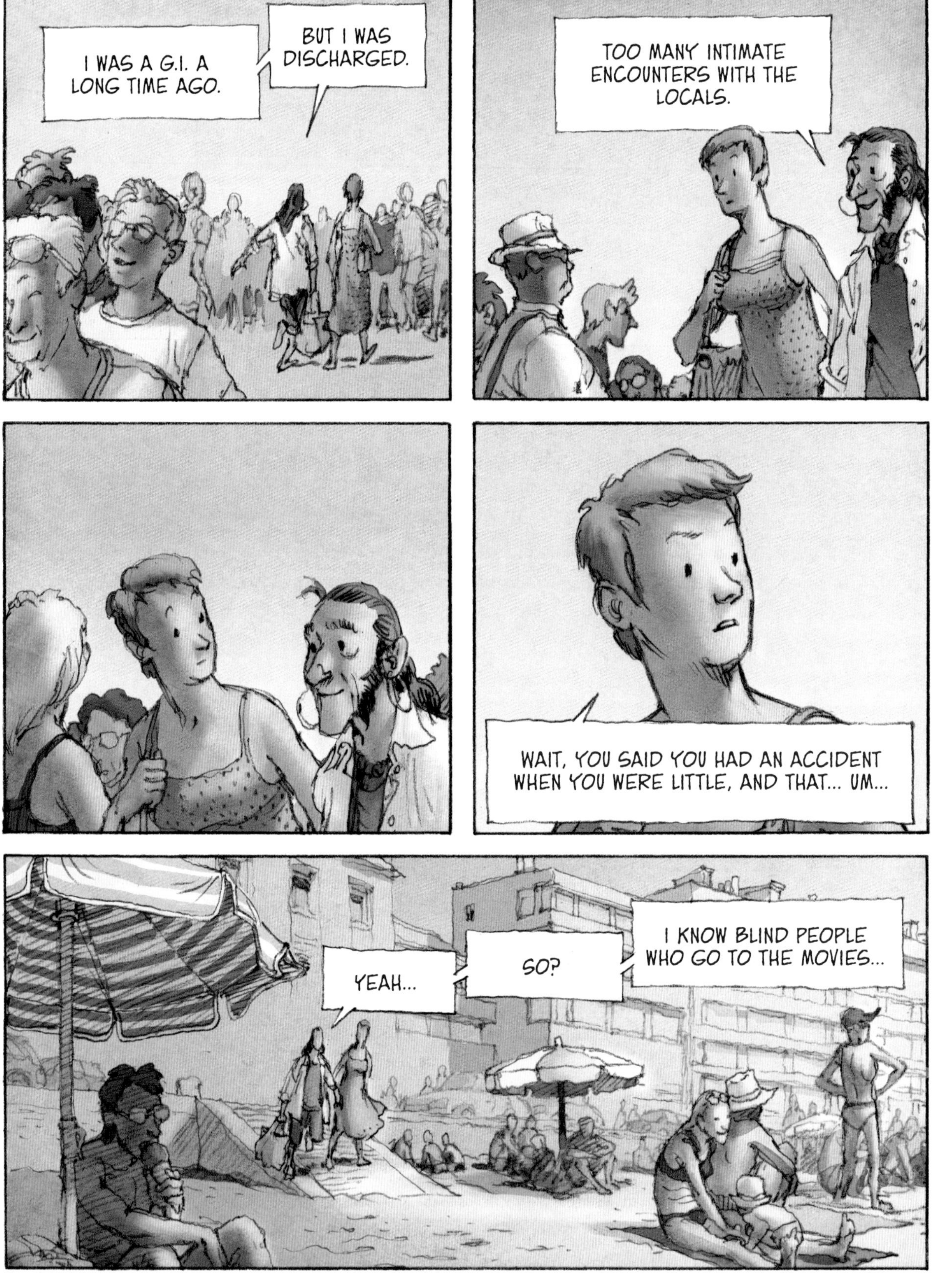
I WAS A G.I. A LONG TIME AGO.
BUT I WAS DISCHARGED.
TOO MANY INTIMATE ENCOUNTERS WITH THE LOCALS.
WAIT, YOU SAID YOU HAD AN ACCIDENT WHEN YOU WERE LITTLE, AND THAT... UM...
YEAH...
SO?
I KNOW BLIND PEOPLE WHO GO TO THE MOVIES...

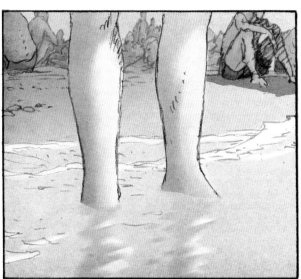

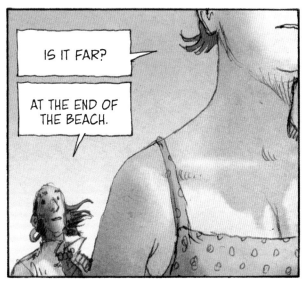

IS IT FAR?

AT THE END OF
THE BEACH.

THERE'S A SMALL TOURIST TRAM THAT GOES THERE...

...BUT FRANKLY I'D RATHER DIE OF ASPHYXIATION IN A MANURE PIT THAN PUT MY BUTT IN ONE OF THOSE SEATS.

LIKE THAT FARMER AND HIS WIFE AND FRIEND IN 1990...?

I...

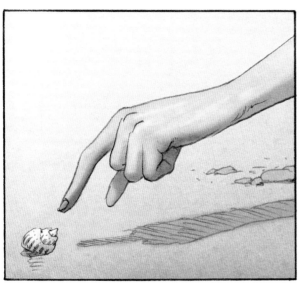

IT REASSURES ME TO KNOW THAT DEATH IS ALWAYS PRESENT, NO MATTER WHEN OR WHERE.

IT'S NOT TO MAKE FUN OF THOSE PEOPLE.

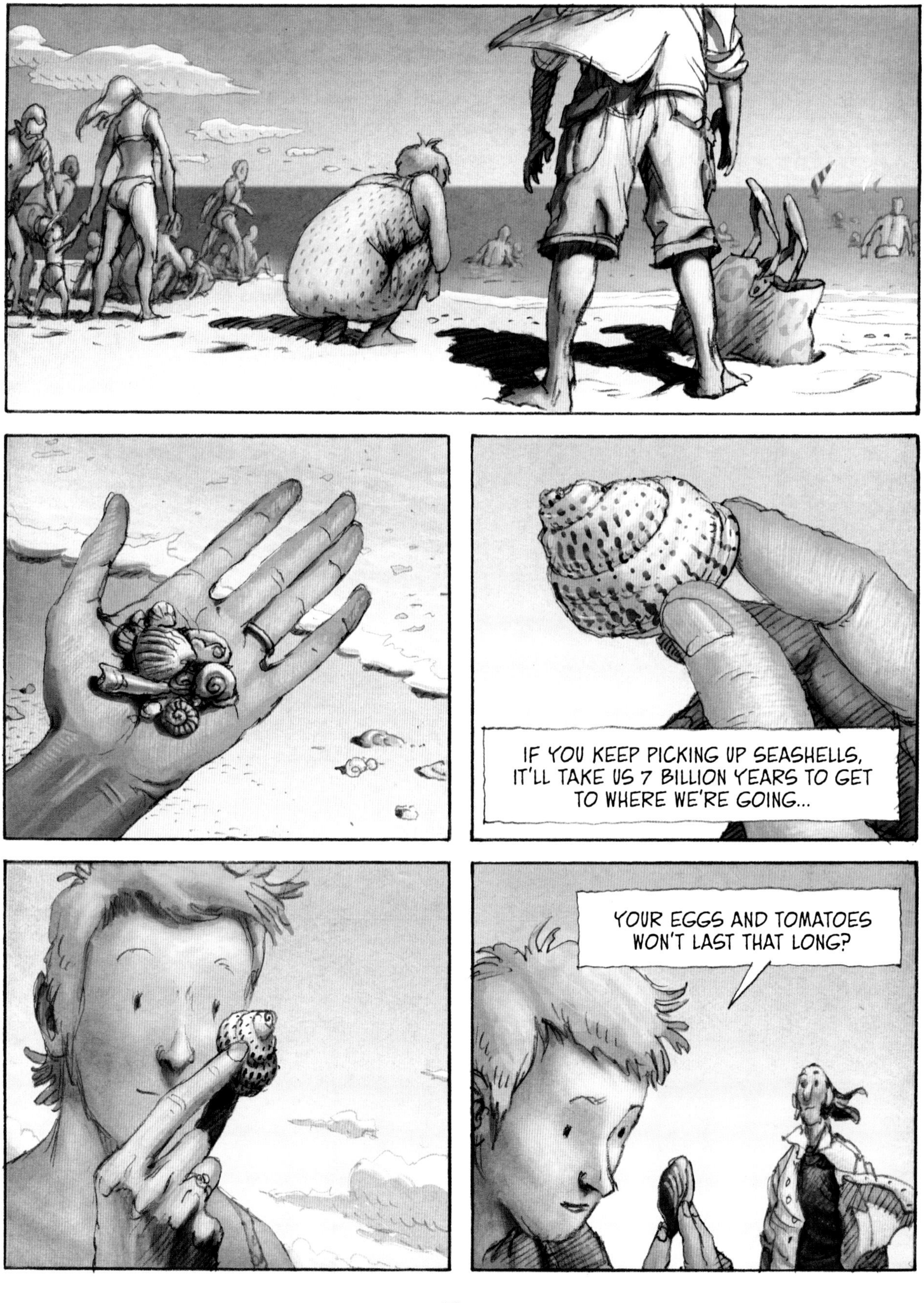

IF YOU KEEP PICKING UP SEASHELLS, IT'LL TAKE US 7 BILLION YEARS TO GET TO WHERE WE'RE GOING...
YOUR EGGS AND TOMATOES WON'T LAST THAT LONG?

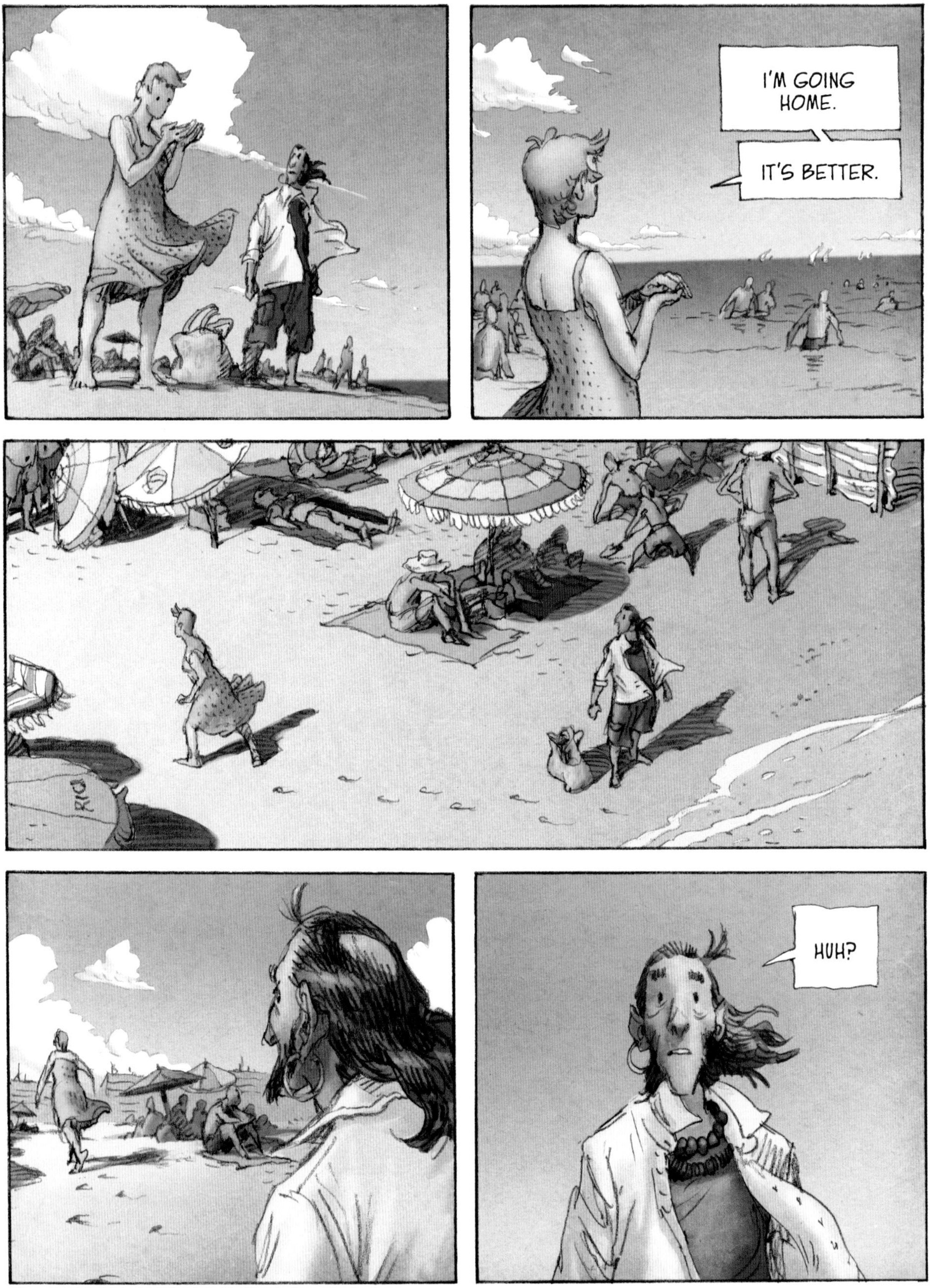
I'M GOING HOME.
IT'S BETTER.
HUH?

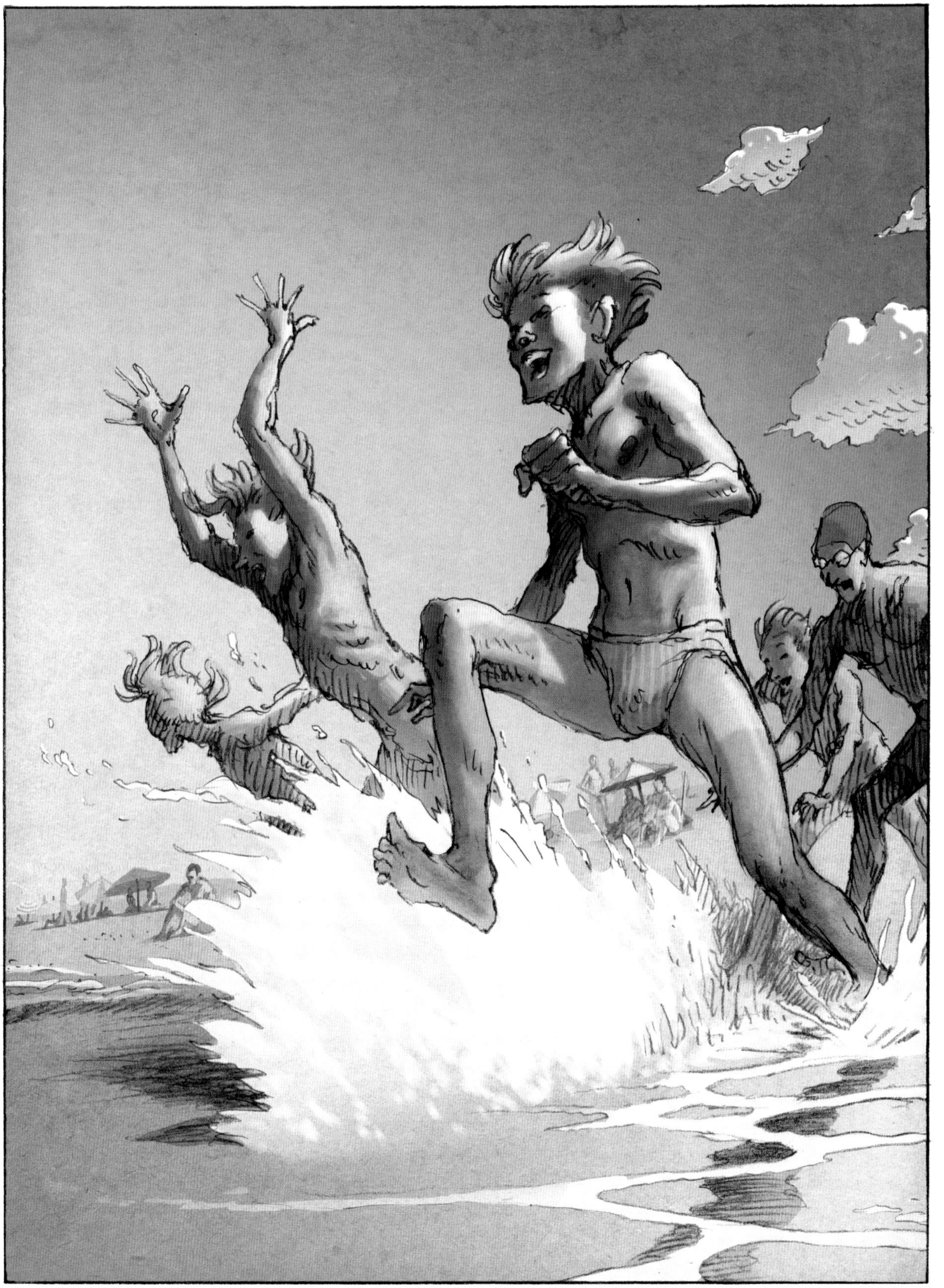

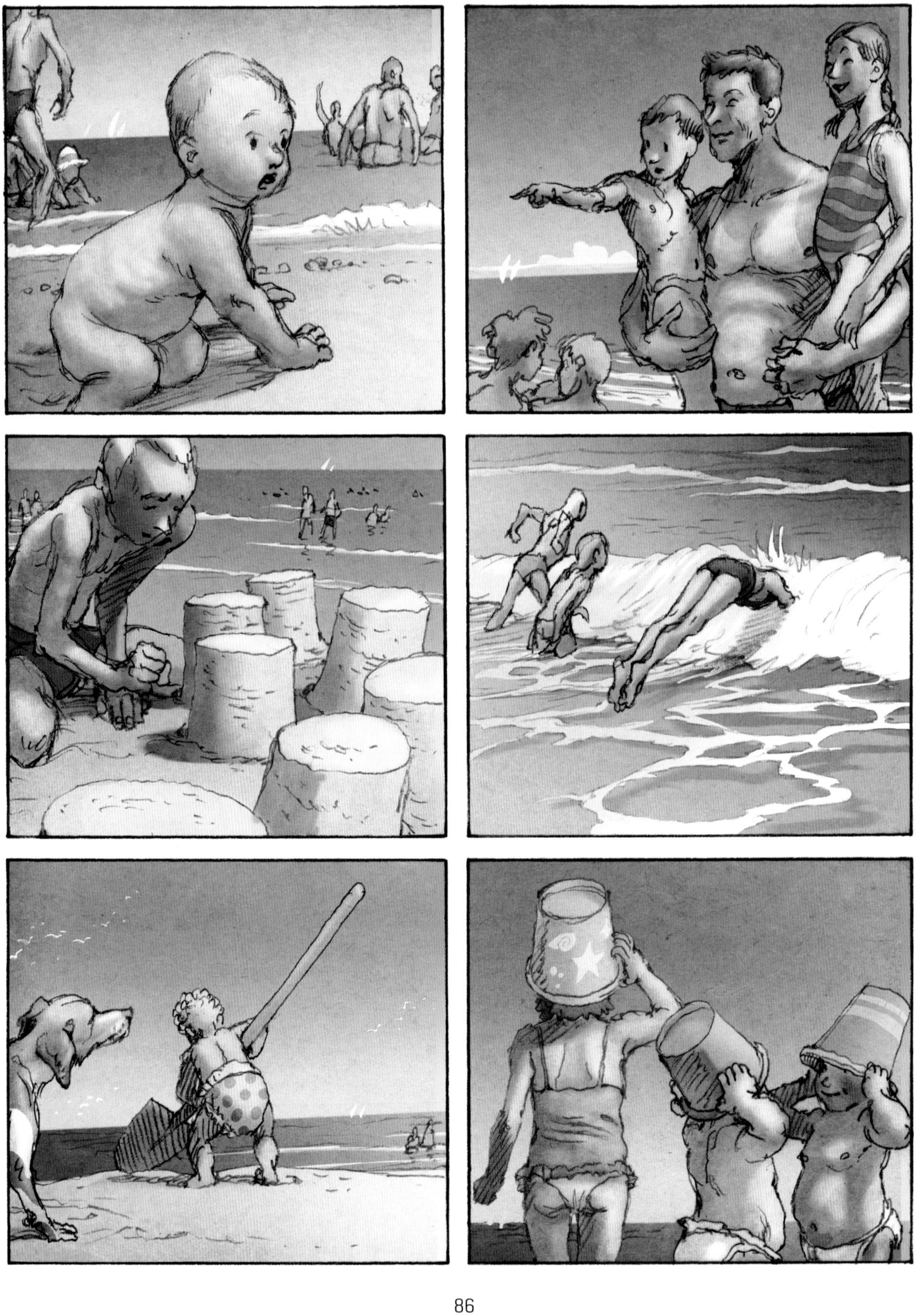

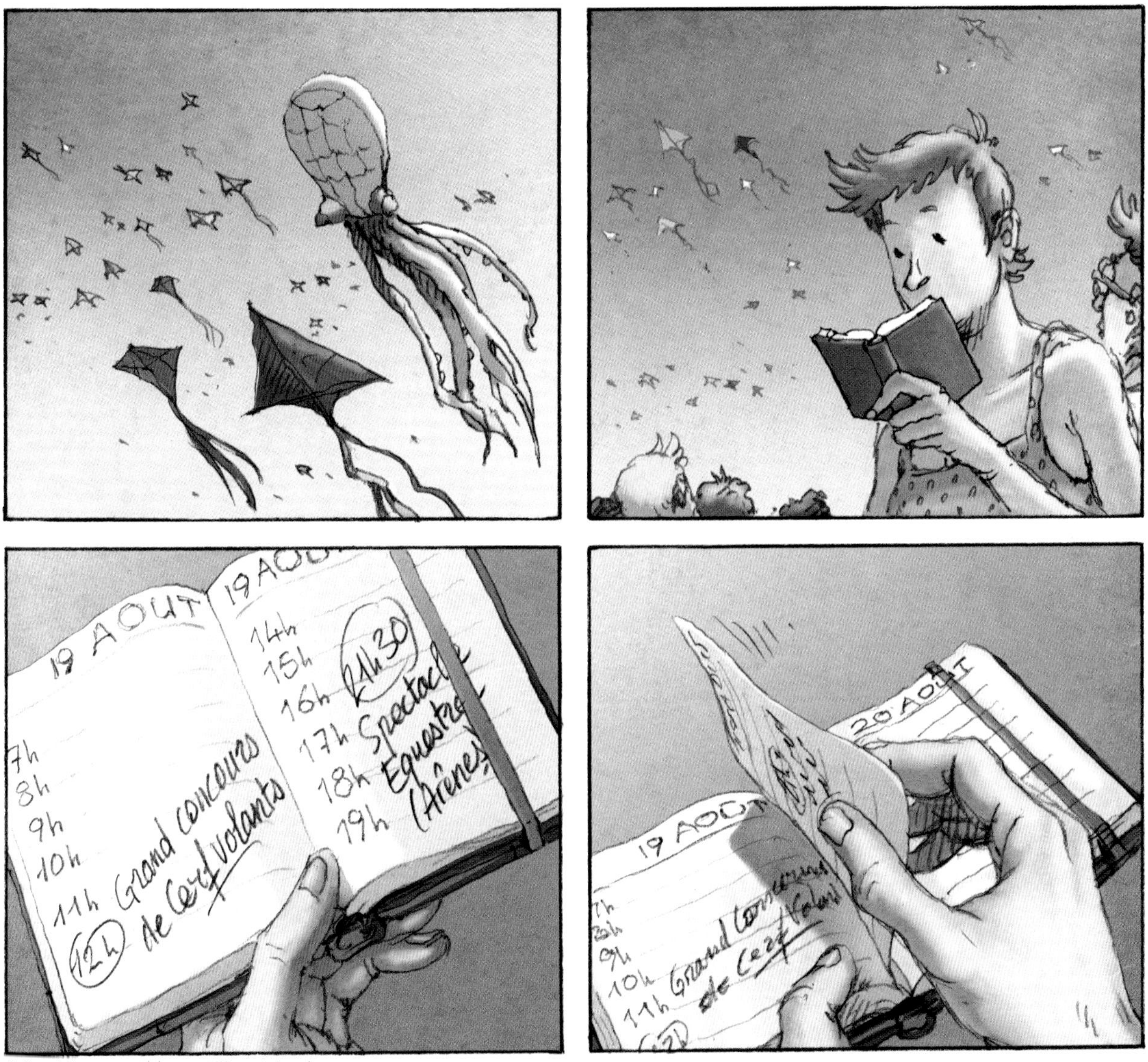
19 AOUT
7h
8h
9h
10h
11h Grand concours de Cerf volants
12h
19 AOUT
14h
15h 21h30
16h Spectacle
17h Equestre
18h (Arènes)
19h
20 AOUT
19 AOUT
7h
8h
9h
10h Grand concours de Cerf
11h

* Grand kite competition **Equestrian show

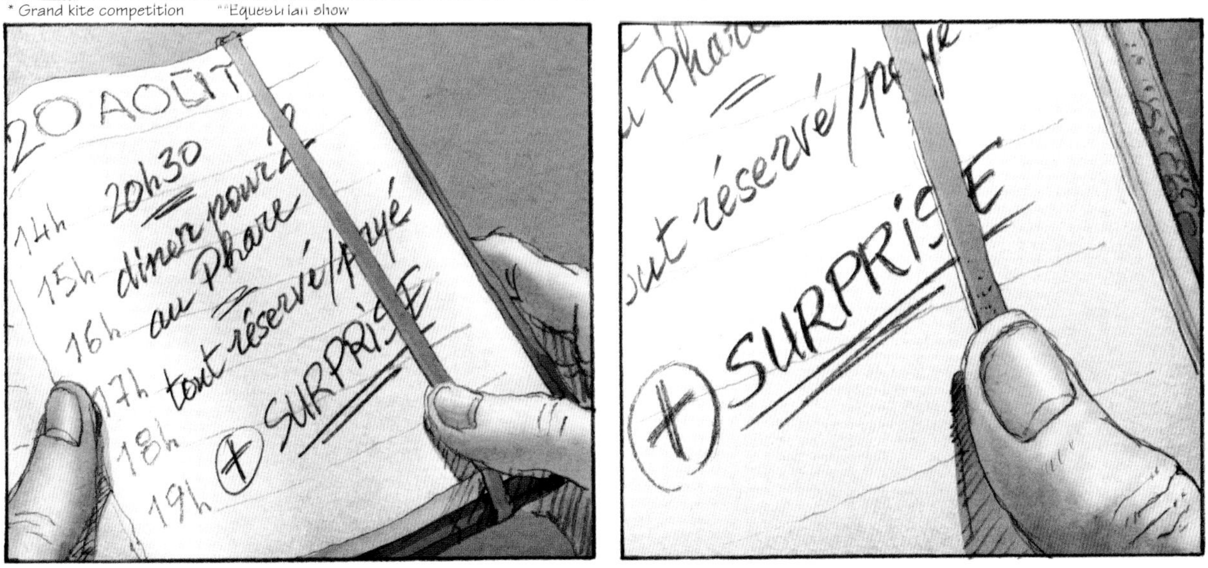
20 AOUT
14h 20h30
15h dîner pour 2
16h au Phare
17h tout réservé/payé
18h
19h + SURPRISE
u Phare
out réservé/payé
+ SURPRISE

* Dinner for two at the Lighthouse, All reserved/paid

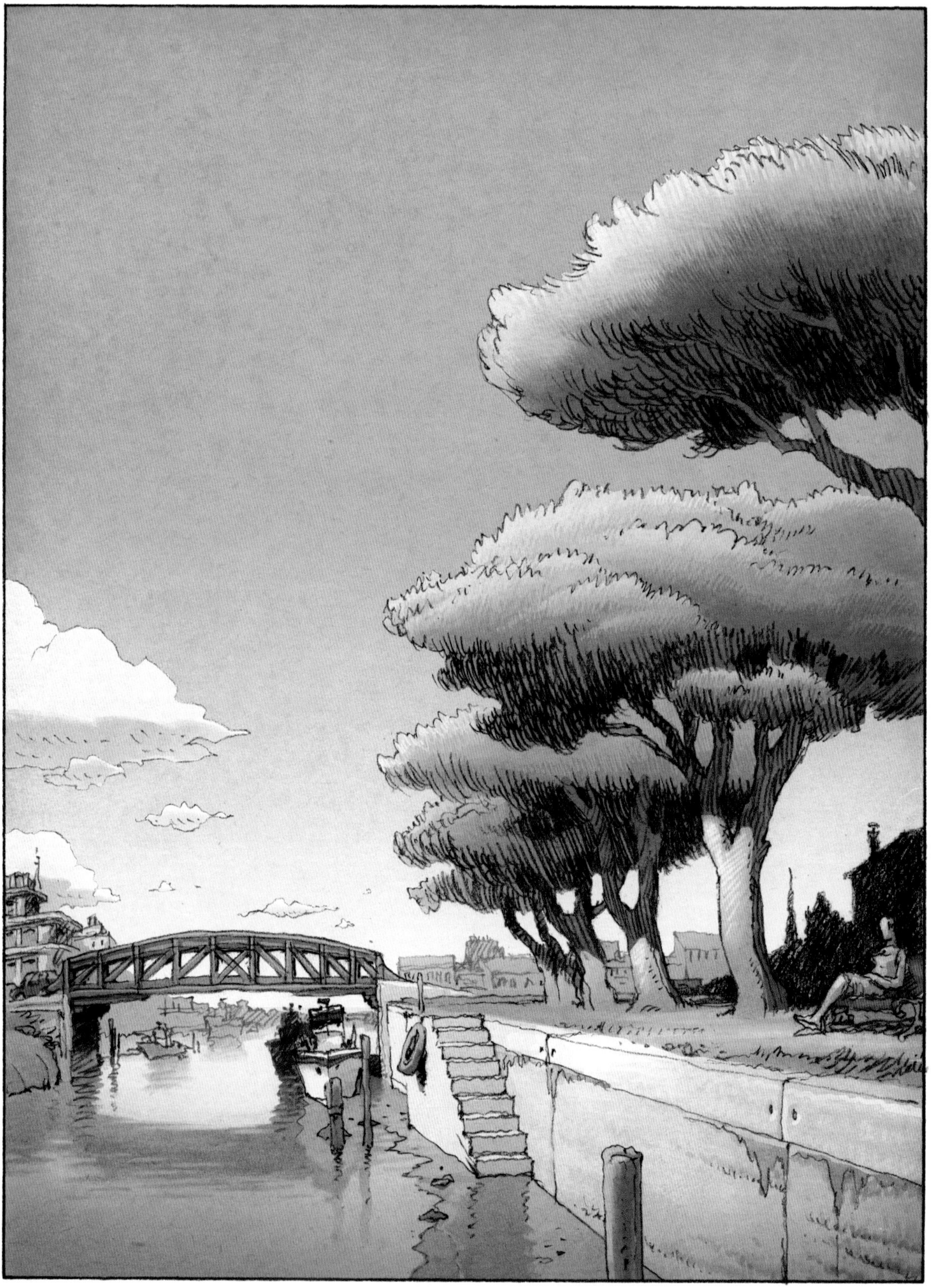

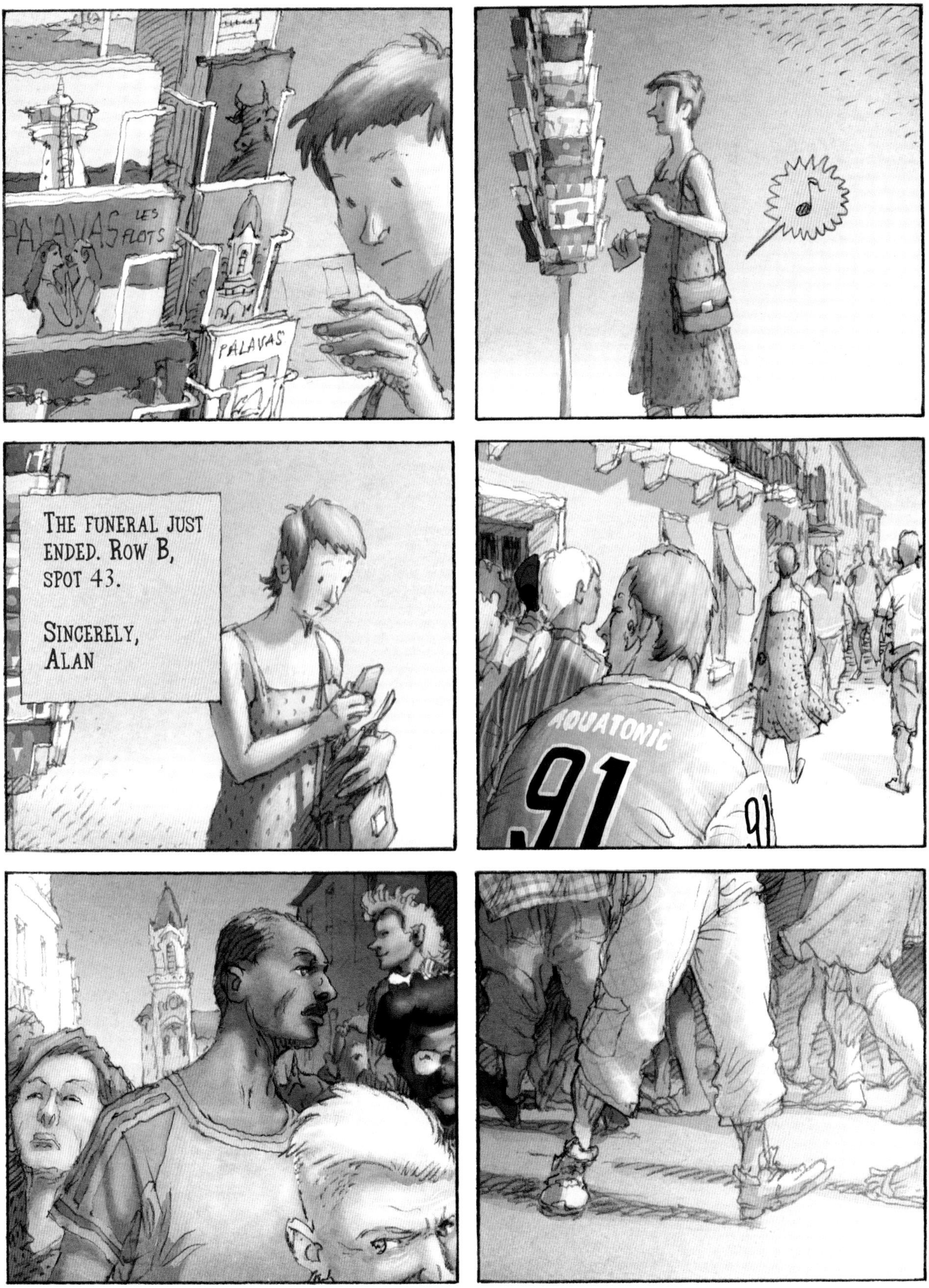
PALAVAS LES FLOTS
PALAVAS
THE FUNERAL JUST ENDED. ROW B, SPOT 43.
SINCERELY, ALAN
AQUATONIC
91
91

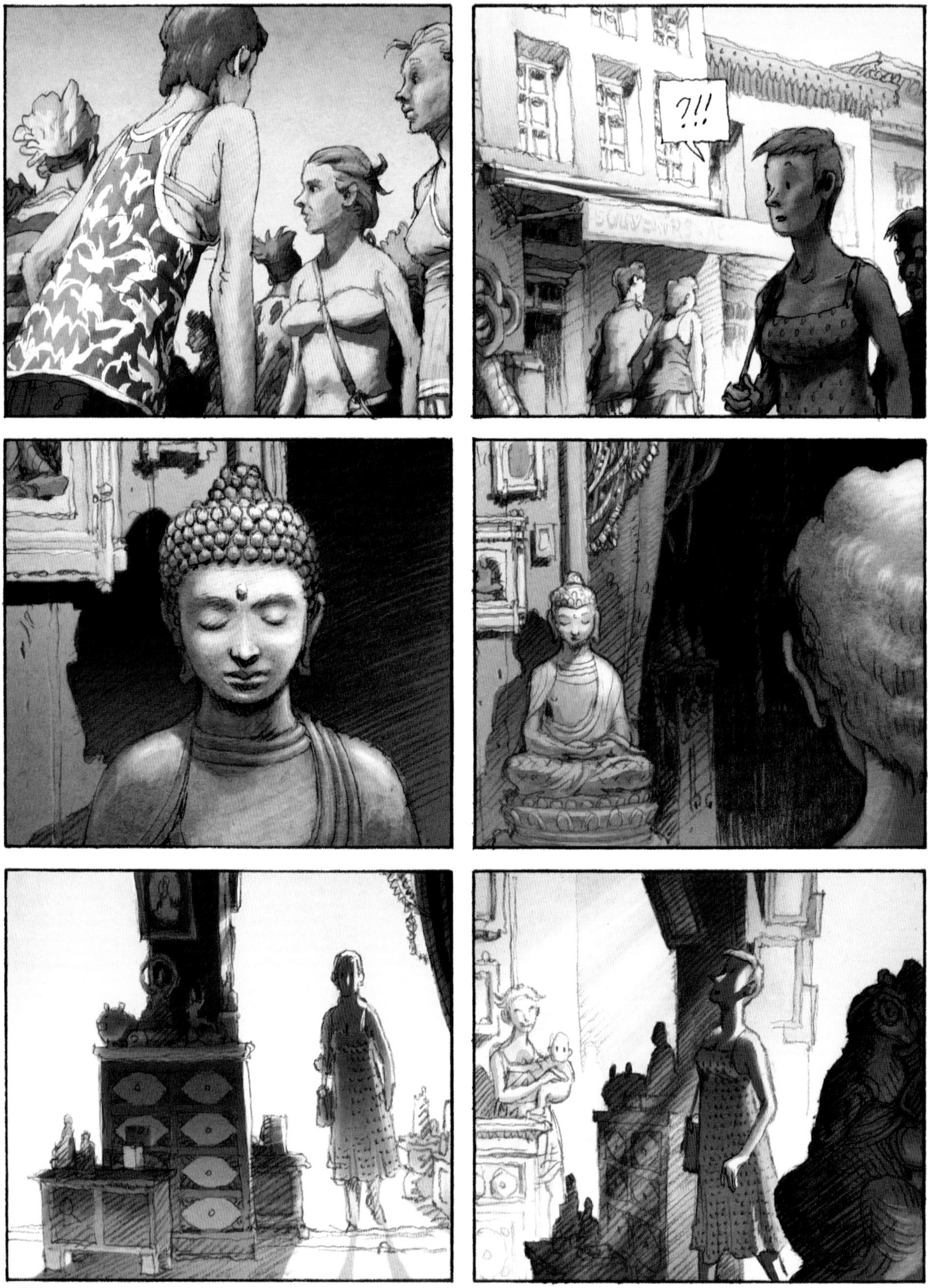
?!!

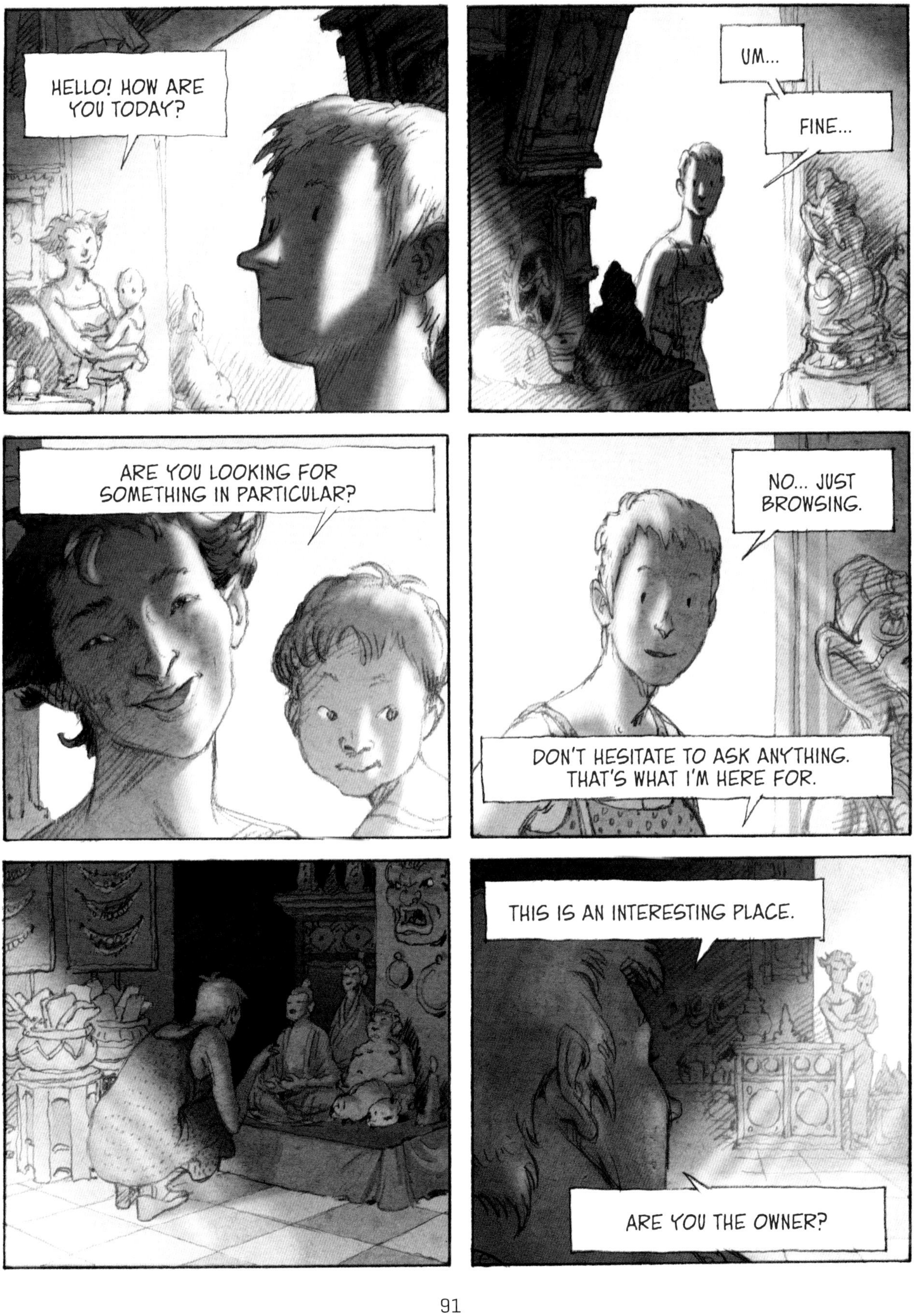
HELLO! HOW ARE YOU TODAY?
UM...
FINE...
ARE YOU LOOKING FOR SOMETHING IN PARTICULAR?
NO... JUST BROWSING.
DON'T HESITATE TO ASK ANYTHING. THAT'S WHAT I'M HERE FOR.
THIS IS AN INTERESTING PLACE.
ARE YOU THE OWNER?

NO, I'M JUST AN EMPLOYEE.

THE OWNER HAS VERY ECLECTIC TASTES.

IS SHE FROM NEPAL OR INDIA?

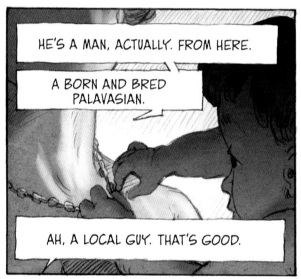

HE'S A MAN, ACTUALLY. FROM HERE.

A BORN AND BRED PALAVASIAN.

AH, A LOCAL GUY. THAT'S GOOD.

DID HE OPEN THE SHOP BECAUSE HE REALLY BELIEVES IN IT OR TO TAKE ADVANTAGE OF THE TOURISTS?

OH, NO. IF PACO SEES A SNAIL ON THE SIDEWALK, HE'LL PICK IT UP AND PUT IT IN THE GARDEN.

THERE ARE MEN LIKE THAT?

HEHEH... HE'S A REAL SWEETHEART.

BELIEVE IT OR NOT, BUT RIGHT NOW, HE'S ON A PICNIC WITH A TOURIST HE DOESN'T EVEN KNOW TO CHEER HER UP.

HA... HE SOUNDS LIKE A REAL FLIRT!

NO, IN FACT, HE TOLD ME THE LADY'S STORY SO THAT I'D FEEL BAD ENOUGH TO COVER FOR HIM THIS AFTERNOON.

I'M NOT KIDDING.

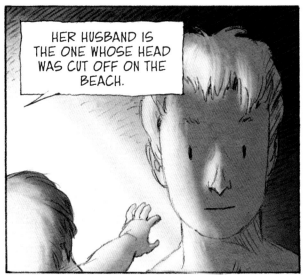

HER HUSBAND IS THE ONE WHOSE HEAD WAS CUT OFF ON THE BEACH.

YOU KNOW, THE OTHER DAY. BY THE WIND.

YEAH...

SO YOU CAN IMAGINE HE'S NOT GOING TO FLIRT WITH HER.

HE SOUNDS LIKE A REAL PEARL, THIS GUY.

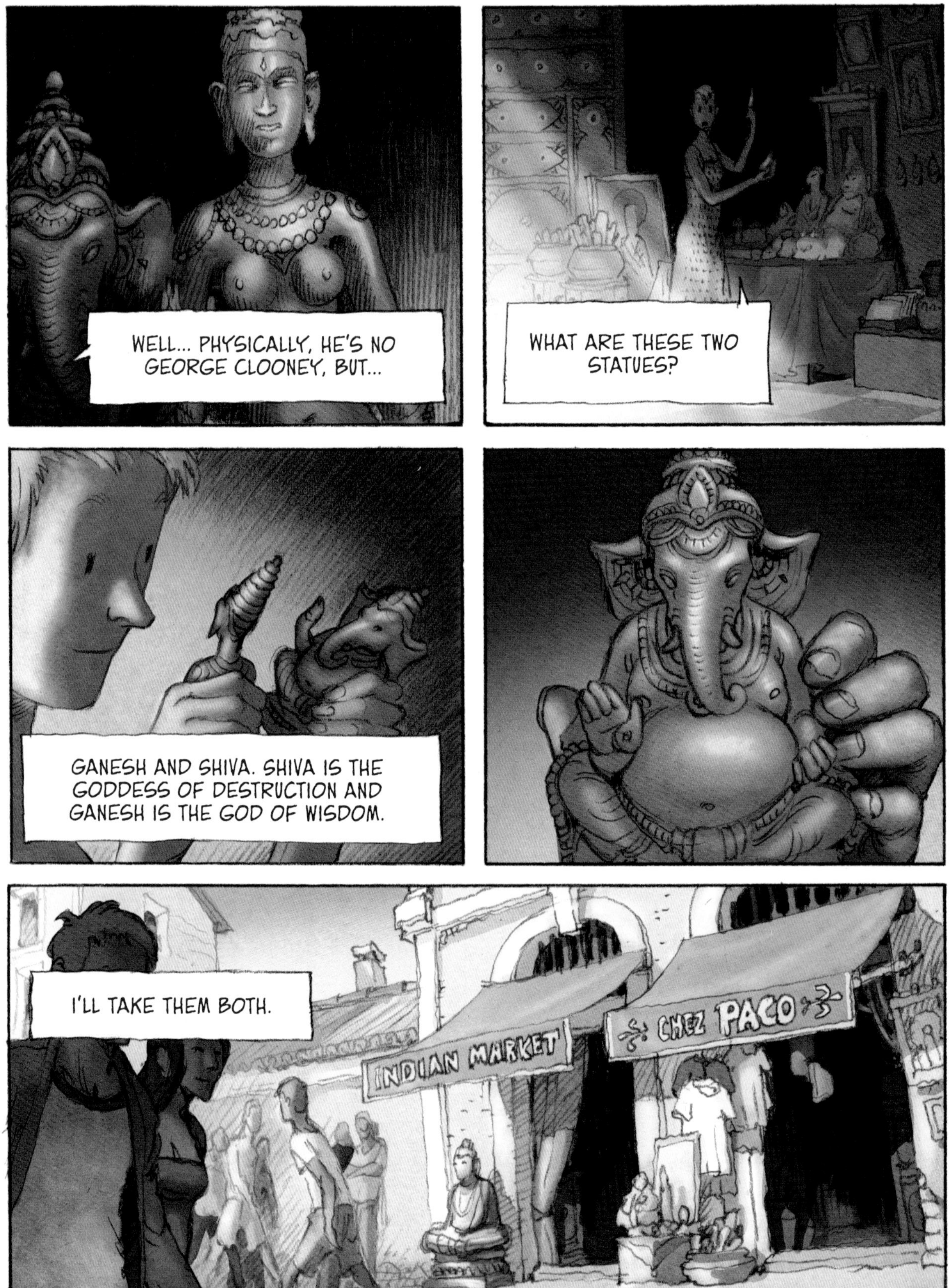

WELL... PHYSICALLY, HE'S NO GEORGE CLOONEY, BUT...
WHAT ARE THESE TWO STATUES?
GANESH AND SHIVA. SHIVA IS THE GODDESS OF DESTRUCTION AND GANESH IS THE GOD OF WISDOM.
I'LL TAKE THEM BOTH.
INDIAN MARKET
CHEZ PACO

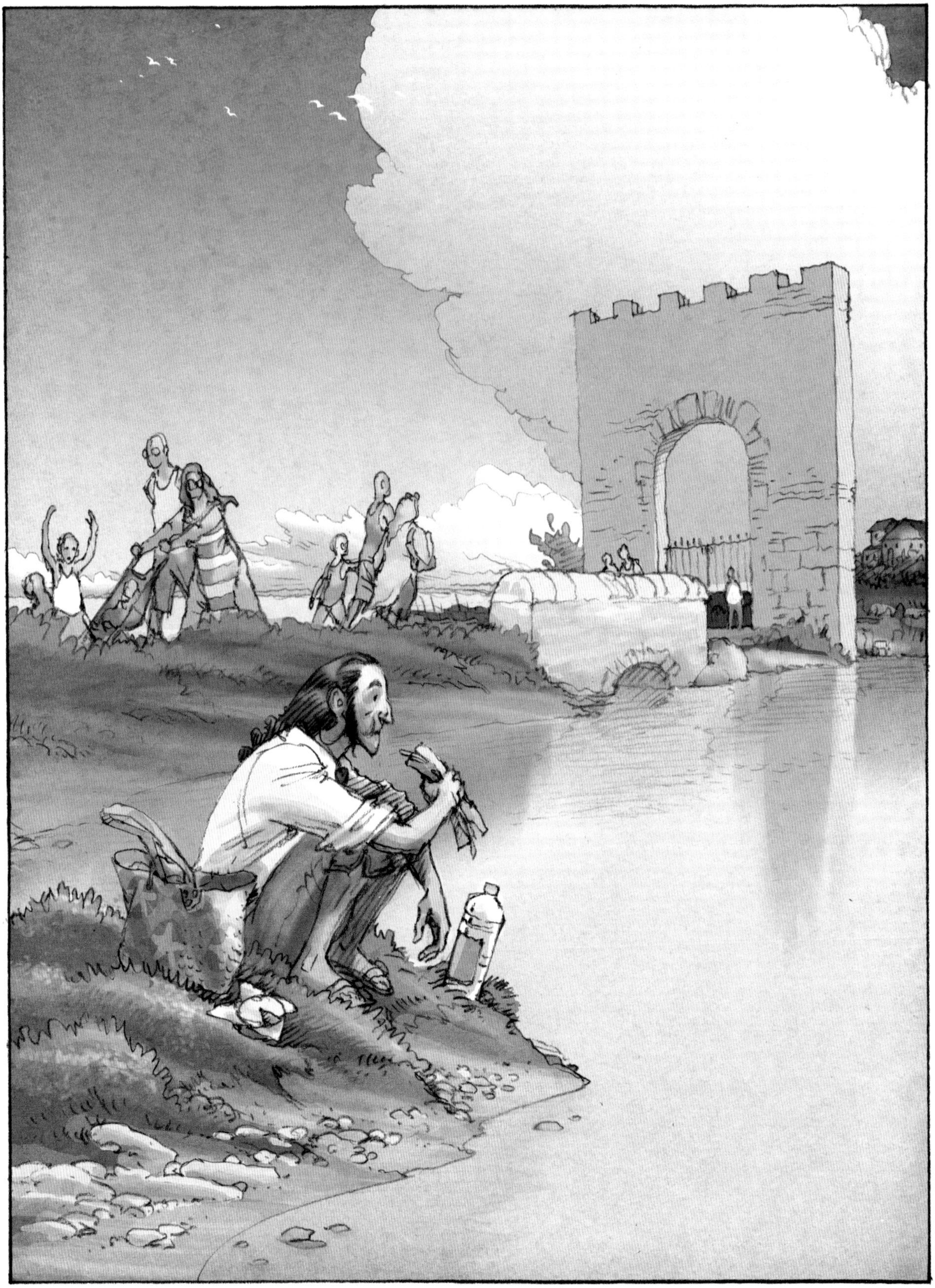

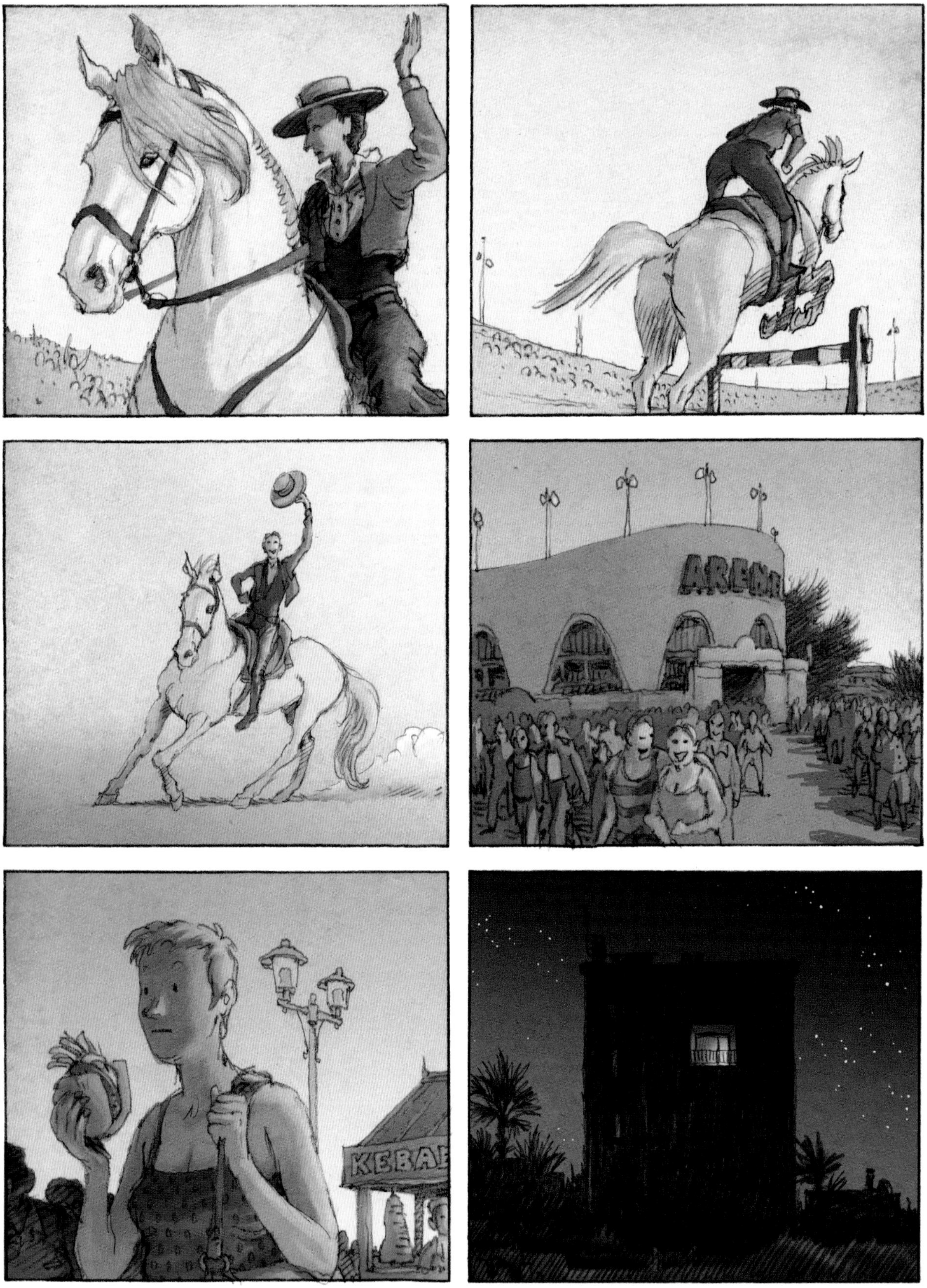
KEBAB

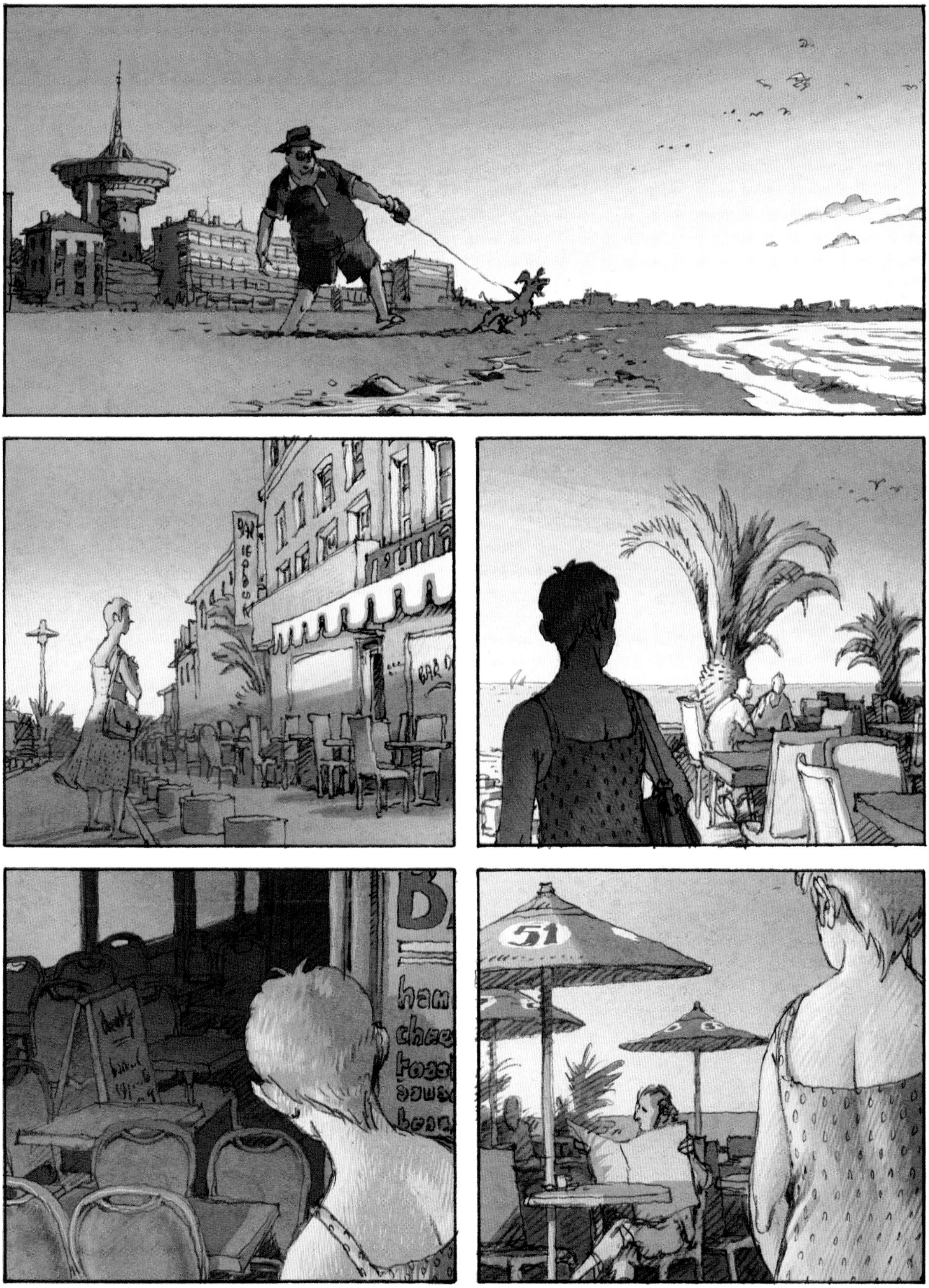
51

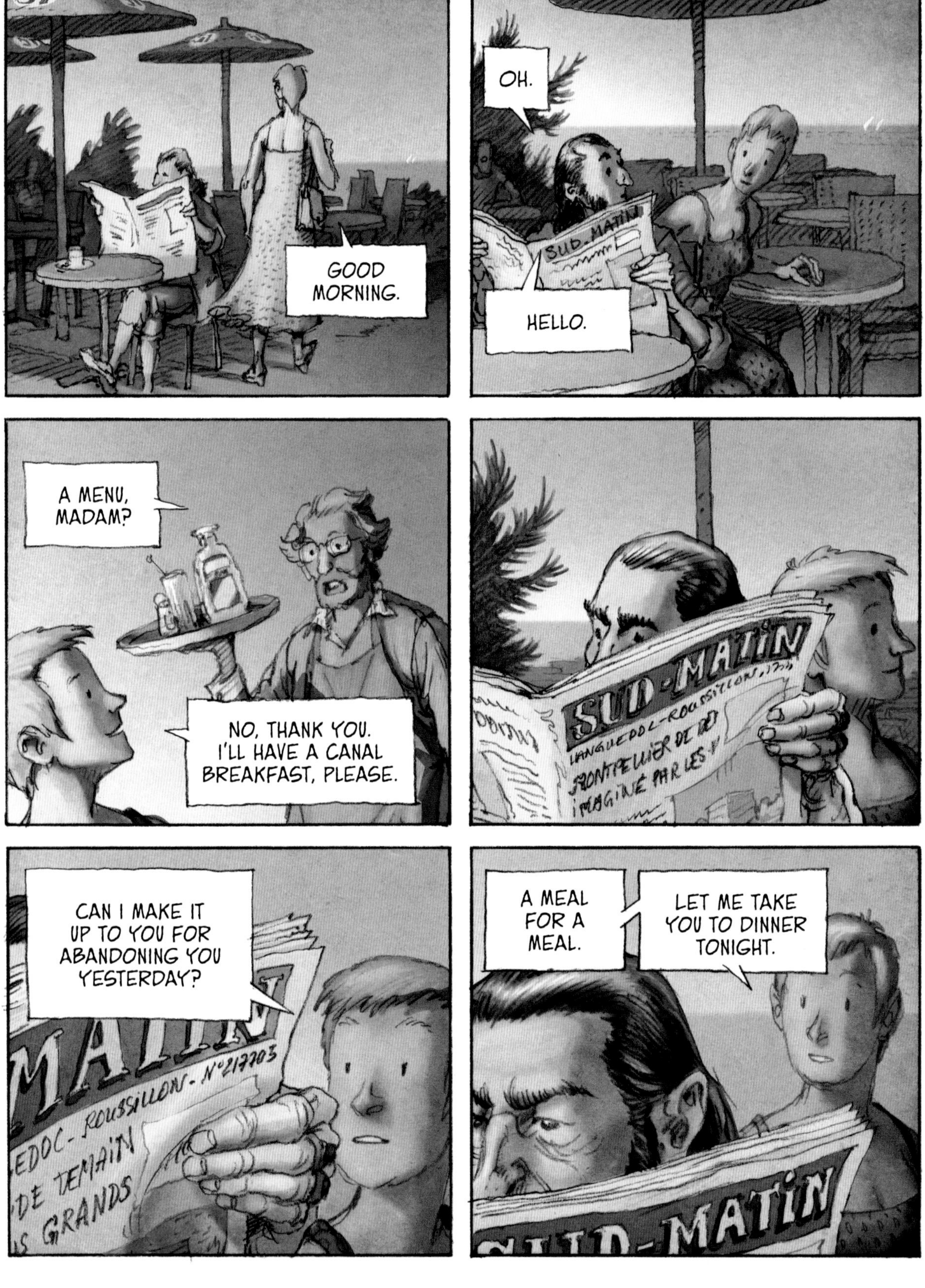
GOOD MORNING.
OH.
HELLO.
A MENU, MADAM?
NO, THANK YOU. I'LL HAVE A CANAL BREAKFAST, PLEASE.
SUD-MATIN
CAN I MAKE IT UP TO YOU FOR ABANDONING YOU YESTERDAY?
A MEAL FOR A MEAL.
LET ME TAKE YOU TO DINNER TONIGHT.

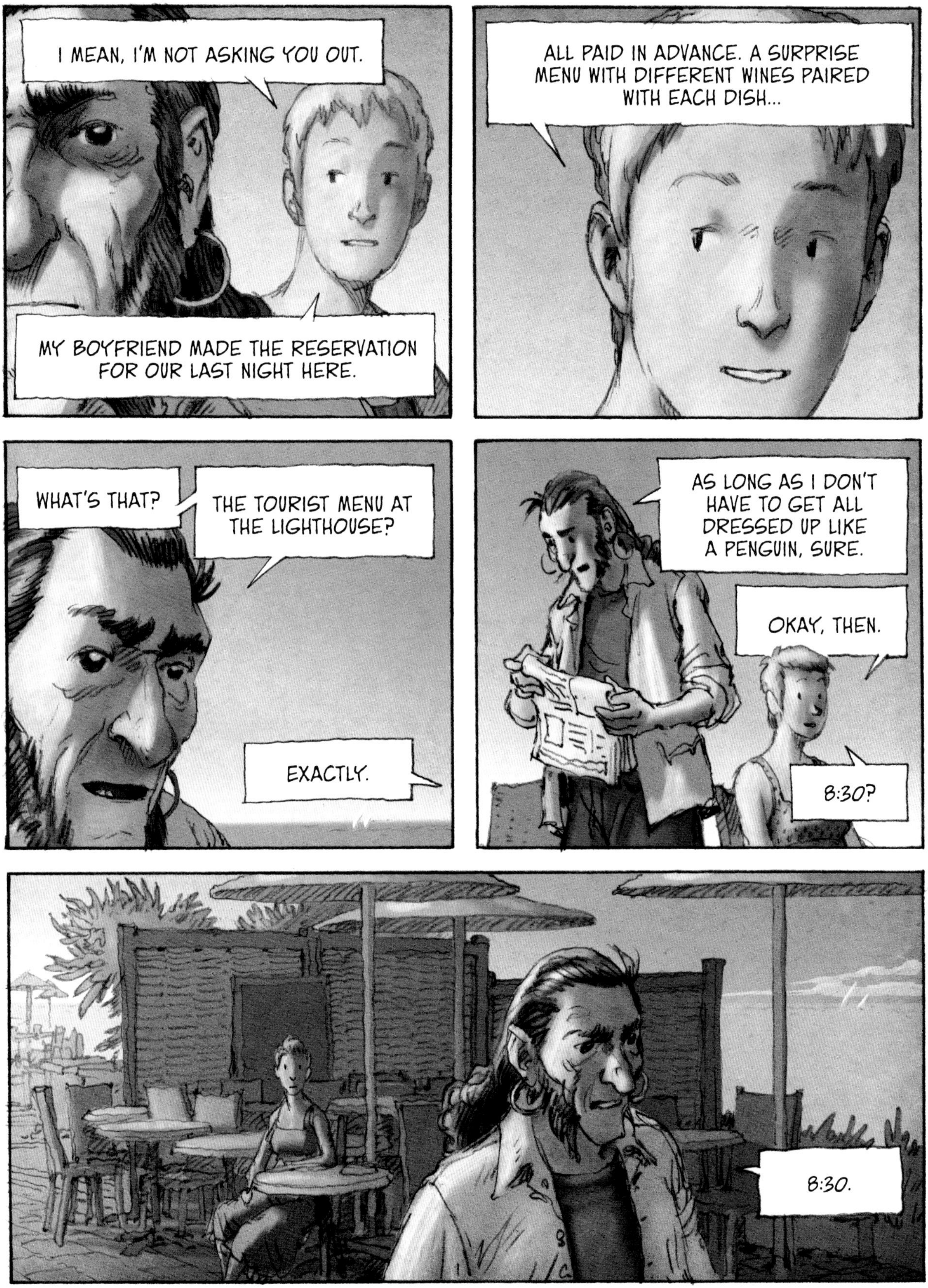

I MEAN, I'M NOT ASKING YOU OUT.
MY BOYFRIEND MADE THE RESERVATION FOR OUR LAST NIGHT HERE.
ALL PAID IN ADVANCE. A SURPRISE MENU WITH DIFFERENT WINES PAIRED WITH EACH DISH...
WHAT'S THAT?
THE TOURIST MENU AT THE LIGHTHOUSE?
EXACTLY.
AS LONG AS I DON'T HAVE TO GET ALL DRESSED UP LIKE A PENGUIN, SURE.
OKAY, THEN.
8:30?
8:30.

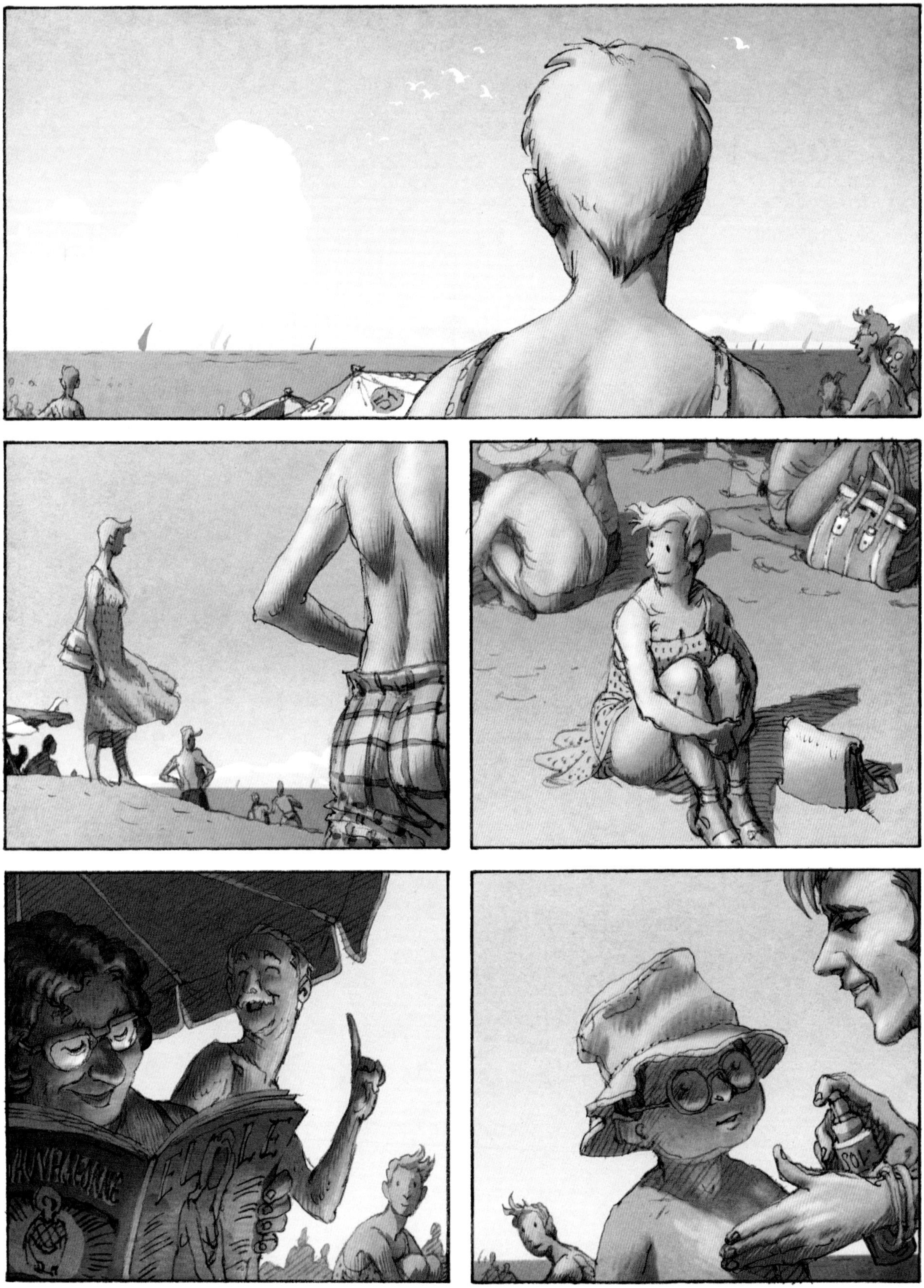

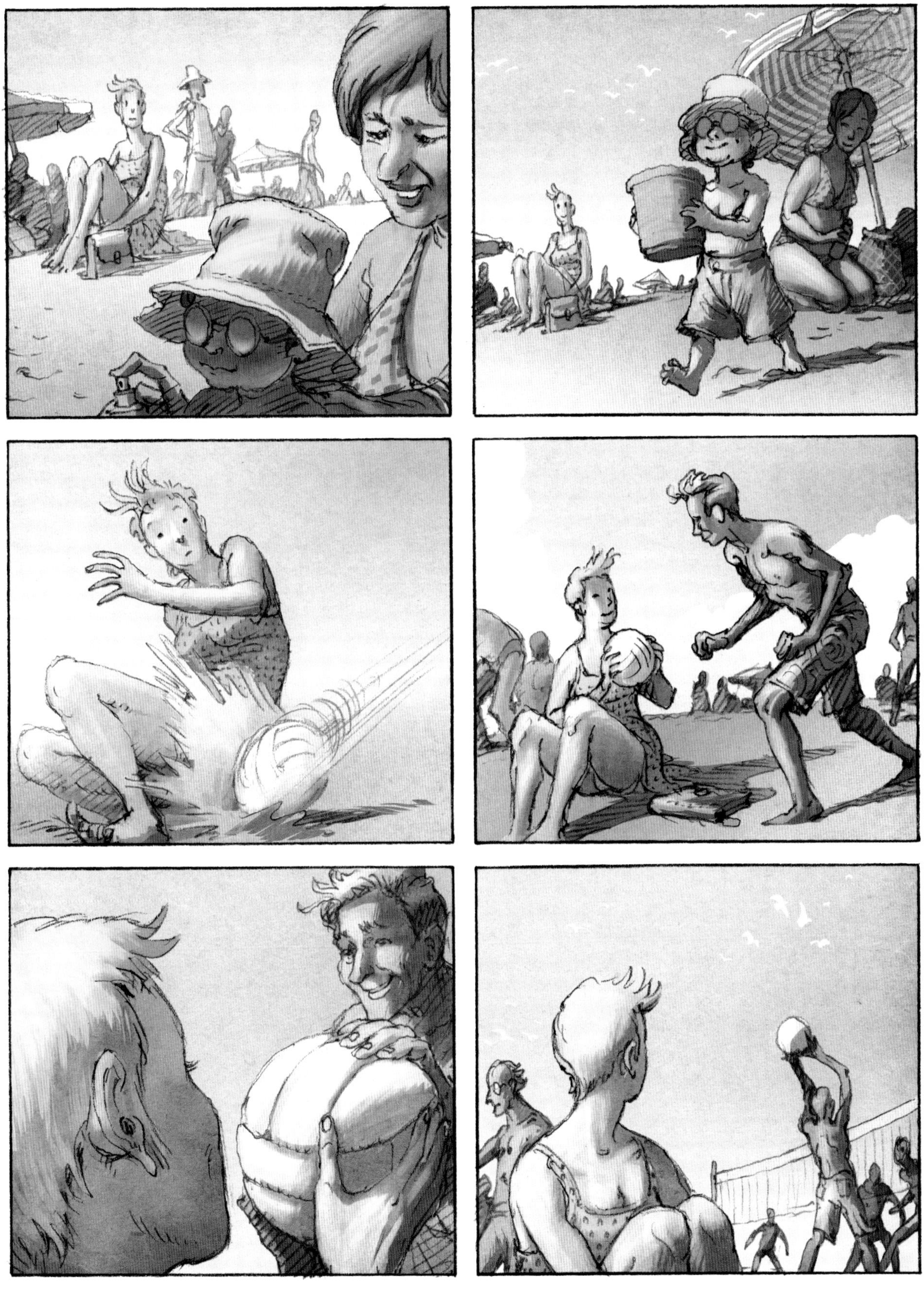

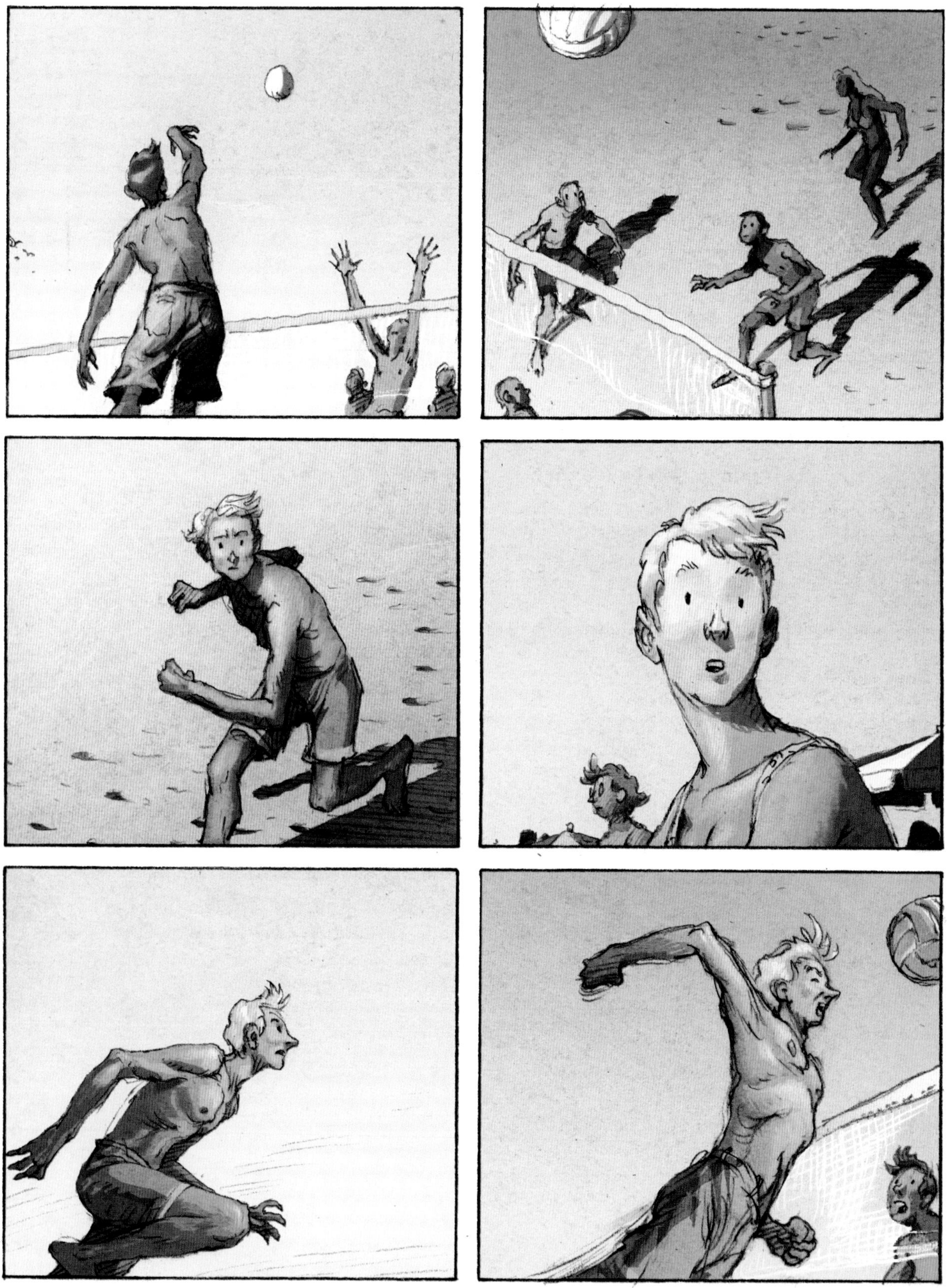

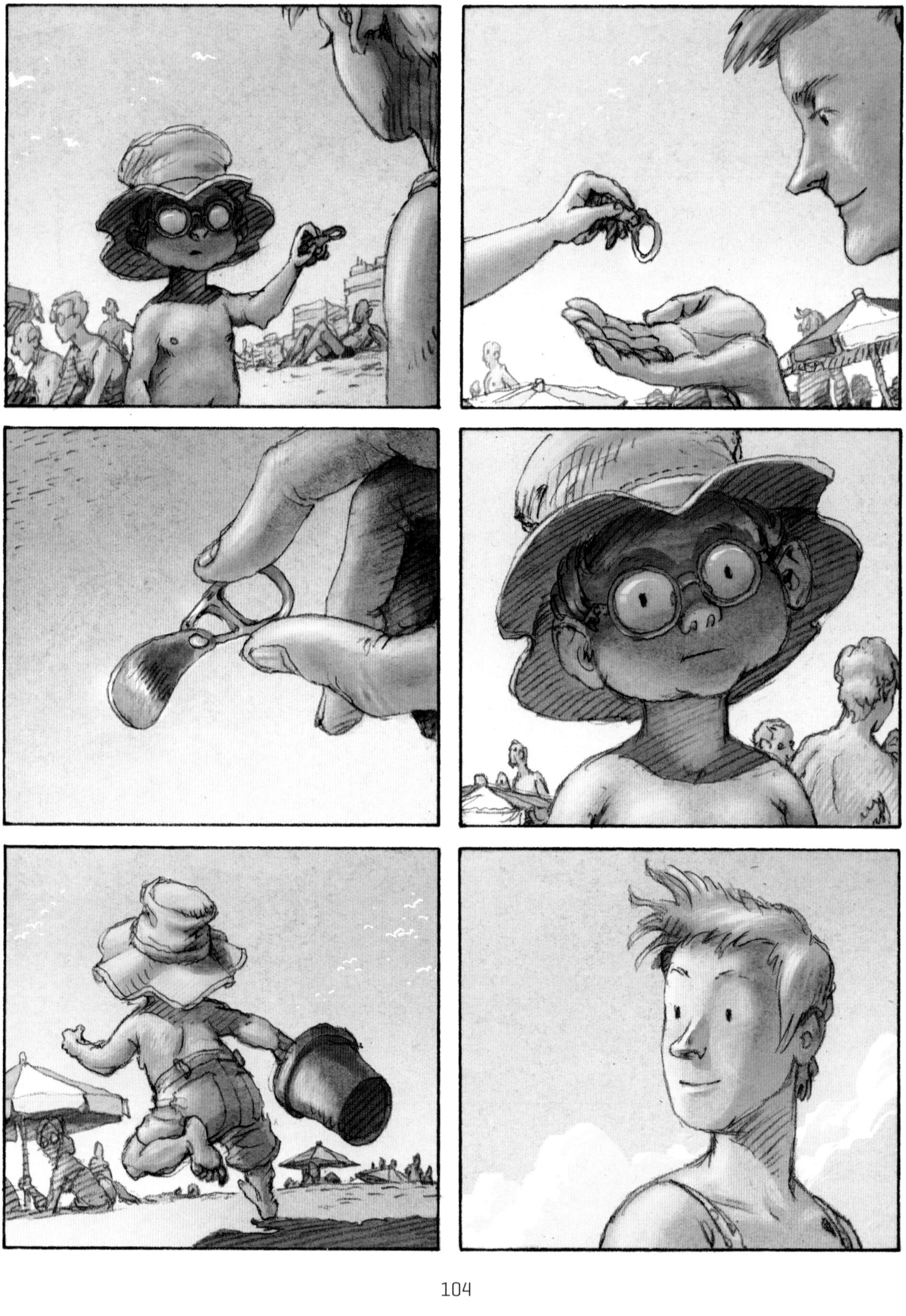

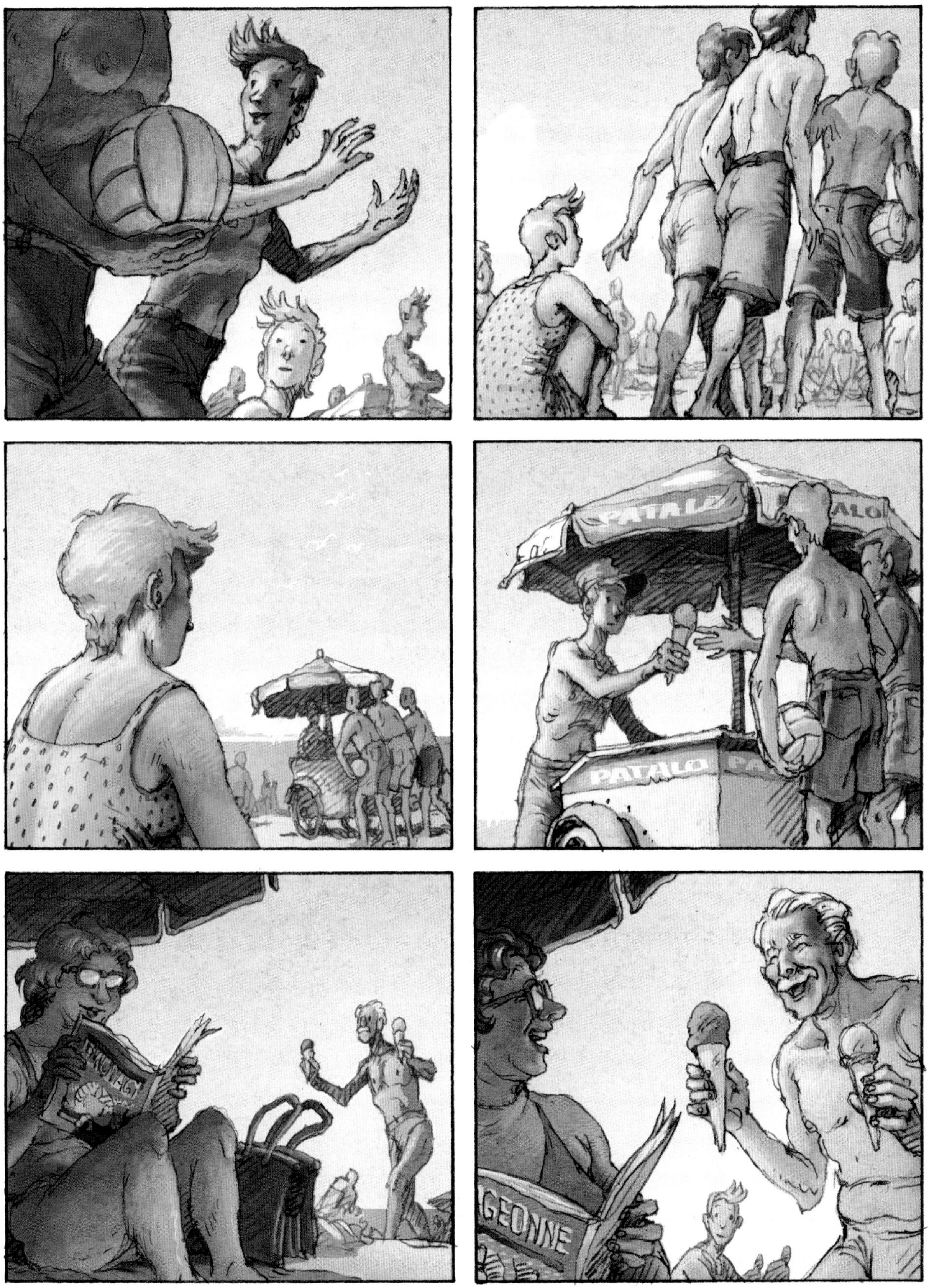
PATALO
PATALO

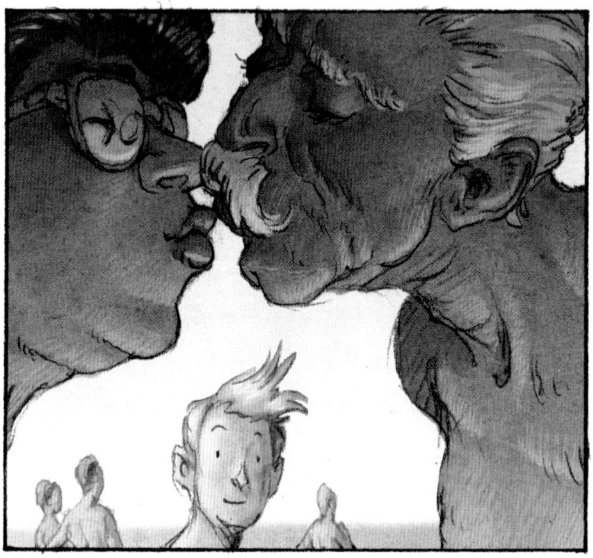

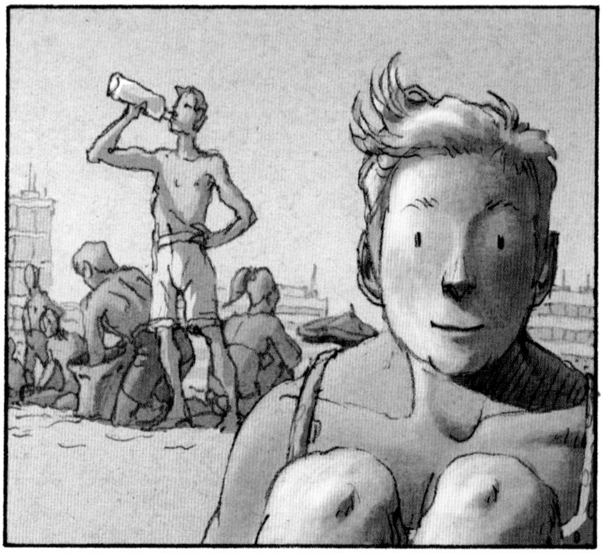

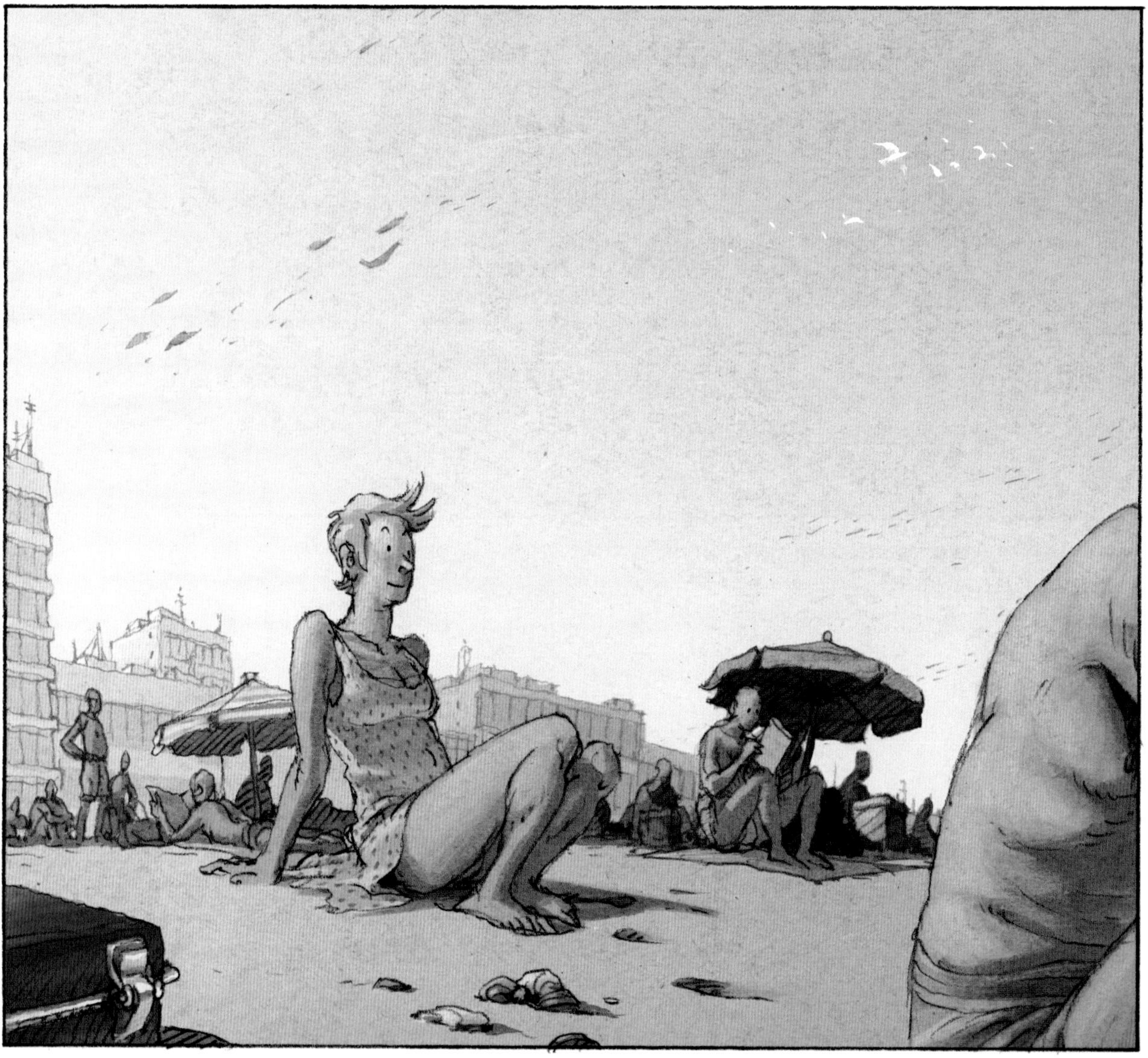

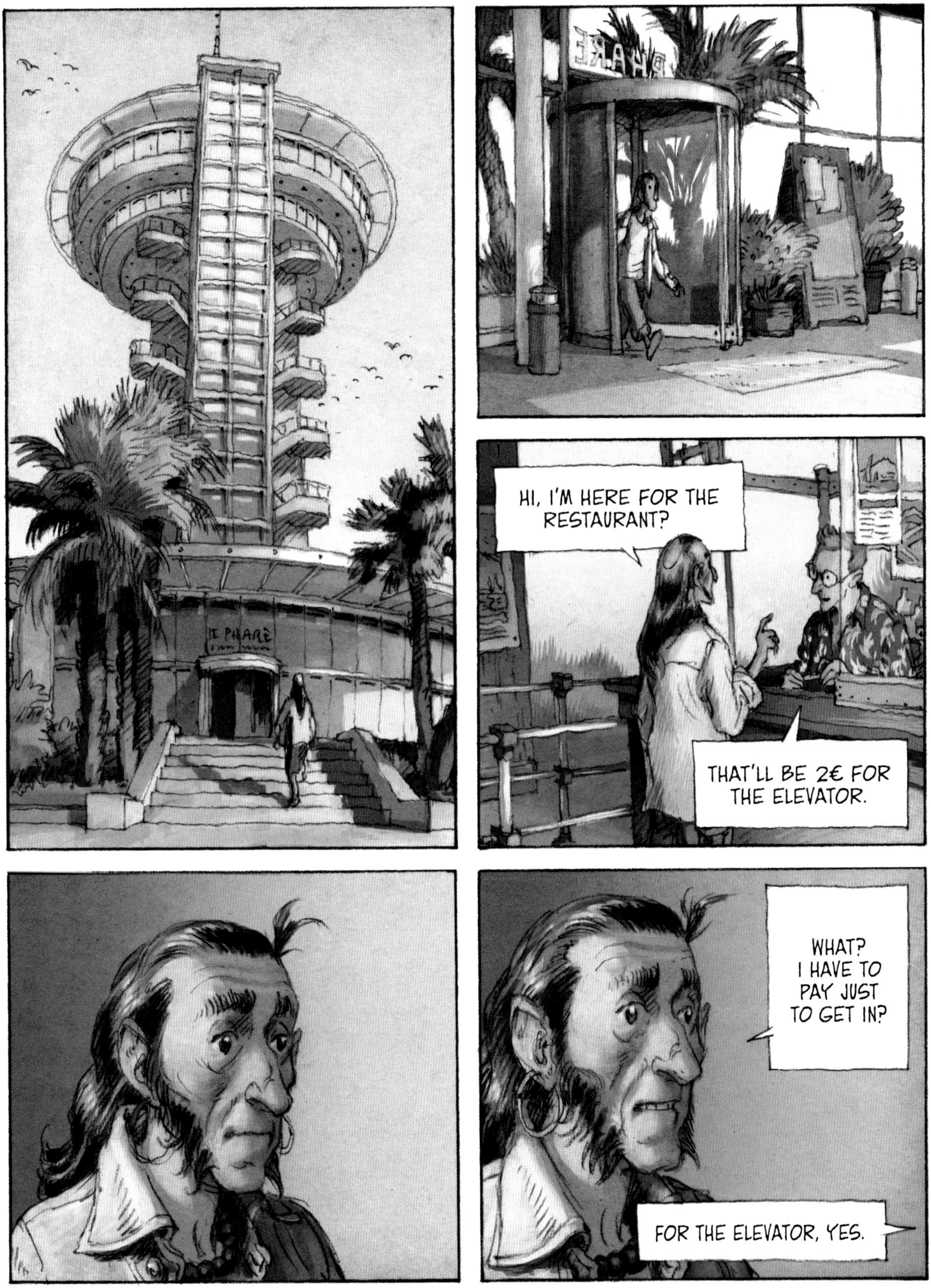
HI, I'M HERE FOR THE RESTAURANT?
THAT'LL BE 2€ FOR THE ELEVATOR.
WHAT? I HAVE TO PAY JUST TO GET IN?
FOR THE ELEVATOR, YES.

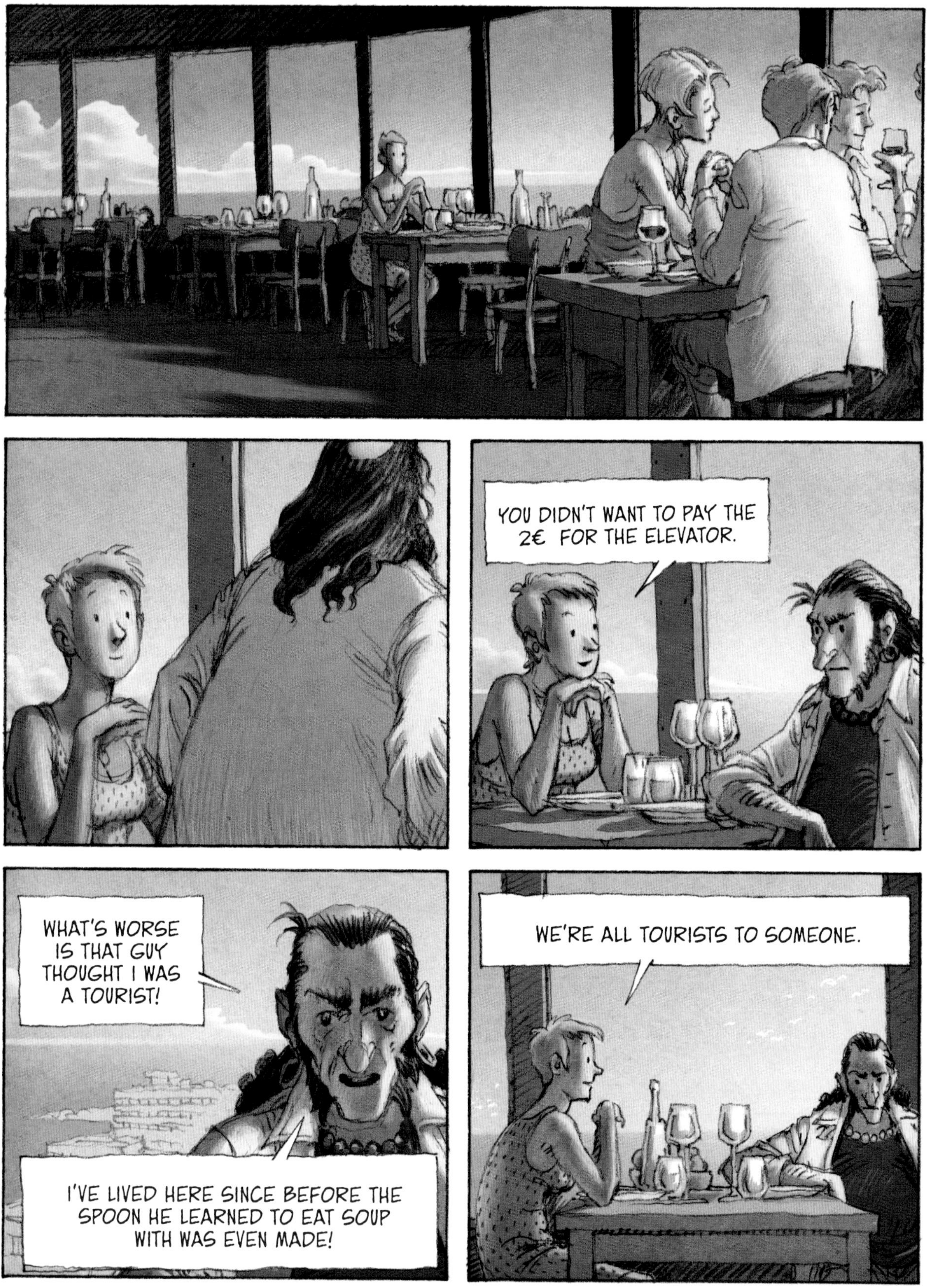
YOU DIDN'T WANT TO PAY THE 2€ FOR THE ELEVATOR.
WHAT'S WORSE IS THAT GUY THOUGHT I WAS A TOURIST!
I'VE LIVED HERE SINCE BEFORE THE SPOON HE LEARNED TO EAT SOUP WITH WAS EVEN MADE!
WE'RE ALL TOURISTS TO SOMEONE.

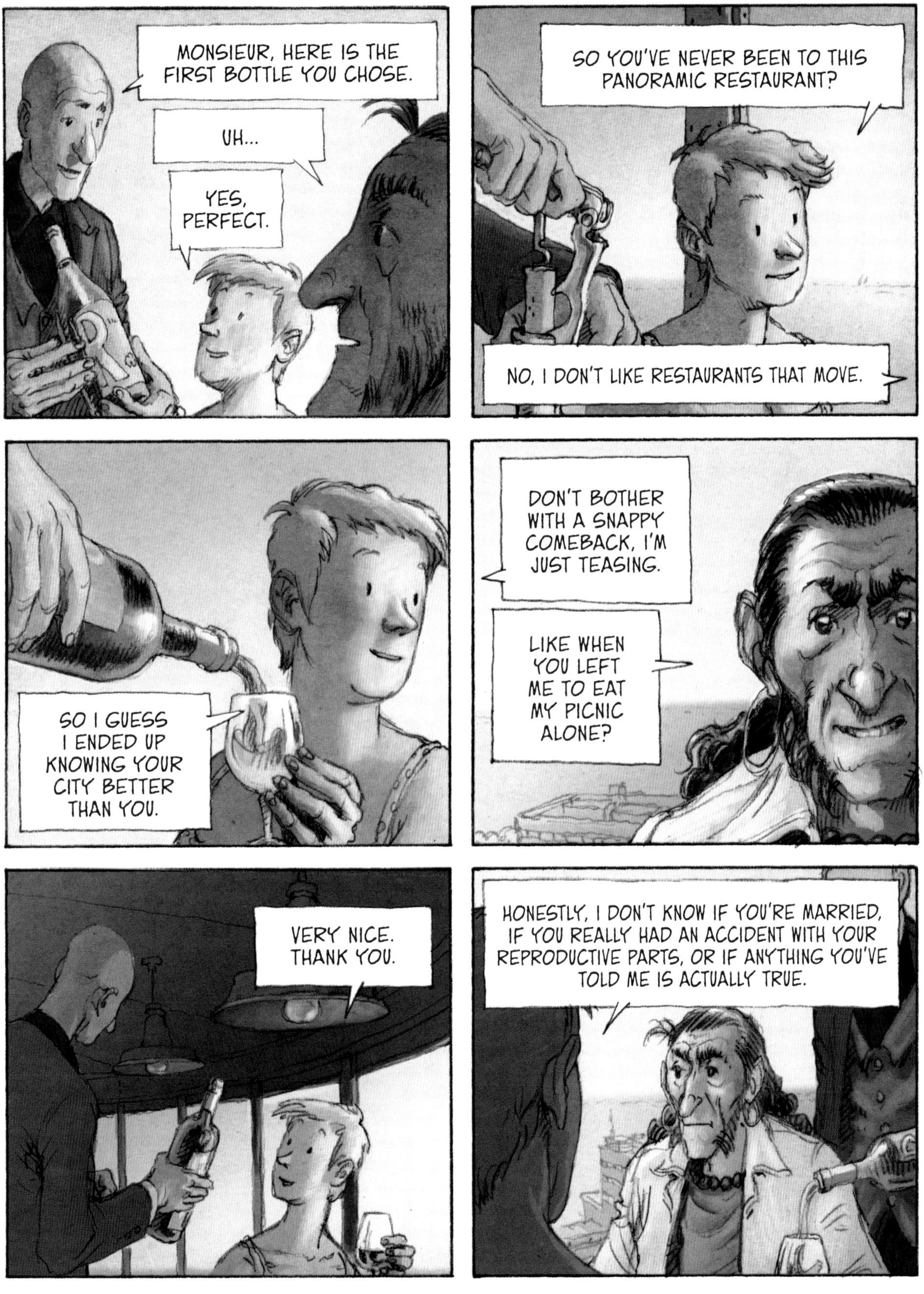
MONSIEUR, HERE IS THE FIRST BOTTLE YOU CHOSE.
UH...
YES, PERFECT.
SO YOU'VE NEVER BEEN TO THIS PANORAMIC RESTAURANT?
NO, I DON'T LIKE RESTAURANTS THAT MOVE.
SO I GUESS I ENDED UP KNOWING YOUR CITY BETTER THAN YOU.
DON'T BOTHER WITH A SNAPPY COMEBACK, I'M JUST TEASING.
LIKE WHEN YOU LEFT ME TO EAT MY PICNIC ALONE?
VERY NICE. THANK YOU.
HONESTLY, I DON'T KNOW IF YOU'RE MARRIED, IF YOU REALLY HAD AN ACCIDENT WITH YOUR REPRODUCTIVE PARTS, OR IF ANYTHING YOU'VE TOLD ME IS ACTUALLY TRUE.

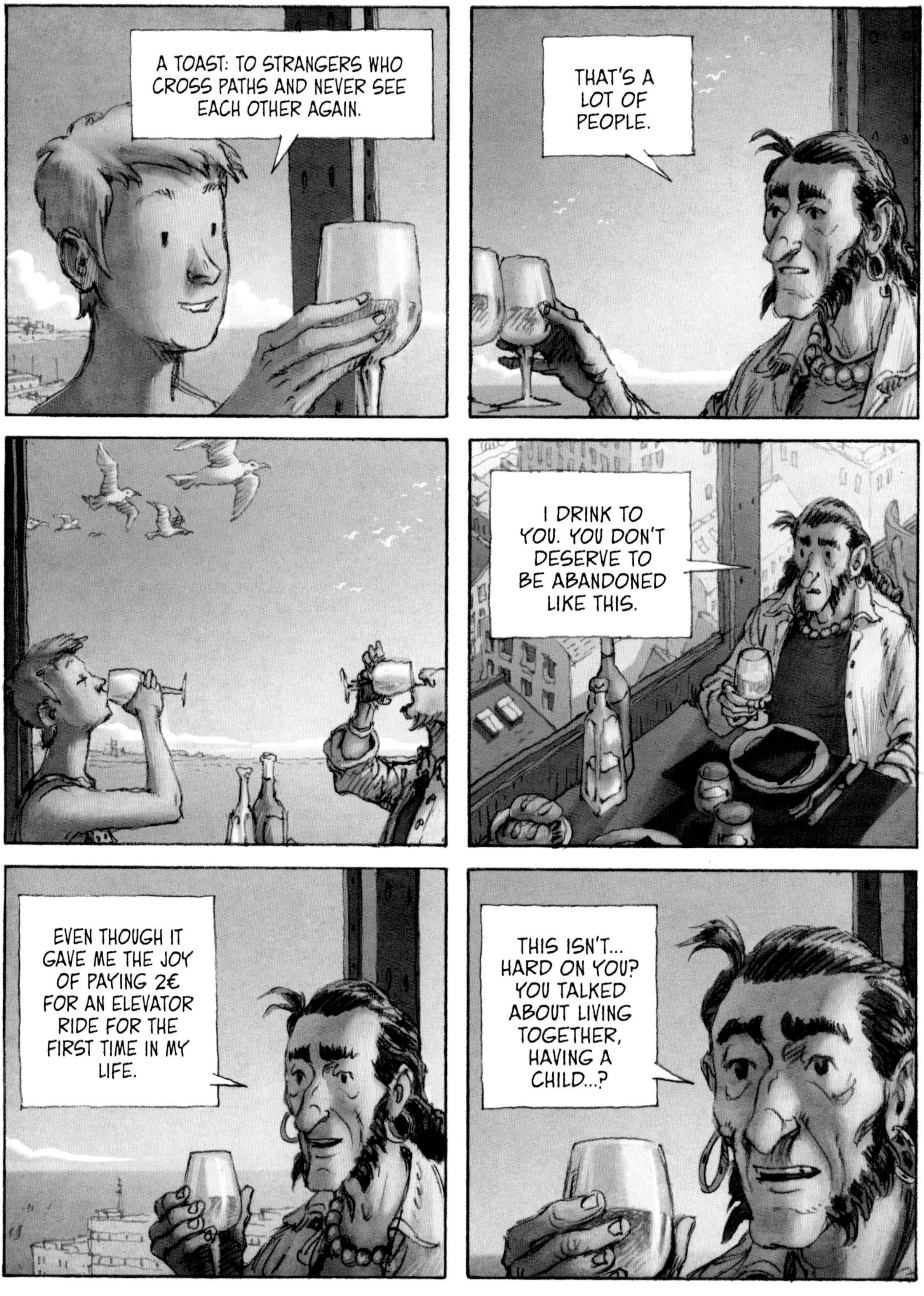
A TOAST: TO STRANGERS WHO CROSS PATHS AND NEVER SEE EACH OTHER AGAIN.
THAT'S A LOT OF PEOPLE.
I DRINK TO YOU. YOU DON'T DESERVE TO BE ABANDONED LIKE THIS.
EVEN THOUGH IT GAVE ME THE JOY OF PAYING 2€ FOR AN ELEVATOR RIDE FOR THE FIRST TIME IN MY LIFE.
THIS ISN'T... HARD ON YOU? YOU TALKED ABOUT LIVING TOGETHER, HAVING A CHILD...?

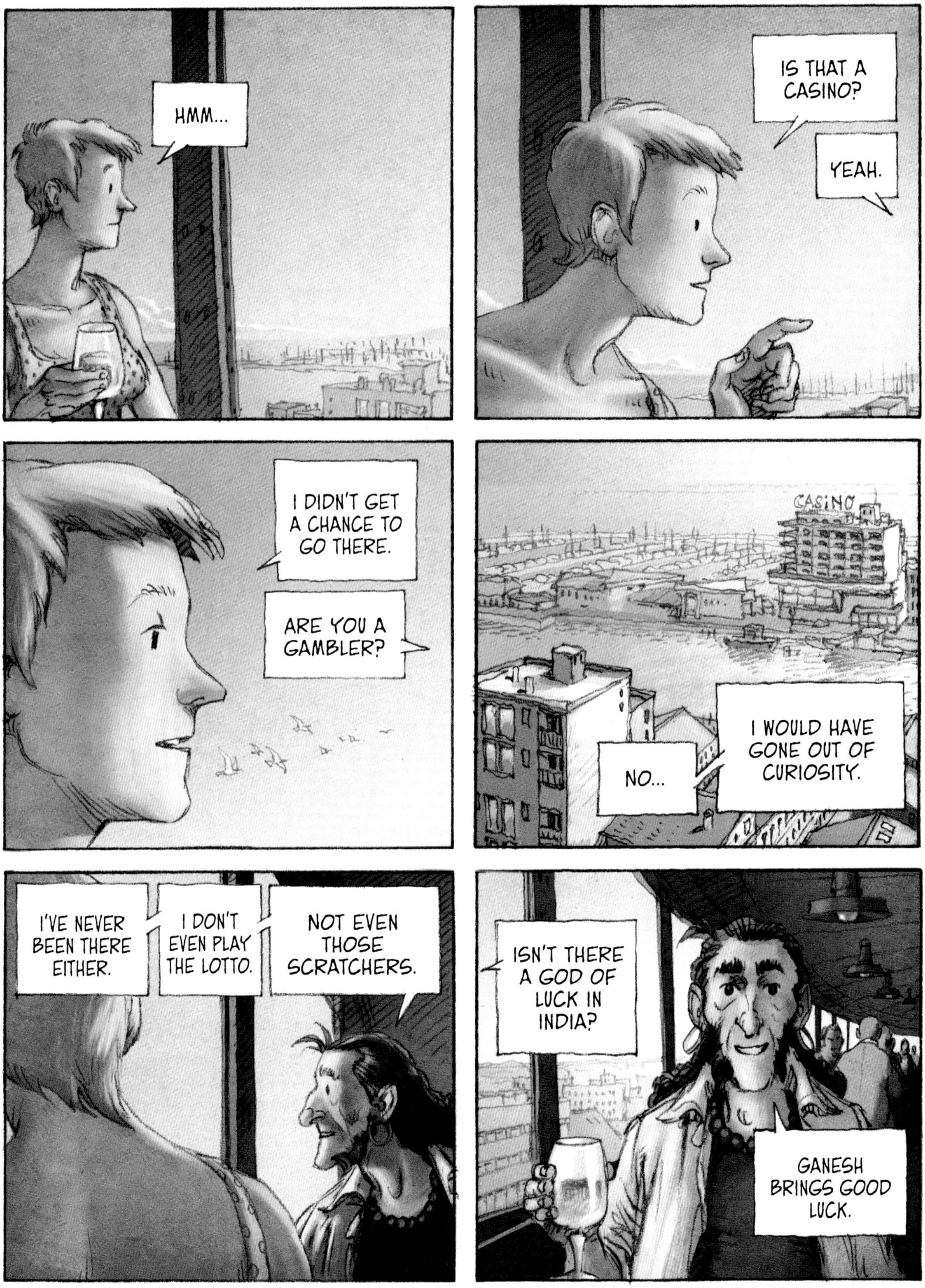
HMM...
IS THAT A CASINO?
YEAH.
I DIDN'T GET A CHANCE TO GO THERE.
ARE YOU A GAMBLER?
CASINO
NO...
I WOULD HAVE GONE OUT OF CURIOSITY.
I'VE NEVER BEEN THERE EITHER.
I DON'T EVEN PLAY THE LOTTO.
NOT EVEN THOSE SCRATCHERS.
ISN'T THERE A GOD OF LUCK IN INDIA?
GANESH BRINGS GOOD LUCK.

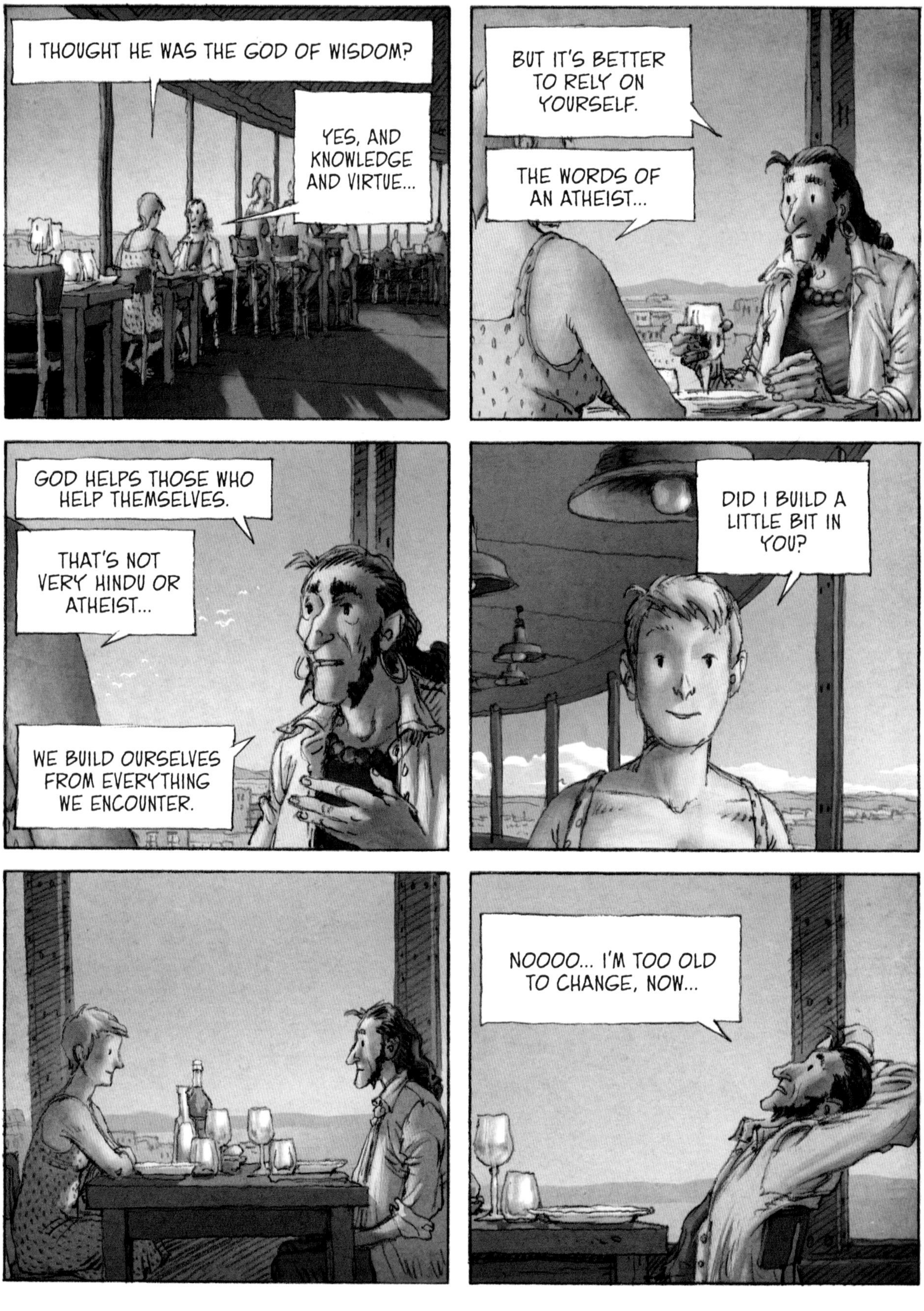
I THOUGHT HE WAS THE GOD OF WISDOM?
YES, AND KNOWLEDGE AND VIRTUE...
BUT IT'S BETTER TO RELY ON YOURSELF.
THE WORDS OF AN ATHEIST...
GOD HELPS THOSE WHO HELP THEMSELVES.
THAT'S NOT VERY HINDU OR ATHEIST...
WE BUILD OURSELVES FROM EVERYTHING WE ENCOUNTER.
DID I BUILD A LITTLE BIT IN YOU?
NOOOO... I'M TOO OLD TO CHANGE, NOW...

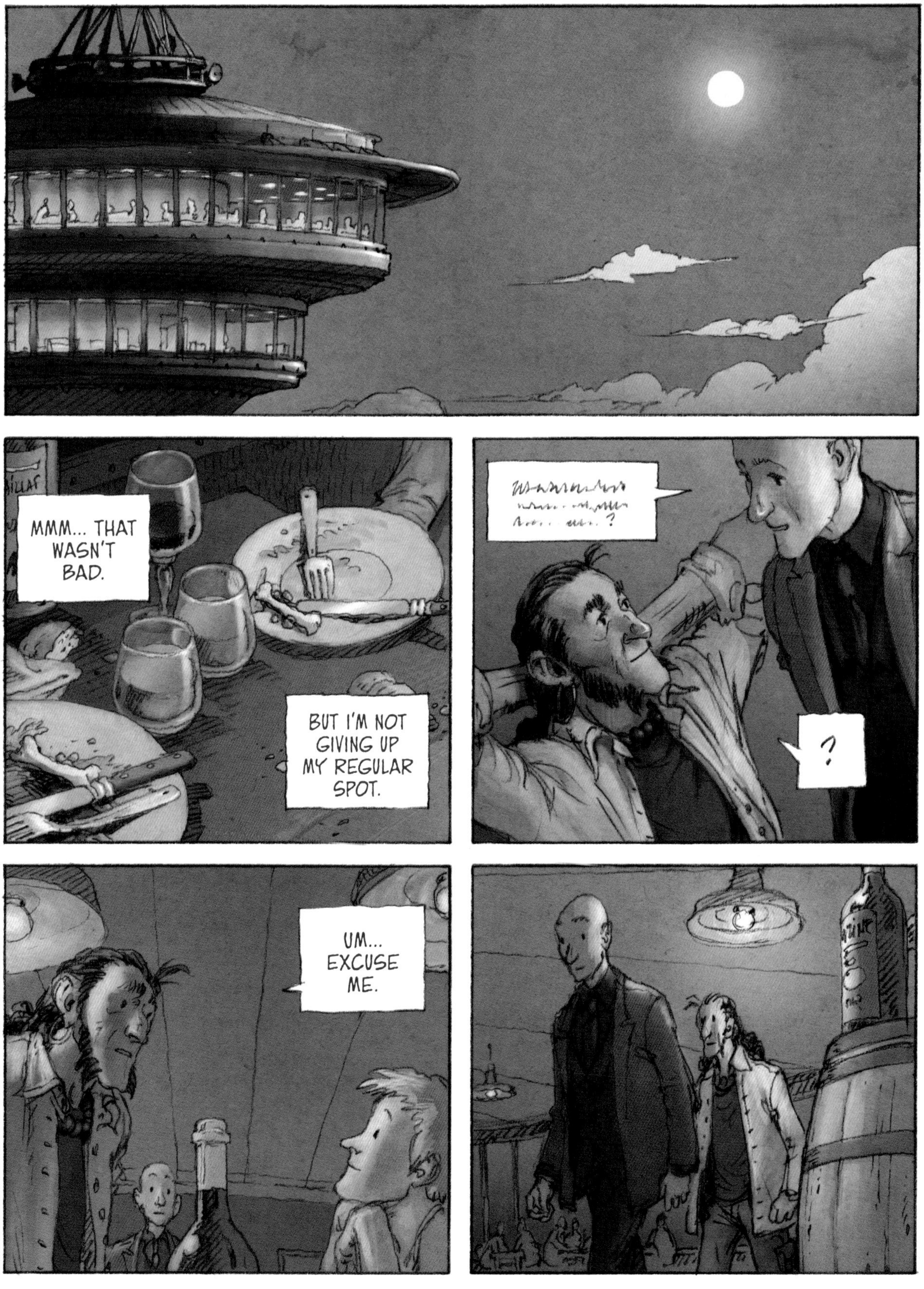
MMM... THAT WASN'T BAD.
BUT I'M NOT GIVING UP MY REGULAR SPOT.
?
UM... EXCUSE ME.

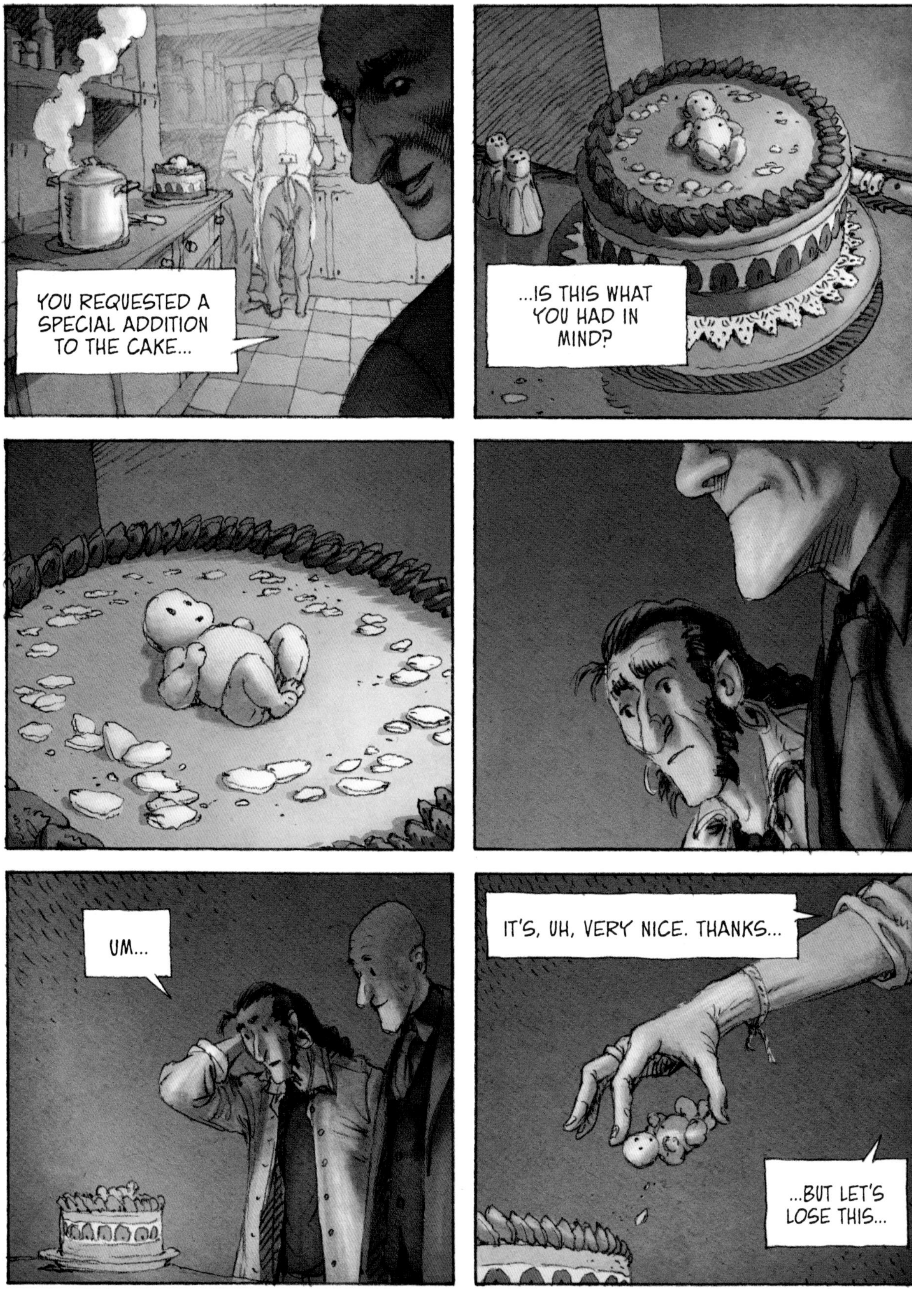
YOU REQUESTED A SPECIAL ADDITION TO THE CAKE...
...IS THIS WHAT YOU HAD IN MIND?
UM...
IT'S, UH, VERY NICE. THANKS...
...BUT LET'S LOSE THIS...

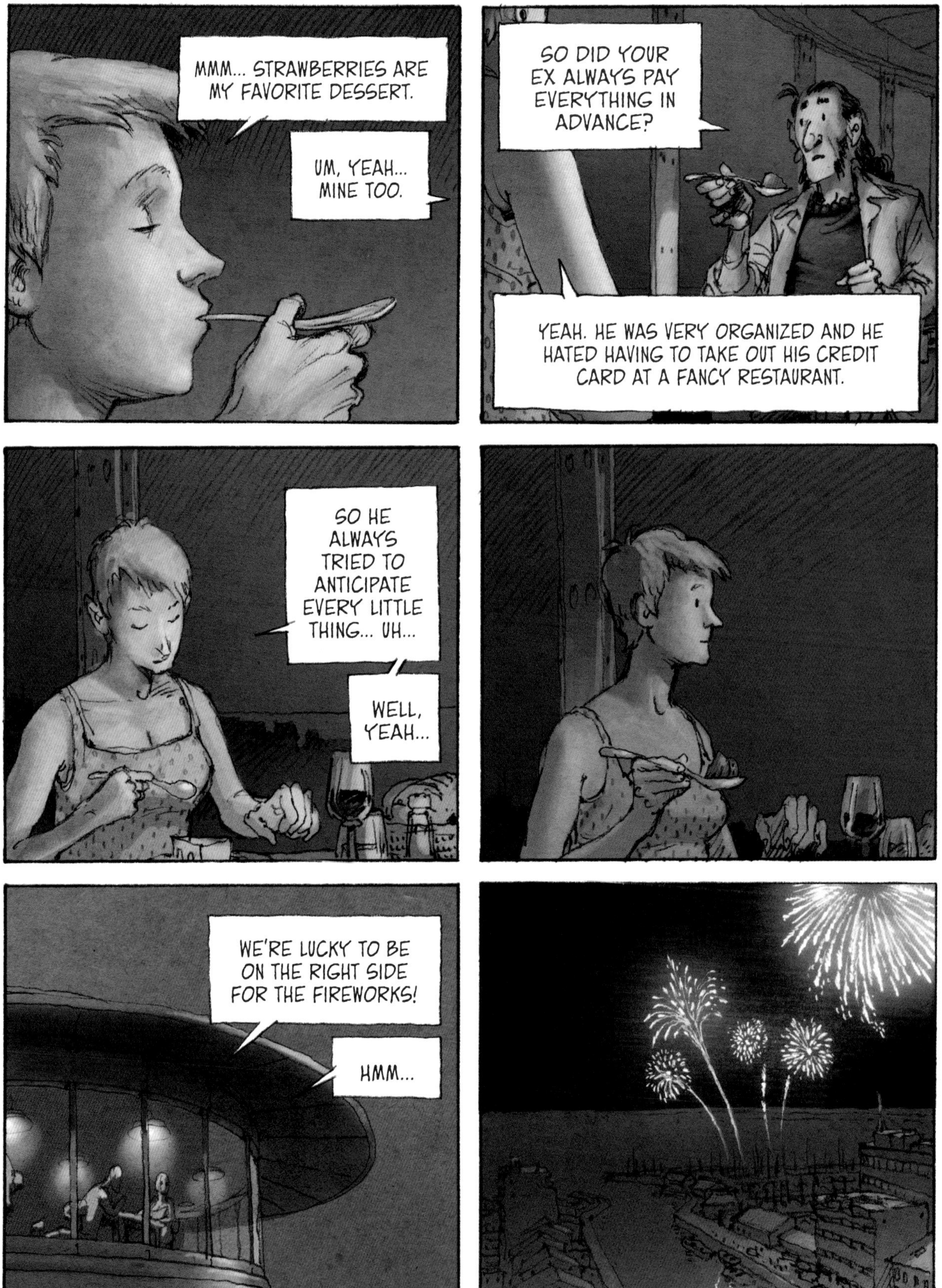
MMM... STRAWBERRIES ARE MY FAVORITE DESSERT.
UM, YEAH... MINE TOO.
SO DID YOUR EX ALWAYS PAY EVERYTHING IN ADVANCE?
YEAH. HE WAS VERY ORGANIZED AND HE HATED HAVING TO TAKE OUT HIS CREDIT CARD AT A FANCY RESTAURANT.
SO HE ALWAYS TRIED TO ANTICIPATE EVERY LITTLE THING... UH...
WELL, YEAH...
WE'RE LUCKY TO BE ON THE RIGHT SIDE FOR THE FIREWORKS!
HMM...

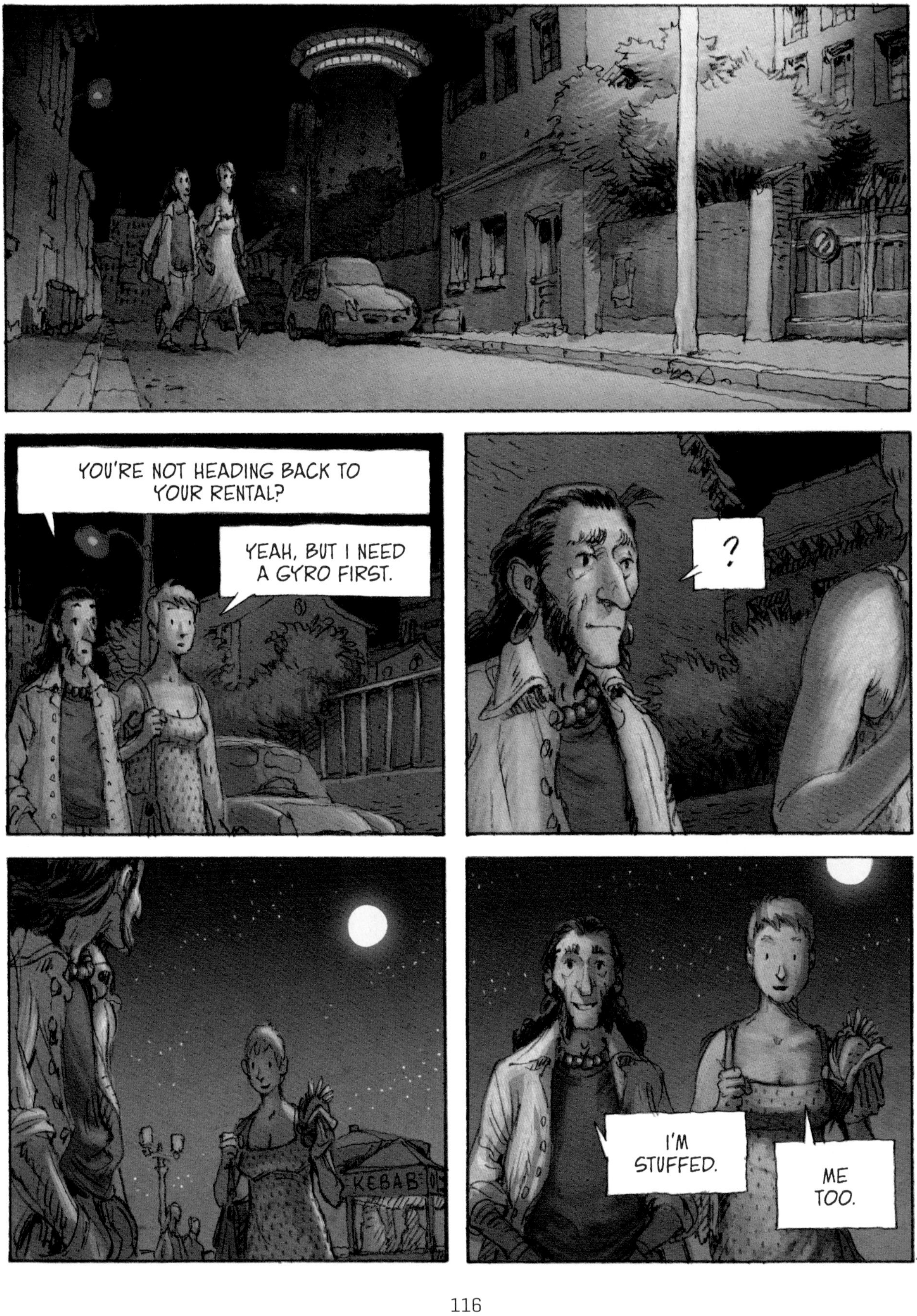
YOU'RE NOT HEADING BACK TO YOUR RENTAL?
YEAH, BUT I NEED A GYRO FIRST.
?
KEBAB
I'M STUFFED.
ME TOO.

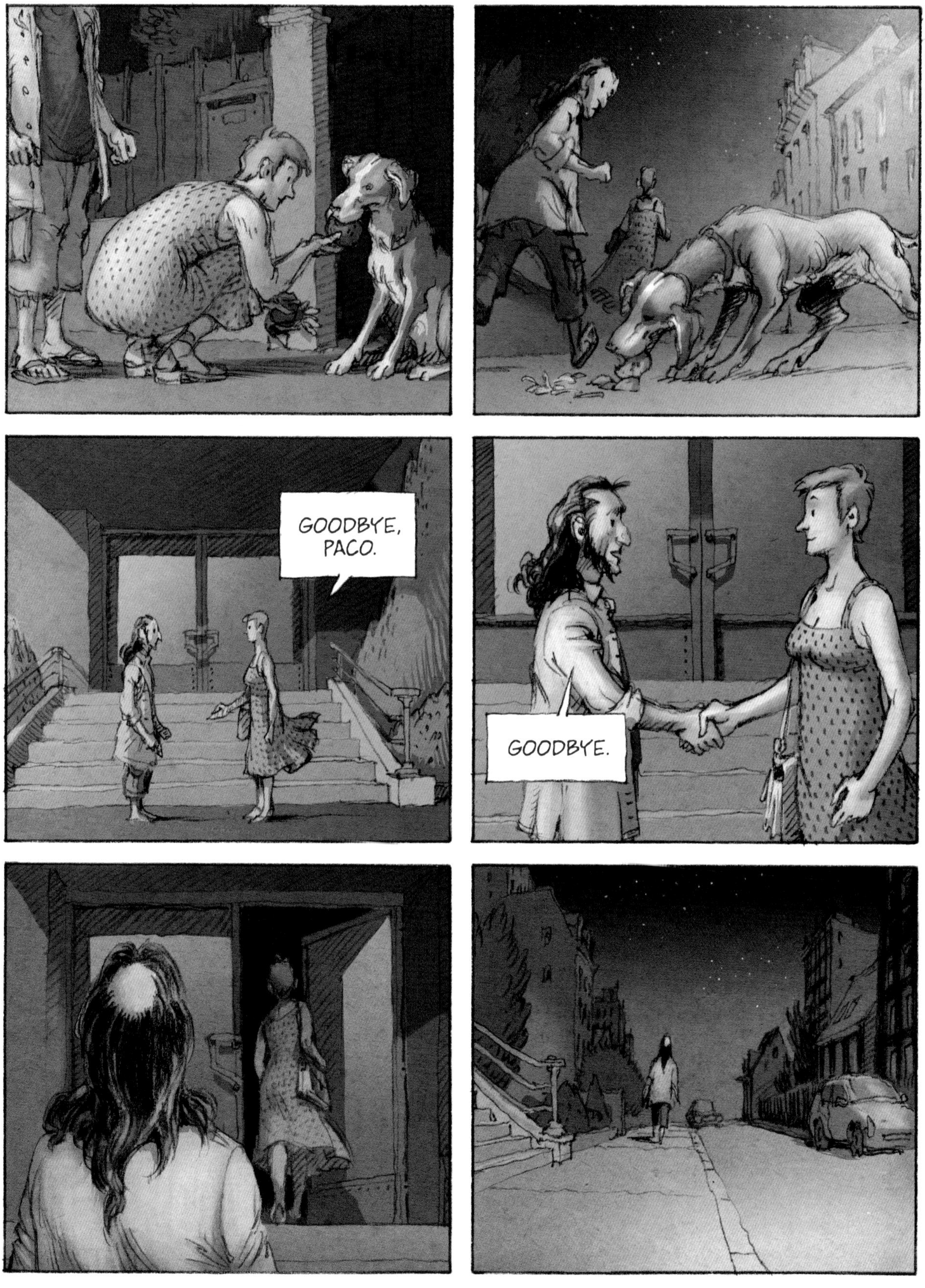
GOODBYE, PACO.
GOODBYE.

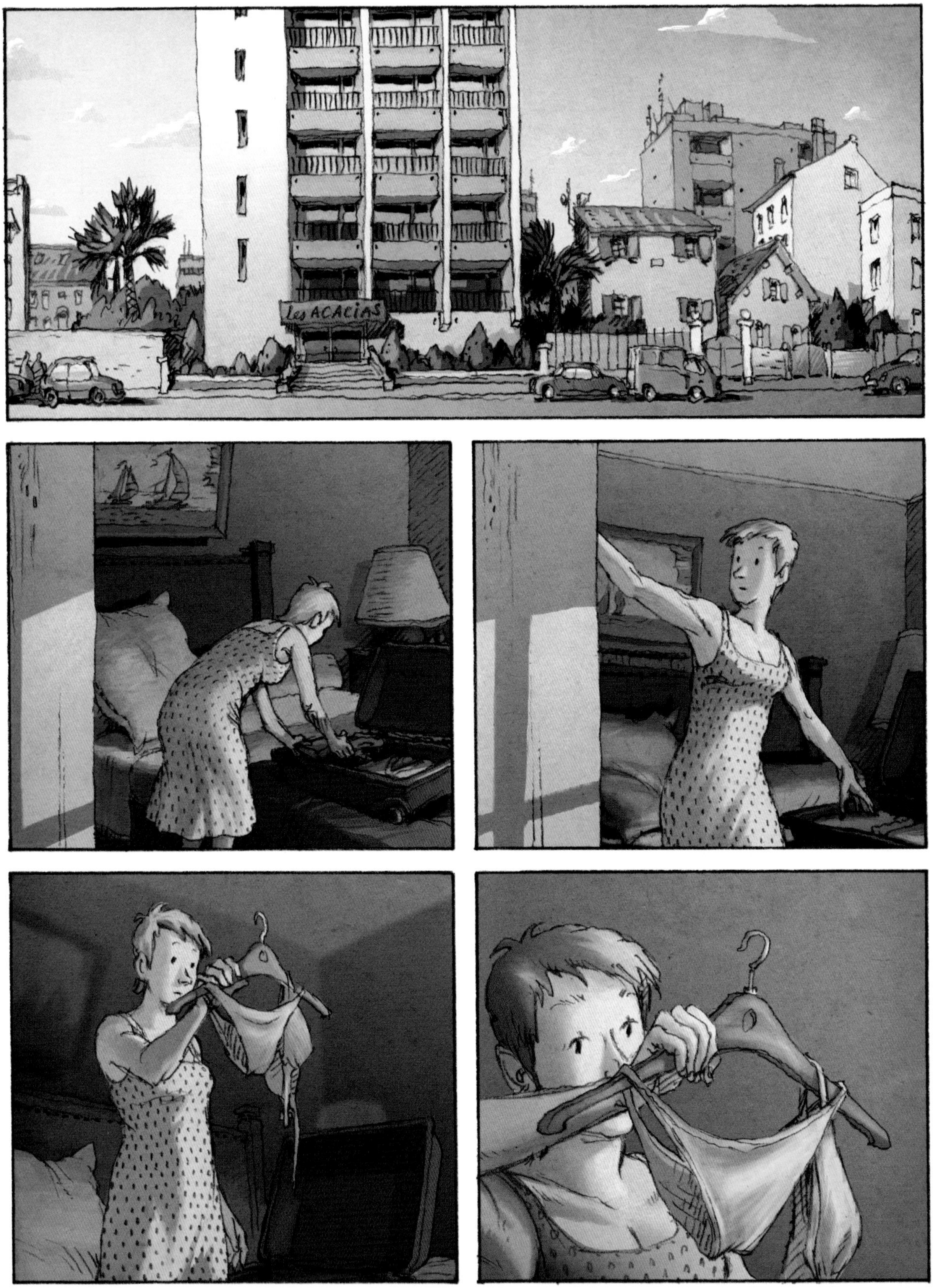
Les ACACIAS

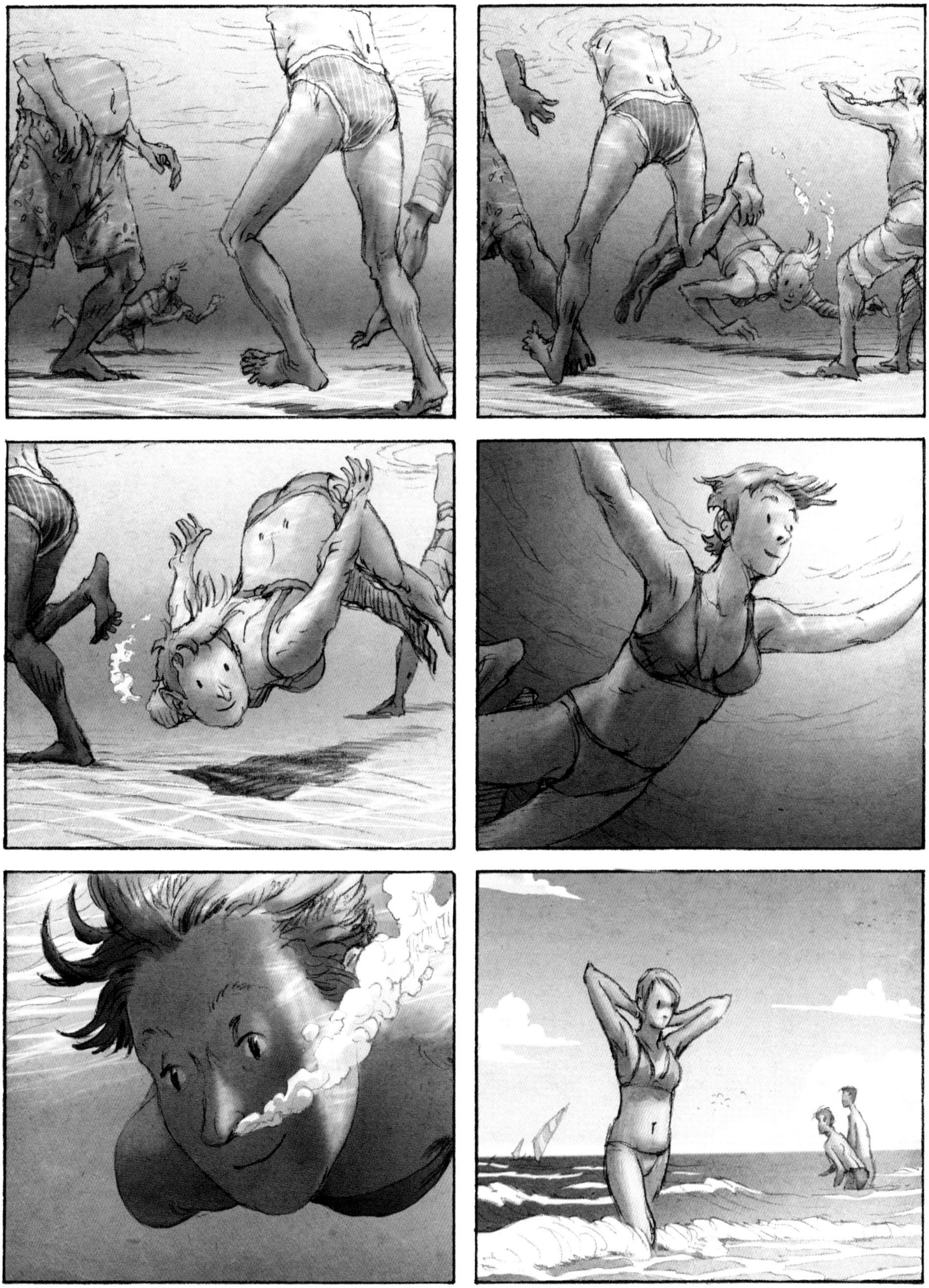

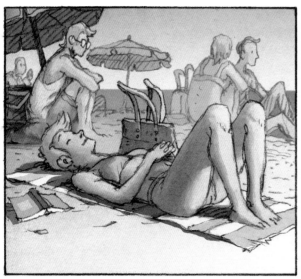

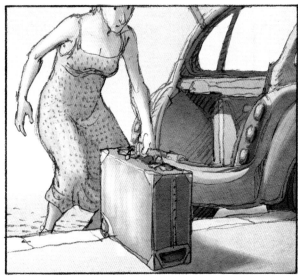

PMU CHAMPION

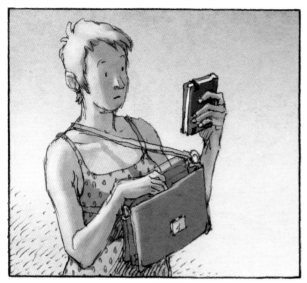

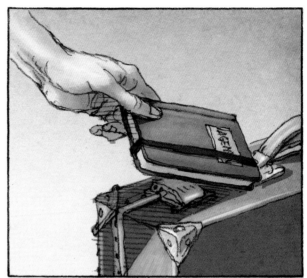

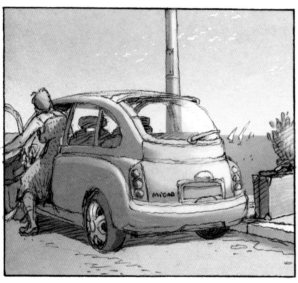

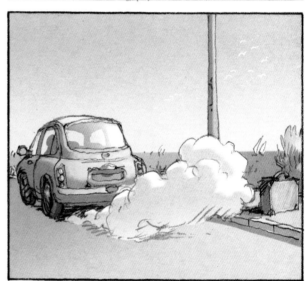

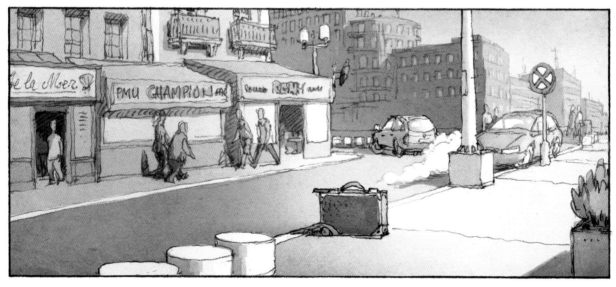

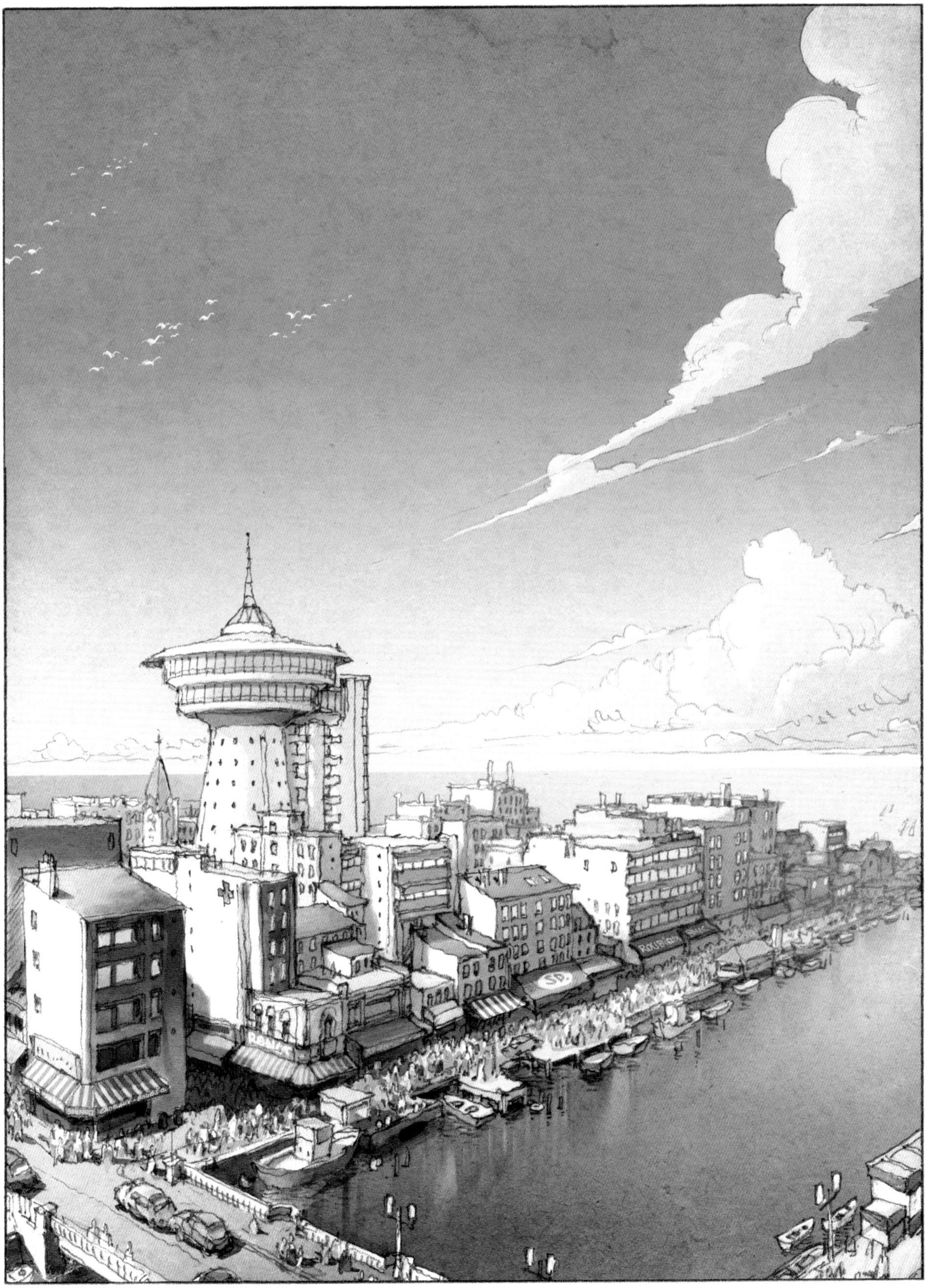

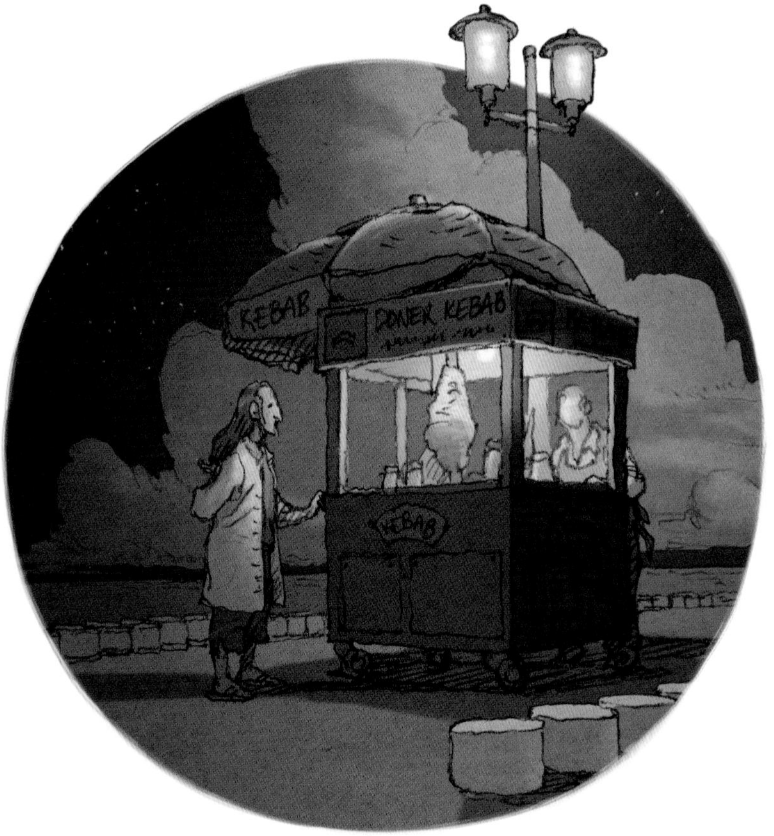
KEBAB
DONER KEBAB
KEBAB

LEWIS TRONDHEIM was born in Fontainebleau, France, on December 11, 1964, and grew up with a rather aimless idea for the future. After a brief stint at a technical college, he ended up graduating with a degree in philosophy and literature. But his real interest was in storytelling. He self-published his first fanzine at the age of 25 before joining five other artists in the creation of the studio **L'Association**. From that point on, his work started to take on a life of its own, first with the popular *Formidables Aventures de Lapinot* (available in English as "The Marvelous Adventures of McConey"), which earned him an award from the Angoulême Festival in 1994, then with a number of collaboration projects, including *Donjon* for Delcourt and *Les Cosmonautes du Future* for Dargaud. Over the years, his works have been adapted for animated television, such as the popular 65-episode run of *La Mouche* and the 35-episode sci-fi cartoon *Kaput and Zösky*. Since then, his recognition has spread far beyond Europe to the rest of the world, and he has collected numerous honors, including several Eisner nominations, Harvey Award nominations, Ignatz Awards, and numerous Angoulême Festival accolades including the top honor bestowed by the festival, the Grand Prix de la Ville in 2006. He is also the co-creator of *Infinity 8* with artist and design director Olivier Vatine.

HUBERT CHEVILLARD was born in Angers, France, in 1962, and he has been drawing stories since childhood. He studied at the School of Fine Arts in Angoulême before starting his career as a cartoonist and comic book artist for *Pilote* magazine. He soon made his mark with the four-volume series *Le Pont dans la Vase* ("The Bridge in the Vase"), written by Sylvain Chomet for Glenat. In addition to illustrating *The Planetary Archives*, a series of short stories in *Fluid Glacial* magazine, he soon applied his talents to both feature animation and video games. He worked as character designer on the animated feature *A Monkey's Tale* in 1999 and directed his own televised animated short *Pantin, la Pirouette* in 2000. In the video game industry, he provided original graphic design to *Rayman 2: The Great Escape* in 1999 and created storyboards for the smash hit *Beyond Good & Evil* in 2003 before going on to art direct the multi-platform releases of Th*e Adventures of Tintin: The Secret of the Unicorn* in 2011 and *Assassin's Creed: Syndicate* in 2015.